101 QUICK AND EASY SECRETS FOR USING YOUR DIGITAL PHOTOGRAPHS

Matthew Bamberg

Course Technology PTR
A part of Cengage Learning

COURSE TECHNOLOGY
CENGAGE Learning™

Australia, Brazil, Japan, Korea, Mexico, Singapore, Spain, United Kingdom, United States

COURSE TECHNOLOGY
CENGAGE Learning™

101 Quick and Easy Secrets for Using Your Digital Photographs
Matthew Bamberg

Publisher and General Manager, Course Technology PTR:
Stacy L. Hiquet

Associate Director of Marketing:
Sarah Panella

Manager of Editorial Services:
Heather Talbot

Marketing Manager:
Jordan Casey

Executive Editor:
Kevin Harreld

Project Editor/Copy Editor:
Cathleen D. Small

Technical Reviewer:
Ron Rockwell

Editorial Services Coordinator:
Jen Blaney

Interior Layout:
Shawn Morningstar

Cover Designer:
Mike Tanamachi

Indexer:
Kelly Talbot

Proofreader:
Melba Hopper

Library of Congress Control Number: 2009933296

ISBN-13: 978-1-4354-5437-8

ISBN-10: 1-4354-5437-5

Course Technology, a part of Cengage Learning
20 Channel Center Street
Boston, MA 02210
USA

Cengage Learning is a leading provider of customized learning solutions with office locations around the globe, including Singapore, the United Kingdom, Australia, Mexico, Brazil, and Japan. Locate your local office at: **international.cengage.com/region**.

Cengage Learning products are represented in Canada by Nelson Education, Ltd.

For your lifelong learning solutions, visit **courseptr.com**.

Visit our corporate Web site at **cengage.com**.

Printed in the United States of America
1 2 3 4 5 6 7 11 10 09

To Richard and Carl

Acknowledgments

I'd like to thank Todd Larson for his endless assessment of my photos and his support and encouragement during the writing process. In addition, I'd like to thank all of the people who have built the wonderful websites available on the Internet. There's so much out there that no one book can cover all of the great photography resources available (but this book sure tries). No book about using photographs could be complete without covering the contribution scrapbookers have made to the photography industry. Heather Landry and Crystal Brothers made fine contributions to the scrapbooking chapter of this book. Also assisting with this chapter were MJ Outcault Hill and her son, Bryce Hill. I'd like to thank Kevin Harreld for reading my proposals and helping to make this photography book series possible. Last but not least, special thanks go to Cathleen Small, who has managed to switch from editing books about how to take pictures to editing books about the myriad resources for using photos.

About the Author

Matthew Bamberg is the author of the *101 Quick and Easy Secrets* photography book series, which covers everything from creating winning photographs to using your photographs and emulating the great twentieth-century photographers. He began his career in the arts as a graduate student at San Francisco State University in 1992. His work in the visual and media arts included video production and software applications. He completed his M.A. in Creative Arts in 1997. After being a public school teacher for 14 years, Bamberg became a photographer and writer. He began to photograph for the articles he was writing while working for the *Desert Sun* and *Palm Springs Life* magazine. He has traveled the world, photographing in the most remote of places, from Burma to Bolivia. His photographs have appeared in international magazines, galleries, and retail stores. Bamberg is also the author of *The 50 Greatest Photo Opportunities in San Francisco* (Course Technology PTR, 2009).

Books in the *Quick and Easy* photography series include *101 Quick and Easy Secrets to Create Winning Photographs, 101 Quick and Easy Secrets for Using Your Digital Photographs*, and *101 Quick and Easy Ideas Taken from the Master Photographers of the Twentieth Century.*

Contents

Chapter 3

Chapter 4

Chapter 5

Chapter 6

Introduction

Millions of people around the world have many photos stored on their laptop and desktop computers, external hard drives, CDs and DVDs, and flash drives. Most images are just sitting there idle, waiting for the world to see them. Some have been unused for years. Up until now there has been no guide to help people find ways to use these photos.

Hidden in various places around the Internet are hundreds of ways to make photos come alive online, in print form, in scrapbooks, on the walls of people's homes, in blogs, on social networking sites, and in many other places.

101 Quick and Easy Secrets for Using Your Digital Photographs takes those who wonder what to do with their photos on a journey where they will immediately discover not only a place to exhibit their work, but also ways to make their photos work for them by selling them online and on the ground.

This book is for using, manipulating, posting, sharing, publishing, managing, and promoting photos that you have taken or plan to take. Online platforms will be introduced so that you can begin navigating through the many free sites to put your photos to use. You'll learn how to use your photos in such online locations as Flickr, MySpace, Photobucket, and Facebook. You'll learn about everything from free downloadable software to manage your photos, such as Picasa (Google's photo management program), to programs that are already on your computer, such as iPhoto on a Mac and Windows Live on a PC.

This book also walks you through the printing process, from learning about the right type of printer for your needs to finding the best paper to make your photos last nearly forever. If you don't want to print your photos yourself, the book shows you the most reasonable ways to outsource your printing.

Using your photos wouldn't be complete for some without mentioning the latest in scrapbooking trends, including extensive how-to instruction on how to build layers in Photoshop to make the most compelling of scrapbook pages. You'll learn about how to use digital kits for making scrapbooks as well as places to find great free materials for making scrapbook pages.

The book doesn't omit on-ground techniques for using your photos. Photos these days usually require significant steps to be performed online and on your computer before you can use the images on the ground. You can order mats, frames, and other photo-framing supplies online; make your framed photos on the ground; and sell them online and host photo shows on the ground—all using your photos that are online or on your computer.

Let's not forget selling your photos and promoting yourself so people can find you and your work. This book details the best ways to make your photos a known commodity, and it brainstorms the best places to sell your photos online and on the ground. You'll learn about how microstock photography, blogs, websites, social networking sites, and photo hosting sites can make or break your photography career.

Dig into the book morsel by morsel, enjoying the rewards that can be had by finding new uses for your photography.

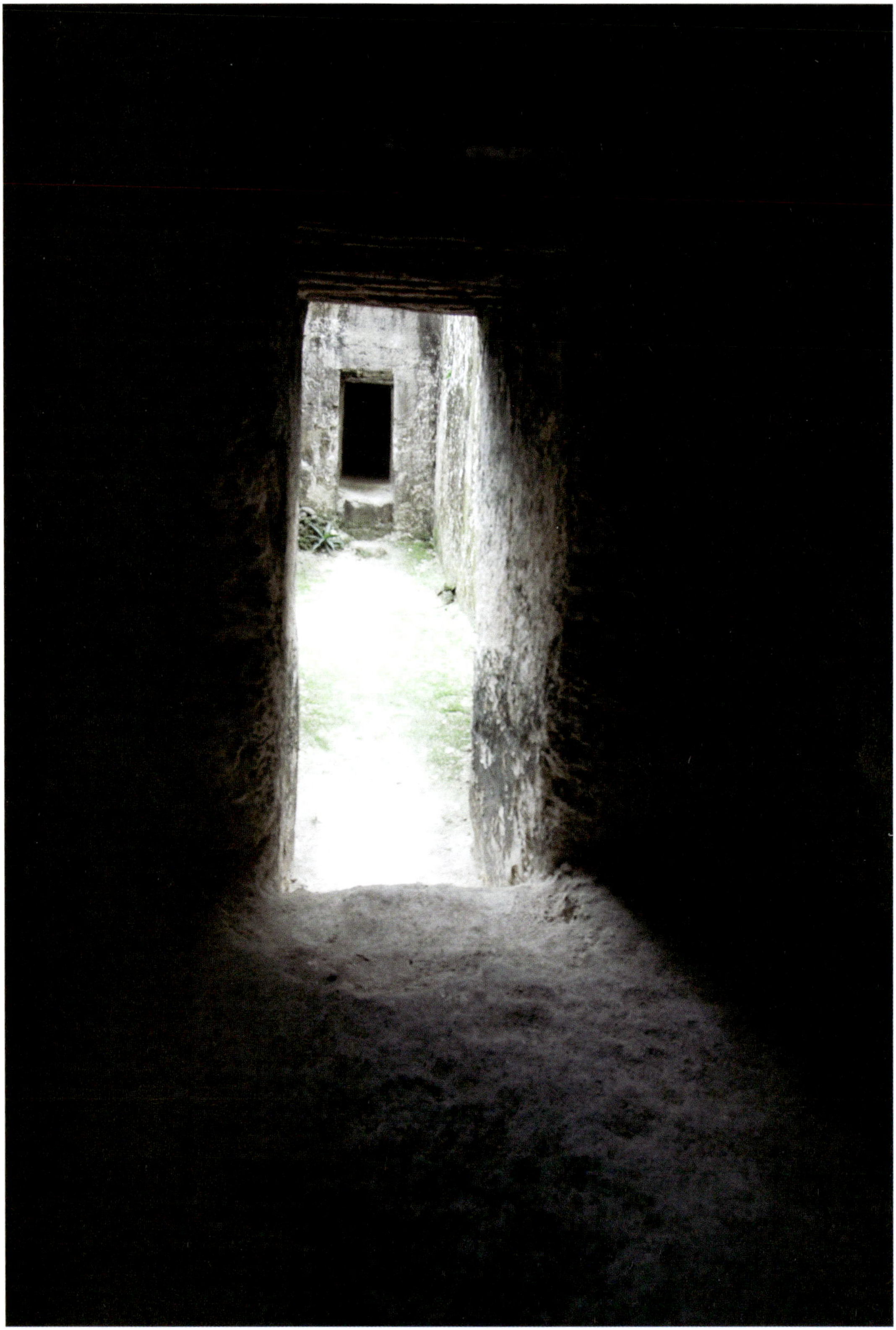

CHAPTER 1

Preparing Your Photos for Use

To easily access your photos in different programs, you'll need to make sure your computer is running efficiently. You don't want to wait for nearly a minute for a photograph to open in Photoshop, nor do you want the programs that process your photos to make your computer crash. There are a few simple things you can do to make your computer run efficiently so that you can access your image files without having to tap your foot waiting for them to come up.

Maintaining Your Computer so You Don't Lose Image Files

On a Mac, if your computer gets sluggish, the first thing you can do is repair disk permissions. To get to the Repair Permissions dialog box, choose Macintosh HD > Applications > Utilities > Disk Utility. Then click on Macintosh HD in the menu on the left side of the window. Finally, click on the Repair Disk Permissions button at the bottom of the window. (There's no need to verify disk permissions.) Figure 1.1 shows what you'll see.

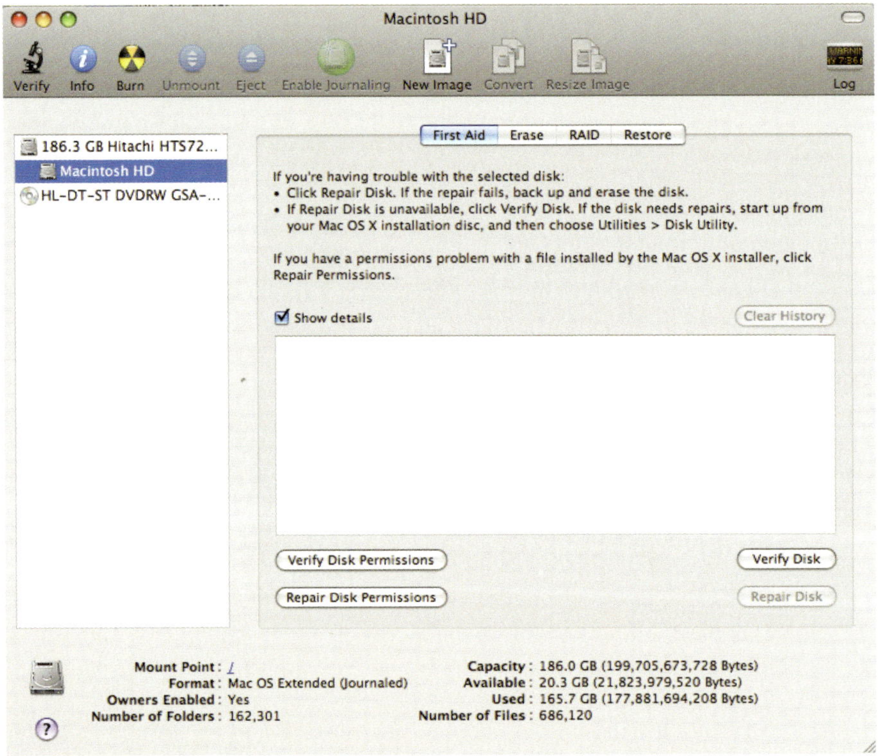

Figure 1.1 Disk Permissions dialog box.

On a PC running Windows Vista, you have an upgraded system maintenance from other Windows versions. You get a report about how your computer is functioning by navigating to Control Panel > System Maintenance > Performance Information and Tools (see Figure 1.2). To improve your machine's score, you can use the Disk Defragmenter and Disk Cleanup (Control Panel > System and Maintenance).

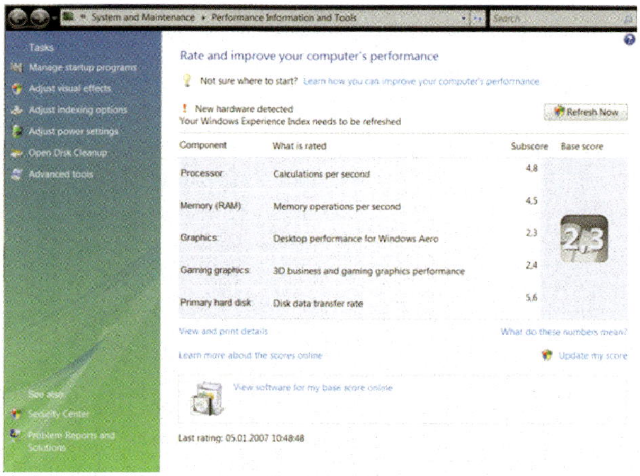

Figure 1.2 Windows Vista gives you a report on how your system is functioning.

WHAT WILL YOUR IMAGES LOOK LIKE IN 10 YEARS?

A good question to ask yourself is, "Where will my images be in 10 years?" Most cameras produce compressed files known as JPEG files. When JPEG files are compressed, data is lost. The most important drawback of keeping your images in JPEG format is that if you open them and then edit and save them, your image will lose quality. If you repeat this process many times, you'll end up with an image of very poor quality. There's a good chance you'll see the little pixels that make up the image. This is called *pixelization*. In order to prevent file degradation, it's best to convert your JPEG files to another format called TIFF, where there is less compression and thus less loss of data.

What happens to your image files over a long period of time depends on what types of files they are and whether you are accessing them and editing them frequently. When you navigate to the File > Save or File > Save As command in a program, you'll have a choice of file formats in which to save your work. If you want to convert a file, all you do is choose what type of file you want in the Save As dialog box. You'll find the choices for file save formats by clicking on the Format drop-down menu in the software application you are working in.

What will happen to your images after 5, 10, or 20 years no matter what the format is? There is no telling. These file formats have only been around for about two decades, and who's to say what new formats might be invented, making existing ones obsolete? You also have to consider storage device options. There are memory cards, hard drives, CDs, DVDs, and online storage. What you choose may affect how long your photos will last. See "Storing Your Photos and Backups Properly" idea in this chapter to learn more about this.

Cropping Photos to Make Them Look Better

Cropping a photo is a world away from resizing one. To be sure, when you crop, you make the size of your image smaller; however, unlike resizing, the picture becomes totally different. If you want to hone in on details of a photo, place a subject at a specific point in the frame (see the upcoming "Cropping and the Rule of Thirds" sidebar), and/or eliminate subjects/objects from a frame, you can crop a photo. The images in Figure 1.3 show how cropping out parts of a photo can enhance the details of it. The texture of the elephant's skin can be seen in the photo where the elephant has been cropped tightly in the frame.

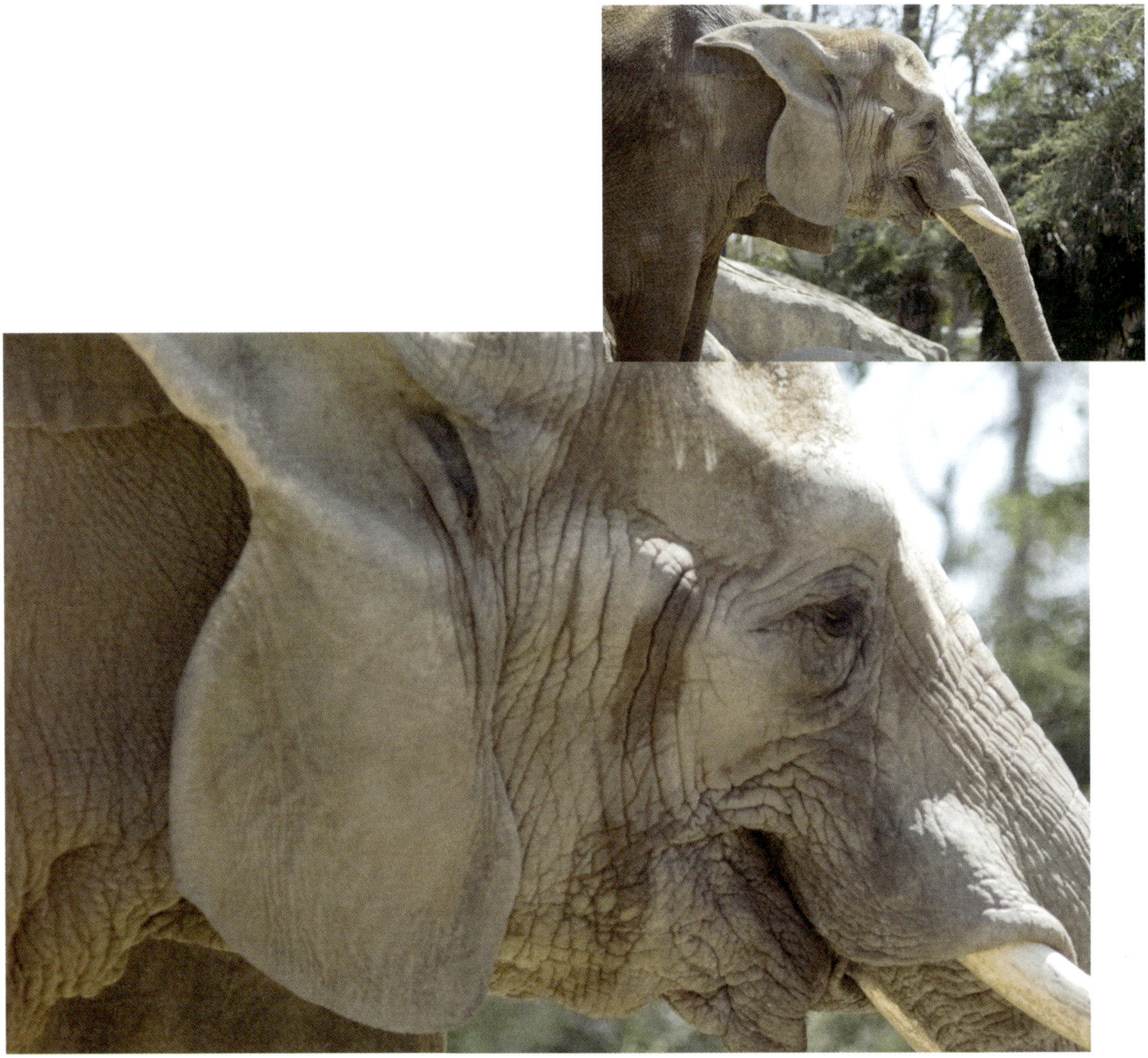

Figure 1.3 Cropping a picture can bring out the details.

CROPPING AND THE RULE OF THIRDS

Painters discovered a long time ago that balance in a painting can be achieved by placing subjects or parts of subjects one-third of the way from any of the four sides of your frame. When you're out in the field, you can easily achieve this, but many times you will forget in the process of capturing that ideal photo-op moment. Also, when you frame in the field, sometimes your estimations of one-third away, say, from the left side of the frame can be off. The first image in Figure 1.4 shows a photograph of a doorway at the ruins of Tikal in Guatemala. In the image, the doorway is smack dab in the middle of the frame—not a good composition option because there is too much black space at the top and the left part of the frame. Cropping the image to what is shown in the second image leaves the frame filled with subtle light around a doorway that sits one-third from the left side of the frame, which follows the Rule of Thirds—a pleasing composition, indeed.

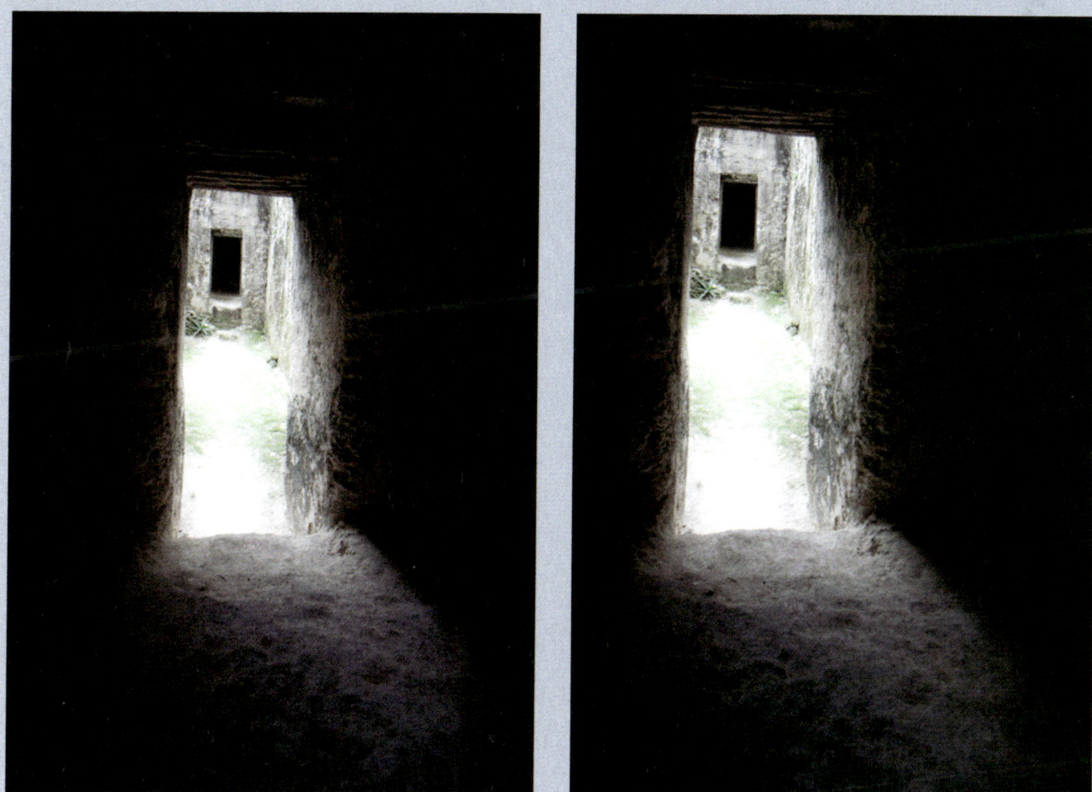

Figure 1.4 Doorway in center of frame and then cropped using the Rule of Thirds.

Attaching Photos to Email (Including the Largest Sizes You Can Send for Each Service)

Email has grown steadily more sophisticated over the two decades or so it has been in existence. There was a time when sending a small JPEG file was a challenge. Today, on most of the free email providers, sending a 12-MB TIFF (or 12 to 15 high-res JPEGs) isn't a problem. And the day is sure to come when you'll be able to send 100-MB files in a flash. As a matter of fact, you can send 100-MB files—or any size, for that matter—on Lycos.

To send an email attachment, you click Attach (or something similar) to prompt the email program to give you a dialog box to browse for the picture you want to attach before you send the email.

Sending email attachments is a breeze if you keep in mind two things. The first thing you need to do is name your file correctly. When you name a file, there should be no blank spaces in the text; if there are, the person you are sending the file to might have trouble opening it. Also, always be sure you put a period/dot (.) and the file type after the name of your file. For example, if you're sending a JPEG picture of a vintage auto, don't name it vintage auto. Use vintageauto.jpg instead.

NOTE

You don't really have to put the file extension at the end of an image. Windows adds the correct extension. But on a Mac, it's a different story—if you don't add a file extension, it won't get done.

The second thing to keep in mind is where on your computer your file is so that when it comes time to navigate to it, you won't have to waste your time scrolling through the file locator dialog box to look for it. I usually put files that I'm going to send via email on my desktop. That way, they're easy to find.

Table 1.1 gives maximum file sizes for email attachments for some of the free email providers on the Internet. Keep in mind that you should send images a bit less than the maximum file size because the size of a file could be larger when transport encodings are automatically added. This means that in some cases, attachments that are 18 to 20 MB in size may push the total message size above 20 MB, for example. When this happens, Gmail lets you know that the message exceeds the 20-MB limit.

You can safely email 18-MB attachments between Gmail users. However, if you are sending an 18-MB file to a Yahoo! mail user, the mail will be bounced back by Yahoo! because they only deal with files up to 10 MB. This is the case for most email providers, except Lycos, which has a setup where other email providers can't read how big the file is, so that files will open when sent to any provider. You'll have to fork over $19.95 annually if you need to send out huge attachments all the time.

TABLE 1.1 EMAIL SERVICE MAXIMUM ATTACHMENT SIZES

Service	Maximum Attachment Size
AOL	16 MB
Gmail	20 MB
Yahoo!	10 MB
Hotmail	10 MB
Lycos Unlimited	Can send unlimited size attachments to any email account at a cost of $19.95/year

Storing Your Photos Online

You can store photos on many sites. The storage sites do a number of other things, too, from making a webpage to display your images to creating cards, calendars, mugs, and mouse pads with your photos on them. Each has specific parameters by which you can store images. Some let you store photos of unlimited sizes, and others have limits. Most free sites don't allow you much space, whereas sites that charge for photo storage/sharing usually can deal with high-resolution photos (JPEGs from 2 to 3 MB and TIFFs of 20 MB and higher).

For example, Flickr only allows 100 MB (10 MB per photo) storage space each calendar month. Their free account is not really the place to store high-resolution photos. You can opt to create a Pro account, which allows you unlimited photo uploads (up to 20 MB per photo). In addition, Flickr will change the format of your TIFF photos to JPEG.

Nikon's mypicturetown.com is a better bet for storing high-res photos. It offers 2 GB of free storage. You can upgrade to a Gold Account, which gives you 20 GB for $2.99/month, and each additional 20 GB is $2.99/month (up to 200 GB).

Files other than JPEGs in mypicturetown.com are Nikon-specific files, so if you have another brand of camera, this isn't the best place to store your files. If you want to store Canon Raw (.CR2) files, you're out of luck, because thus far there are no online storage options for this type of file.

Table 1.2 shows some parameters of free photo storage options on the Internet. It also gives the cost of upgrading to a premium account.

TABLE 1.2 FREE PHOTO STORAGE OPTIONS ON THE INTERNET

Site Name	Storage Space	Types of Files	Max File Size	Cost for Premium	Uses
ImageShack	5 GB	JPEG, PNG, TIFF converted to PNG	1.5 MB	No Premium	Photos mostly for Web
Flickr	100 MB/month	JPEG, PNG, TIFF converted to JPEG	10 MB	Pro account $24.95/year: unlimited uploads, 20 MB file size limit	Photos mostly for Web
MyPicturetown	2 GB; can upgrade to Gold Account —20 GB for $2.99/month, and each additional 20 GB is $2.99/month	JPEG, TIFF, Nikon Raw files—NEF, NRW	No max file size	Gold Account	Photos for professional Nikon users, storage for high-res JPEGs
Photobucket	1 GB	JPEG, PNG	1 MB	Pro account $39.95/year: 10 GB storage, 5 MB file size limit	Photos mostly for Web
Shutterfly	Unlimited	JPEG	Unlimited	No Premium	Photos for Web and print (high-res)
Snapfish	Unlimited for low-res images	JPEG	Low-res indefinitely; high-res stored for only 3 months	No premium	100 MB file size limit

Storing Your Photos and Backups Properly

If you're inclined to store backups for all your photographs on an external device, you're off to a great start to preserving your photographs for a long time. The best way to store your photos is to make backups from those on your computer and put them on an external hard drive. If you want to make room on your computer for more photos, you can delete the photos that you have saved on the external storage device.

Some people store their photos on CDs and DVDs. I can tell you that I become one frustrated photographer when I give a client a DVD, and he can't read it on his computer. (I burn my DVDs on a newer Mac, and some clients' older PCs won't read DVDs.) That's just the beginning of the challenges of using these shiny storage discs for both business and personal use. Part of the problem is that these storage devices weren't really designed for photography. CDs are meant for music, and DVDs are meant for video.

The two discs have many contrasts between them. CDs burn quickly but don't have much capacity, while DVDs burn slowly but have a high capacity. CDs hold about 700 MB of data, while DVDs hold 4.7 GB. That's a big difference! I'd love to use DVDs as storage, but because they burn slowly, they become time consuming as a storage device.

For high-capacity storage, a mechanical external hard drive is the way to go (see Figure 1.5). High on the list for photographers who like to take oodles (I'm talkin' millions) of photographs is the LaCie d2 Quadra 1.5 Terabyte Hard Disk ($280). You can see some shots of this model in Figure 1.5. If you don't think you'll be storing quite that many photos, you can go with the 500-GB model ($200). You probably noticed the prices for these products next to each model, but do take into consideration that the prices are dropping quickly.

> **NOTE**
>
> If you're looking at the word *terabyte*, and you haven't a clue what it means, see the upcoming "What's a Terabyte?" sidebar.

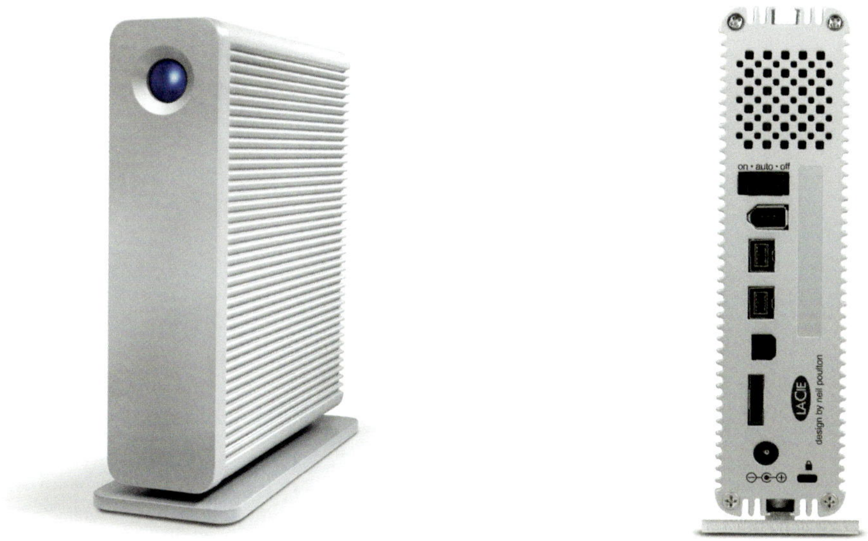

Figure 1.5 Some high-capacity mechanical hard drives hold millions of high-resolution images.

NOTE

Even though they're cheap, 250-GB-or-less capacity hard drives are not worthy of consideration because they fill up too fast.

We now have several possibilities for where to store your photos. But wait—there's one more. I think of this one in terms of a storage device that is used to transfer a few images from one computer to another. But as the years pass, this device has grown in capacity, making it a viable alternative for storing photos. The device is called a *flash drive* (see Figure 1.6). At the time of this writing, a 64-GB Corsair Flash Voyager cost $199. You can get flash drives with 8-GB memory capacity for less than $20. These devices are a little larger than an adult's thumb. It won't be long before flash drives will compete with mechanical hard drives as high-capacity storage devices.

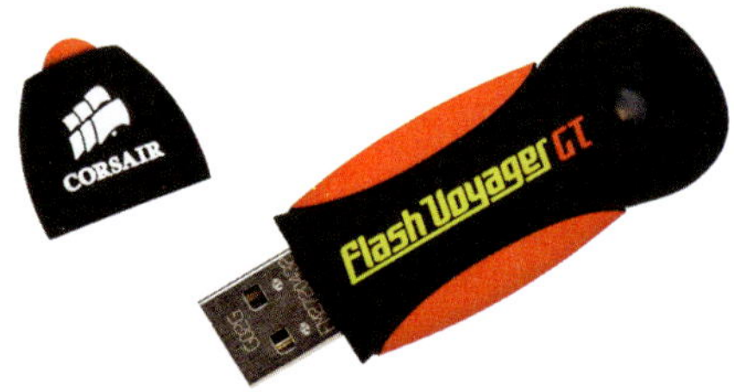

Figure 1.6 Flash drives are about the size of an adult's thumb.

WHAT'S A TERABYTE?

Big numbers make the news every day. I mean, we don't even have to look further than the trillion-dollar budget deficits with which the United States is burdened. Just as we see numbers today on the order of trillions (one trillion is a thousand billion, or $1,000,000,000,000) today, we also see similar big numbers when talking about computer memory.

Just a few short years ago, when people talked about computer memory, the word *megabyte* was pervasive. Today we hear of *terabytes*. To put this in perspective, we need a chart.

Table 1.3 shows the memory capacities of various storage devices. Today we have an external hard drive with a 1.5-TB capacity (1,500 GB or 1,000,000,000,000 bytes). So what's next? I mean, these numbers are getting bigger all the time. How about a petabyte, which is 1,000 terabytes?

TABLE 1.3 MEMORY CAPACITY OF VARIOUS STORAGE DEVICES

Media	Size
One page Microsoft Word document	1 kilobyte (KB)
Small JPEG photo for Internet	20 kilobytes
High-res JPEG photo	1,000 kilobytes or 1 megabyte (MB)
High-res TIFF photo	24 megabytes
CD capacity	700 megabytes
DVD capacity (single-sided)	4,700 megabytes or 4.7 gigabytes (GB)
Flash drive	500 megabytes to 64 gigabytes
Average computer hard drive	100 gigabytes
Large external hard drive	1,000 gigabytes or 1 terabyte (TB)

Organizing Photos on Your Computer

The first thing you have to do before you organize your photos on your computer is get them there. For methods of transferring your photos from one electronic device to another, see the "Using a Memory Card Reader to Transfer Photos" section later in this chapter. After you get your photos on your computer, you have to rename them and then back them up.

NOTE

Please back up your photos. Machines live and then they die!

You'll probably want to keep all of your original pictures in one folder on your computer. If you're using a PC, that folder is called My Pictures. On a Mac it's called Pictures.

Each time you download pictures from your camera to your computer, you can opt to create a folder inside your Pictures or My Pictures folder with the name of the place where the pictures were taken. For example, I took a Caribbean cruise in 2008. I took pictures at each port I visited. When I got back from the port, I downloaded my pictures into a folder named Caribbean inside my folder for 2008 (which is in my Pictures folder). I added a folder inside the Caribbean folder and downloaded the images into it for each port I visited. When I got home, my pictures were organized as shown in Figure 1.7.

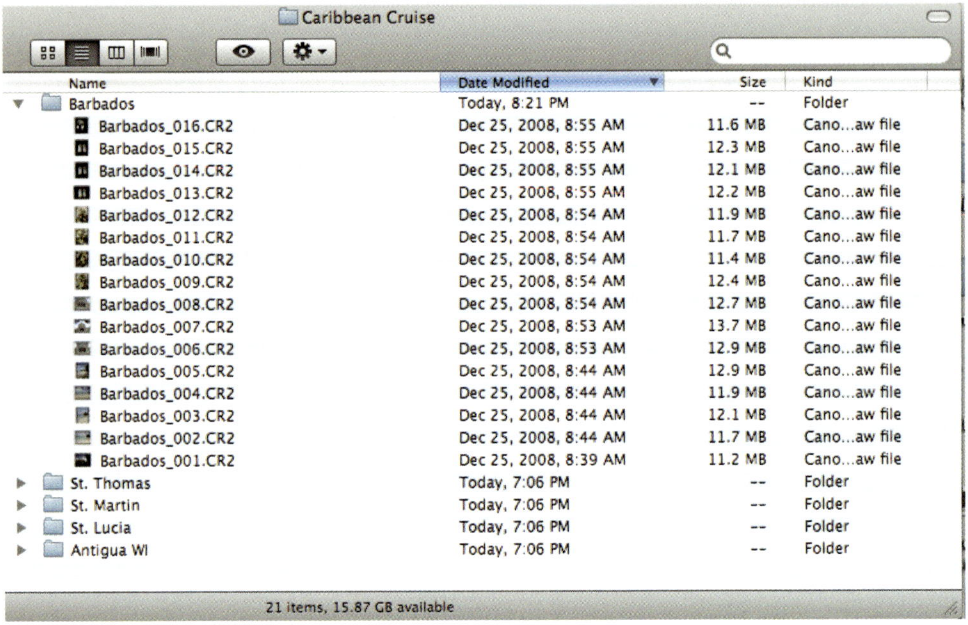

Figure 1.7 The organization of my Caribbean cruise images.

Windows Vista and XP let you rename files with a common name and sequential numbers by batch-renaming files. In Mac OS X, you can rename files using the Automator application.

To rename files in Windows, navigate to the folder with the files you want to rename in My Computer, select the files (select the first file, hold down the Shift key, and then click on the last file) and choose File > Rename. Type in a new name for the first file in the folder and press Enter. To undo the change, press Ctrl+V.

To rename files on a Mac, you use the Automator (see Figure 1.8), which is a bit trickier, but once you get the hang of it, it's a cinch. First you open the Automator. A window will come up, giving you several options. Choose Custom. You'll now see the window in which you build a workflow. (It sounds dreadfully painful, but it's actually fun after you see how it works.) There's a huge selection of commands from which to choose. You are going to pick three, one by one, and click and drag each from the right side of the window to the blank space on the left side of the window. The first one you'll choose is Get Specified Finder Items. The second is Sort Finder Items, and the third is Rename Finder Items.

Next, click on Add in Get Specified Finder Items. A navigation menu will come up, in which you navigate to the images whose filenames you want to change. While holding down the Shift key, click on the first and last files. Click on Add. Select the same settings for each action as you see in Figure 1.8 except for New Name. For New Name, type in the name you want for the file list.

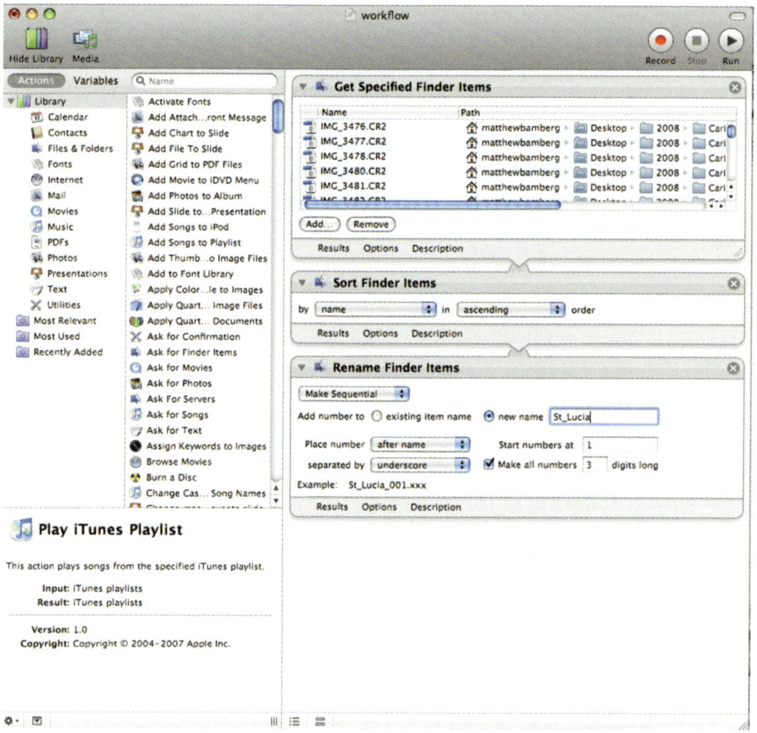

Figure 1.8 This is how your workflow should look to change filenames on a Mac.

In Figure 1.8 I chose St_Lucia because that's the port I visited on the Caribbean cruise. Finally, click Run at the top of the window. Your files' names will now be changed.

NOTE

Other programs, such as Picasa, also let you rename files quickly and easily. (See the "Managing Your Photos in Picasa" section.)

WHAT ABOUT STORING PRINTS?

If you want to make it in the on-the-ground photography world, you're going to need to know how to both store and present your print photographs. First, let's begin with the question of what is the best way to store your photos. This question can be dicey when it comes to the technology that is used today for photo storage. The best way to keep your photos for generations is to have them printed (see "Outsourcing Your Printing" in Chapter 4) or to print them yourself. (For printing tips, see the ideas in Chapter 4.)

Safeguarding prints so they last more than a lifetime is more than just throwing them into a shoebox and shuffling though them when you want to use some. Cardboard boxes contain acid and lignin (a complex polymer), which can cause your photos to yellow and deteriorate over time. If you do choose a box, there are acid- and lignin-free boxes you can buy online. There are compartmentalized boxes so that you can divide up your photos by category. Get Smart Products has boxes of various sizes up to 22×30 inches.

You have to be careful when you store prints in photo albums and binders, too. The best albums to get are ring-binder notebooks with archival-quality polypropylene photo pages.

Last, but most important, are the presentation tools you'll need to show off your photographs to galleries and other venues. There are presentation portfolio cases and portfolio books for displaying your photos that you can buy on the Internet. (One such place is portfolios-and-art-cases.com.) Each portfolio usually comes with 10 individual page archival protectors, which can hold 20 photographs (one photograph on each side). You can also buy extra page protectors if you need more.

Managing Your Photos in iPhoto

When I use iPhoto, the first thing I want to do is import my image files to my iPhoto library. Because I've already put my images in the Pictures file of my Mac, iPhoto can take those pictures and put them in its Library if I select File > Import to Library.

NOTE

You can also download your pictures directly from your camera into iPhoto.

When you move pictures from your computer (not your camera) into iPhoto, iPhoto will make a copy and a thumbnail of the picture. The copy and thumbnail will be put into an iPhoto Library. The original will remain where you put it on your computer. When you download images into iPhoto from your camera, the photos go directly into the iPhoto Library with no copies anywhere else on your computer.

NOTE

When you're importing folders into iPhoto, iPhoto will make an album with the same filename as the folder on your computer.

Creating a new album is a snap. You can create one by clicking on the + sign on the bottom of the window or by selecting File > New Folder. Once you create a new album, you can click and drag pictures from the right side of the window onto the album icon on the left side of the window. When you do this, iPhoto will duplicate a new thumbnail of the picture so it shows up in the new album. The thumbnail of the original will remain in place.

The next thing you'll want to know about iPhoto is what the Smart Albums are all about. Suppose I have a group of random images that I pulled from my external hard drive that are not organized. I want them organized by the year I took them. Since most of them (all the ones I downloaded from my camera) are dated with internal scripts, iPhoto will be able to arrange them by date. To do this, I need to use a Smart Album.

Say, for example, I want to find all the images from 2008. I'd make a Smart Album (File > New Smart Album) whose search criterion is a date that is after 12/31/2007 and before 1/1/2009. Figure 1.9 shows the dialog box with this info. All files with a capture date (digital cameras) or a created date (scanned) in that year will be in the 2008 folder after I click OK in the New Smart Album box.

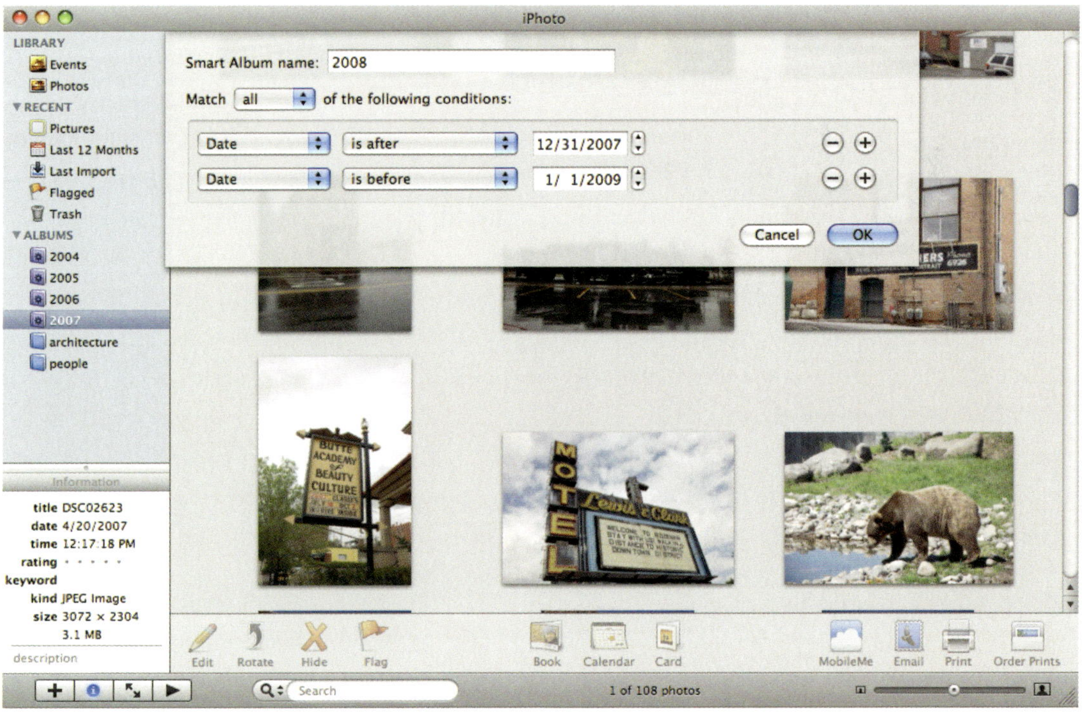

Figure 1.9 You can create an album for any time period in iPhoto.

Make sure you include some info about your photo (title, date, time, rating, and keywords) in the Information box at the bottom left of the iPhoto window. iPhoto uses this information to categorize your image files.

You can also create Smart Albums by words from the text you've included in your photo descriptions in the Information box. The Smart Albums can then be images with any, some, or all of the following specifications: dates, events, keywords, filenames, your ratings of the photographs, and/or any aperture or shutter speed you shot at.

Oh, and if you make a mistake with an album, you can delete it by using Photos > Delete Album.

Managing Your Photos in Picasa

Do you have photos that are everywhere on your computer—so many places that you can't seem to find what you want? If that describes you, the best solution for viewing your photos is Google's Picasa. It's a program you download onto your computer that automatically scans your hard drive for folders with images in them, sorts them by date (or other parameters), and displays them in a window on your computer. To get the program, go to picasa.google.com. In this photo-use idea, I'll go over how to use Picasa to manage your photos. In the next photo-use idea, I'll explain how to edit your photos in Picasa. In Chapter 2, I'll go over how to share your photos using Picasa web albums, an online platform that works in tandem with Picasa.

If you look at Figure 1.10, you'll see that Picasa lists folders handily by the date they were created, listing the most recent folders first. The program can categorize the folders/pictures by the year they were taken, listing the most recent year first. The contents of folders can be sorted by name or by size (Folder > Sort By). In the figure, you see the list of folders in a frame on the left side of the window and the images in that folder on the right. You can click and drag one or more photos from the right frame and put them into any folder on the left. Unlike in iPhoto, when you move an image from one folder to another, it is eliminated in the folder that you're moving it from and inserted into the new folder. The image also will be moved on your computer. If you want to delete an image, you select it in the right frame and press the Delete key. You can select more than one photo by holding down the Apple key on a Mac or the Ctrl key on a PC. You can also move photos into an Album in Picasa (File > New Album). When you do, your photo is copied to the album, and the original remains where it was.

Picasa gives you some great info about your pictures and/or folders. For images, it gives you the name of the image, the date it was created, and its size in pixels. For folders, it gives you a range of dates from the date the first image was created to the date the last image was created. You can also search images by typing the name of the file or image into the Search field (that has the magnifying glass in it) at the very top right of the Picasa window.

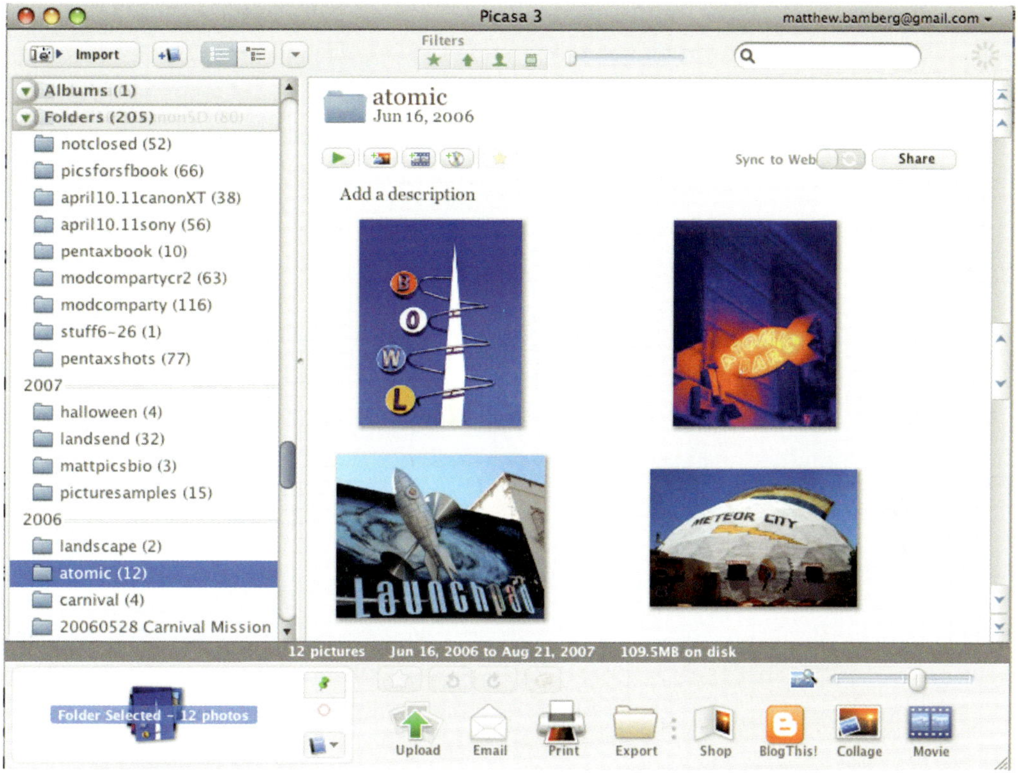

Figure 1.10 Click and drag a photo from the left frame into a folder on the right.

Picasa has a face recognition system where the program can find all the pictures of people you have in a folder. If a folder has images of people in it, a face button will appear among the other buttons right under the picture of the folder and the folder name. When you click on the face, all of the images with faces on them will appear.

There's a lot more Picasa can do, too, especially when you include its online partner, Picasa Web Albums. You'll notice a Sync to Web button (under where it says Save to Disk) in Picasa in the top-right part of the window. When you click that, everything you do will be put online into Picasa Web Albums as you do it. To get set up with Picasa Web Albums, see Chapter 2, "Sharing Your Photos Online."

NOTE

You can export copies of a picture (this converts all copies to JPEGs with a choice of resolutions) to other folders on your computer using the Export button at the bottom of the window. You have the option of putting a watermark on the photo when you do this.

Finally, you can create collages and slideshows with images from any one folder. To make a collage, see Chapter 3. To create and save a slideshow movie, see Chapter 12, "Working with Slideshows." If you're in a hurry, move your cursor over the rest of the buttons under the folder name to get a description of what the button will do. Then you can get started with slideshows and collages.

Using Image Processing Programs to Tweak Your Photos

There are dozens of image processing programs in which you can tweak your photographs to make them look better or change them altogether. There are many options for minor tweaks within the platforms of online photo hosting sites. And you can purchase more sophisticated image processing programs. The most popular are Photoshop and Photoshop Elements. Finally, there is one high-end program you can download from the Internet for free, called GIMP.

Flickr

On Flickr, there is an Edit option in a list of options that spreads across the top of each photo. The first time you click on it, you find out that Flickr has partnered with Picnik so that Flickr users can edit their photos online. Once you go through the hoops of approving the Flickr/Picnik agreement, you're on your way to using some nifty editing tools. Figure 1.11 shows the tools you can use to tweak your photos.

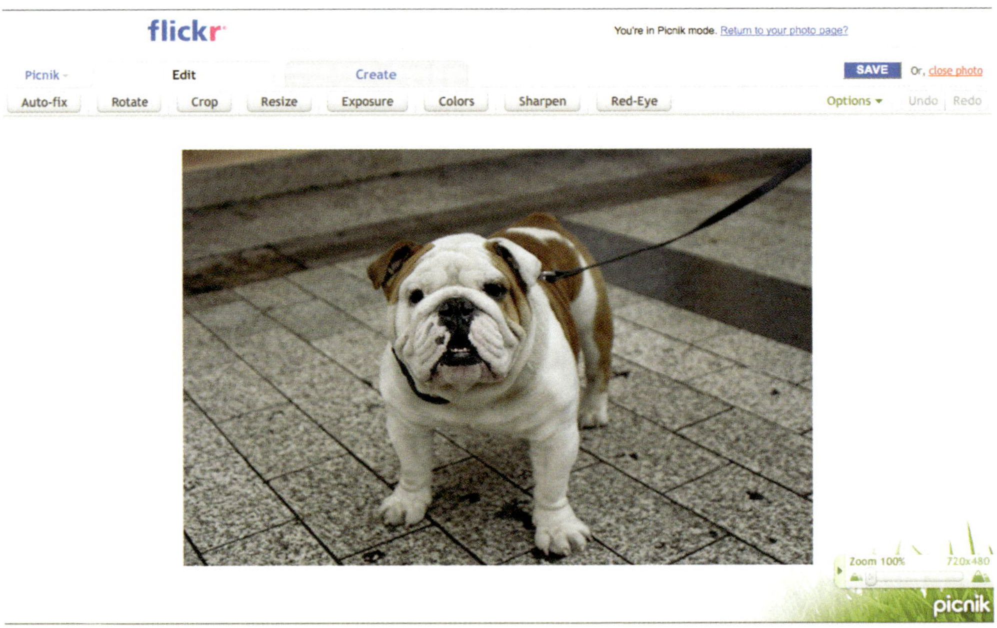

Figure 1.11 Flickr has teamed up with Picnik to let you edit your photos online.

Picasa

When you double-click on a photo in Picasa, a window appears with a host of editing options (see Figure 1.12). There are three tabs you can choose from for your editing options—Basic Fixes, Tuning, and Effects. When you click on the Basic Fixes tab, there are numerous buttons —some of which take you to new menus for the adjustments—to crop, straighten, adjust red eye, adjust auto contrast/color, and retouch. In the Tuning tab, there are sliders you can use to adjust the fill light, highlights, shadows, and color temperature, as well as a color picker, which changes the colors of your image when you click on it. Finally, there's the Effects tab, where you can apply a variety of effects, from sharpening your photo to giving it a sepia tone.

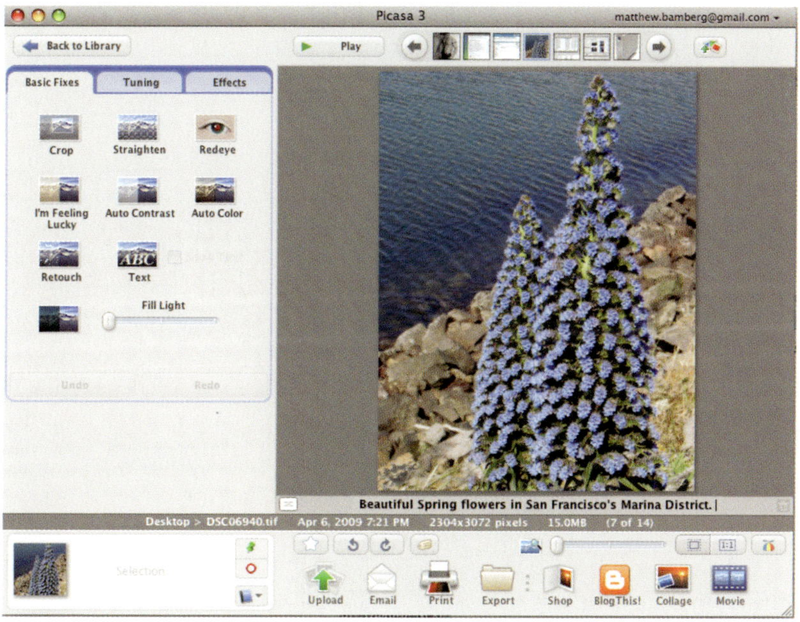

Figure 1.12 Picasa has a variety of editing options.

Photoshop/Photoshop Elements

Photoshop and Elements (for short) have to be the two most popular image processing programs around. If you're using these programs, it's likely you have a dSLR (*digital Single Lens Reflex*) camera, and you are taking pictures in Camera Raw format. Camera Raw is a different format from JPEG and TIFF in that it stores extra information about the picture. The format allows you to "develop" the file before you open it in Photoshop or Elements. That is, you tweak the image in a kind of pre-processing before you put it in either Photoshop or Elements.

Most of the time, you'll find that tweaking using the sliders in the Camera Raw dialog box is all you have to do to process the image. Figure 1.13 shows you what the Camera Raw dialog box looks like. Another good thing about Camera Raw is that you can always revert the image back to the way it was, because you really never save the file outright (like you would a JPEG or TIFF file)—you just save all the data that was used to take the picture.

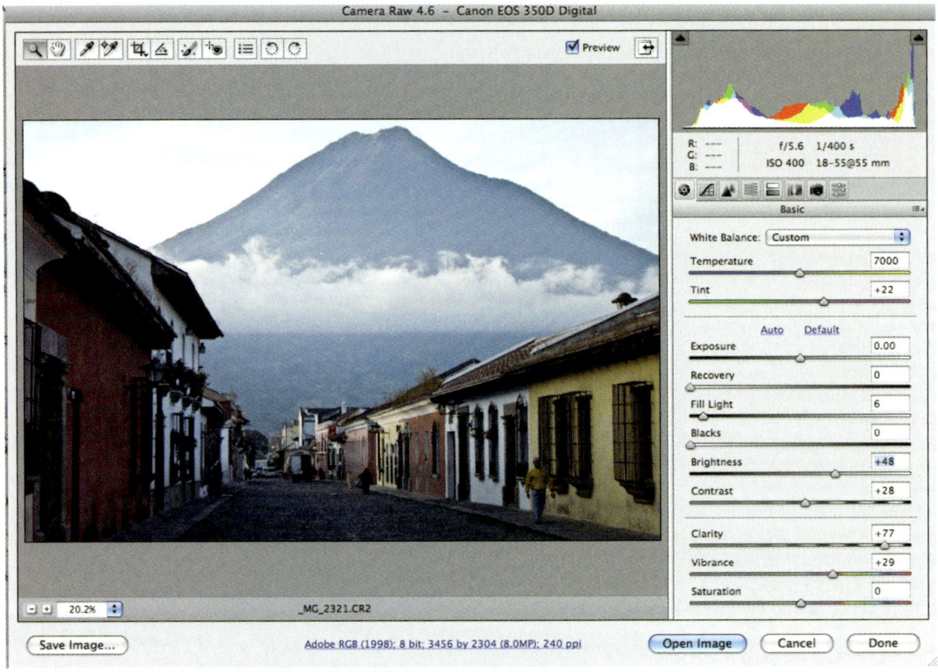

Figure 1.13 The Camera Raw window in Photoshop.

> **NOTE**
>
> If you don't need custom CMYK separations, 16-bit support, animation, slice exports, and other high-end options that perhaps you haven't even heard of, go with Photoshop Elements instead of Photoshop. It will probably have everything you need for your post-processing needs (including the Camera Raw window). It's cheaper, too. Elements is about $99, and Photoshop is about $650.

GIMP

The best thing about GIMP is that it's free. How cool is that? You can download it at www.gimp.org/downloads. It's not a bad program, either. It can do most things Photoshop can do, but the interface is a bit more complex than that of either Photoshop or Elements.

Figure 1.14 shows you the Camera Raw dialog box for GIMP. The options are a bit ambiguous, as shown in the figure, but if you slide your cursor over any button, there's pop-up text to tell you what it will do.

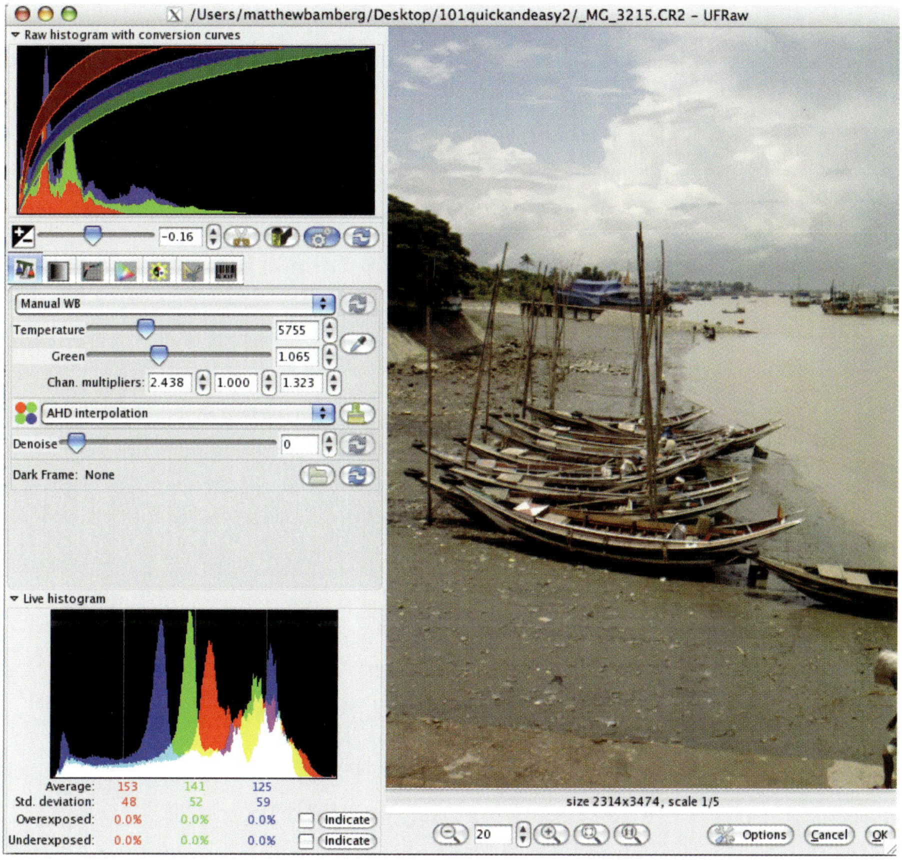

Figure 1.14 The GIMP Camera Raw dialog box.

Many photo management programs have photo editing built into them. Many use slider and button features with which to tweak hue/saturation, exposure, exposure compensation, and most options to change photos to black and white or sepia tones. The possibilities for tweaking your photos appear to be endless. At blibs.com, you can create animation and reflections in your photos. In iPhoto (for Mac), you can use editing options (click on the pencil at the bottom of the window), such as crop, straighten, enhance, red eye, and effects, and sliders to adjust exposure, highlights/shadows, and hue/saturation. There are also controls for noise reduction and special effects. Finally, there's Windows Live, a free program for Windows in which you can crop, fix light levels, and adjust colors. Download it from download.live.com/photogallery.

Resizing Your Photos for Different Uses

Whether you want to print out a wall-sized photo (a full-resolution photo or an enlarged photo) or insert a thumbnail (a very small photo around 8 KB) into a website, resizing the photo probably will be part of the job. Most of the time when you resize, you'll want to make a picture smaller. A good size to make a picture for the Internet is from 50 to 150 KB (as a JPEG file). The Internet only handles JPEG, GIF, and PNG files; most of the time, JPEGs are the name of the game for uploading files to websites.

If you try to make a picture bigger, it's best to get a program that works with Photoshop to do the job. Photoshop alone doesn't do a great job with this task. There's a Photoshop plug-in program called Genuine Fractals by onOne Software that does a great job of enlarging photos.

If you're going to print using a workflow in Photoshop/Photoshop Elements, print from a TIFF file of about 24 MB. (Resolution and image size are used to calculate file size. Don't go under 200 dpi with the image size you want. If it goes under 200 dpi, you won't get a sharp print at the image size you want. You'll have to make your image smaller.) Make sure the size is a bit smaller than the paper on which you are printing. If you try to print larger-size files, the processing time for a consumer-type computer will be lengthy, and the photo won't look that much different than when it's printed at about 24 MB.

Creating a workflow means tweaking the image you see on the monitor to closely match the one you'll see in print. There are entire books on workflow for Photoshop. One such book is *Photoshop CS4 Workflow: The Digital Photographer's Guide* (Sybex, 2008). If you don't want to use a workflow (if you're not making gallery-quality prints), and you want to print out photos, most printers/image processing software will let you do this automatically, after you choose from an assortment of paper options and print qualities in the Print dialog box.

For the purposes of this book, we'll work in inches when thinking about resizing a photo. To resize in Photoshop, you navigate to Image > Image Size (File > Resize > Image Size in Elements). A dialog box such as the one you see in Figure 1.15 will come up.

The most important box to check or uncheck in this dialog box is Resample Image. When Resample Image isn't checked, you can change the values of Width, Height, or Resolution, and Photoshop/Elements will proportion the photo accordingly without changing the file size (the number you see right next to where it says Pixel Dimensions at the top of the box). When Resample Image *is* checked, Photoshop will resize the image according to the values that you've put in for the width and height of the document size. When Resample is checked, the photo's file size will change. Because most of the time you'll want to make a file smaller, you'll choose Bicubic Sharper. The values will be up to you. Just remember that the resolution for most web photographs is 72 pixels/inch. For most print jobs, you'll want a resolution from 200 to 300 pixels/inch.

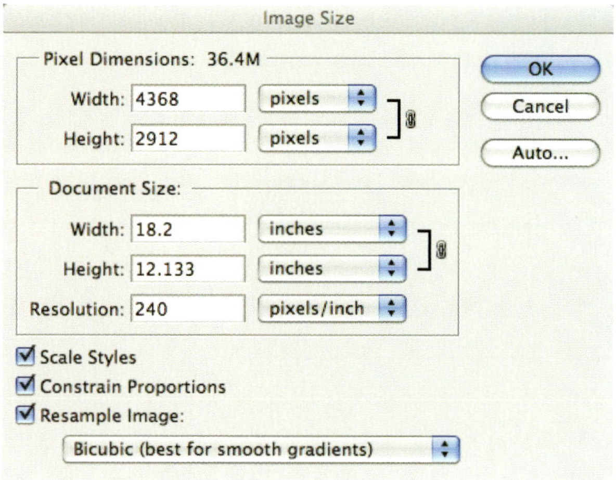

Figure 1.15 The Image Size dialog box.

Finally, Scale Styles has to do with layer styles. This setting, checked or unchecked, will have no effect on your resizing.

When you're working with programs other than Photoshop/Elements, resizing is a similar process. For example, to resize photos in iPhoto, you navigate to File > Export. The Export Photos dialog box will come up. If you open the Kind drop-down menu, you'll have a choice of photo formats. Navigate to JPEG and choose Small if you're going to use the images on the Internet or Full Size if you are going to print them. You have choices for the quality and size for exporting your files. The smallest file you can make is about 8 KB—that's if you choose a small, low-quality photo. The sizes go up from there.

Using a Memory Card Reader to Transfer Photos

There are a couple of ways to share photos by moving them from one electronic device to another. One of the most common ways people move pictures from their camera to their computer is by connecting the two directly using a USB cable. The images move very slowly through this connection, especially if the files are large (such as a Raw photo from a 12-MP camera). A faster way would be to use a memory card reader. Most digital cameras (and some cell phones; see the upcoming "From Phone to Computer" sidebar) have memory cards (also called *SD* cards or *CompactFlash* cards) that you can remove from the device. A memory card reader can read a memory card once the reader is connected to a computer. The reader reads files quickly, which means the transfers are fast—faster than if just a USB cable was connected from the camera to the computer.

To use a memory card reader, you first have to take it out of the device you want to be read. I'll use an example of a Canon dSLR camera. You would first have to turn off the camera. Then push on the arrow on the right side of the camera to open the compartment where the memory card is located. You take out the card by pushing gently on it and then pulling it out. Next, you insert the memory card into the memory card reader (see Figure 1.16). Finally, you connect the reader to the USB port of your computer. The installed software on your computer usually detects the camera, and a window will pop up on your computer, asking whether you want to download the images. Or the camera may appear on your desktop as a mass storage device, enabling you to click and drag the files to your computer.

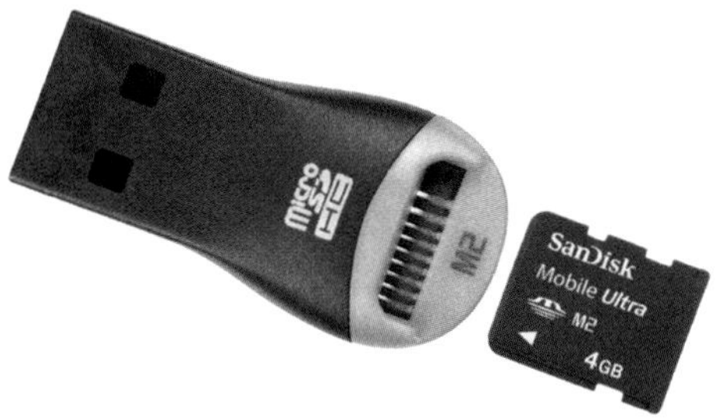

Figure 1.16 Using a memory card reader is a fast way to get photos from one device to another.

Sometimes you'll want to move photos from one computer to another. You can use a USB flash drive for this. A USB flash drive should not be confused with an SD or a CompactFlash card, which is a memory card for a camera. The USB flash drive is a removable and rewritable device weighing less than 2 ounces (56g), with storage capacities that run from 64 MB to 32 GB or more.

To move images from one computer to another on a Mac, all you do is insert the flash drive into the USB port of one computer, double-click on the drive icon that comes up, and click and drag the images or folders you want into the drive window that comes up.

In Windows, after the flash drive is inserted into the USB port, copy the images or folders by right-clicking on them and selecting Copy. Then right-click on the flash drive and select Paste.

To dismount the drive on a Mac, drag the drive icon to the Trash. In Windows, right-click on the flash drive and then select Safely Remove USB Mass Storage Device.

Next, you move the flash drive to the other computer and insert it into the USB port. When the drive comes up on this computer, you can double-click on it (select Open when prompted in Windows) and then click and drag the images to the desktop. Finally, dismount the flash drive as described in the preceding paragraph.

NOTE

After you remove the USB flash drive from your computer, put it in its "house"—a place where it's stored—so you won't lose it.

FROM PHONE TO COMPUTER

You can connect most cell phones to your computer with a USB cable. After you connect your phone to the computer with a USB cord, a disk drive will come up on your desktop. If you double-click on the disk drive (if it's a Blackberry phone, the folder will say Blackberry), you'll find the Pictures folder inside. To move the pictures, all you do is select them from the Pictures folder and click and drag them to the desktop. Another way to move your images from your cell phone to your computer is to use a memory card reader.

Note, though, that some cell phones disable the feature that enables you to move images from the phone to your computer. They'd rather have you email them so they can charge you for sending the emails.

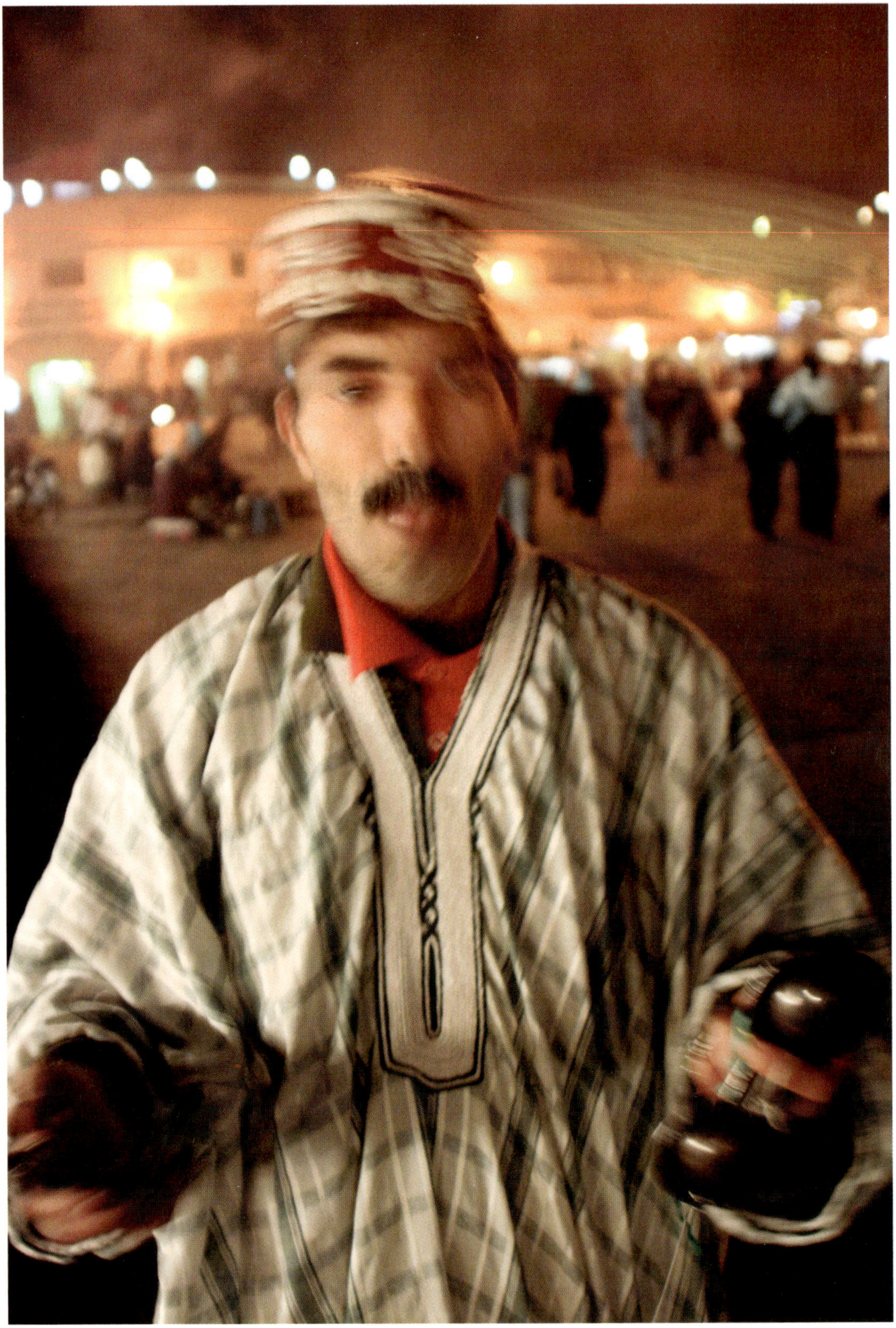

Chapter 2
Sharing Your Photos Online

Free is definitely the name of the game when it comes to posting and sharing your photos online. Nowhere in the world will you find so much that's free as you do in cyberspace. There are a slew of options for sharing your precious moments or your adroit photography skills with others. Photo sharing and social networking sites can host hundreds of your photos. Some have photo editors; others have slideshows. Each site has its own limits on file size and number of photos you can upload, as well as access options for connecting with other Internet sites. Navigating these sites can be tricky. This chapter spells out all the bells and whistles of managing your photos on different photo sharing and social networking platforms.

Posting and Sharing at Flickr

How easy is it to join and post to Flickr? Well, let's see…

1. Go to www.flickr.com and click on Create Your Account.
2. Sign up for a Yahoo! account (it's free) or sign in to Yahoo!
3. Click on Create a New Account.
4. Click on Upload Photos and Video.
5. Click on Choose Photos and Videos.
6. In the window that appears, navigate to the folder where your photos are.
7. While holding down the Shift key, you can select contiguous images to upload. To upload non-contiguous images, hold down the Command (Mac) or Ctrl (Windows) key while selecting.
8. Click on Select.
9. Click on Upload Photos and Videos.

After you've uploaded your photos, you can either sign out or add descriptions by clicking on the prompt: Next, Add a Description, Perhaps? If you select Add Descriptions, you'll also be asked for titles, descriptions, and tags.

When you decide to come back to Flickr for some more uploads or to find friends to share your photos with, you'll have to log in again using your Yahoo! ID and password. When you do, you'll be taken to your homepage. On that page you have options to upload photos, or you can just view, organize, and share the ones you have.

To view your photos, you can click on Your Photostream. After you do, your images will come up (see Figure 2.1). You have myriad choices here. You can add or change captions or delete photos.

To change or add tags and to see editing options, you have to click on a photo. You'll be taken to a new window with only one photo in it (the one you clicked on). Above the photo, there is a host of options for editing the photo or changing/adding information about it. To the right of the photo, there are options to add, change, or delete a tag, to make the photo public or private, and to add a map to your photo (which is really cool). When you click on one of these options, a new dialog window comes up in which you can make your choices.

At the top of the window, below where it says Your Photostream, there are options for Sets, Tags, Archives, Favorites, Popular, and Profile.

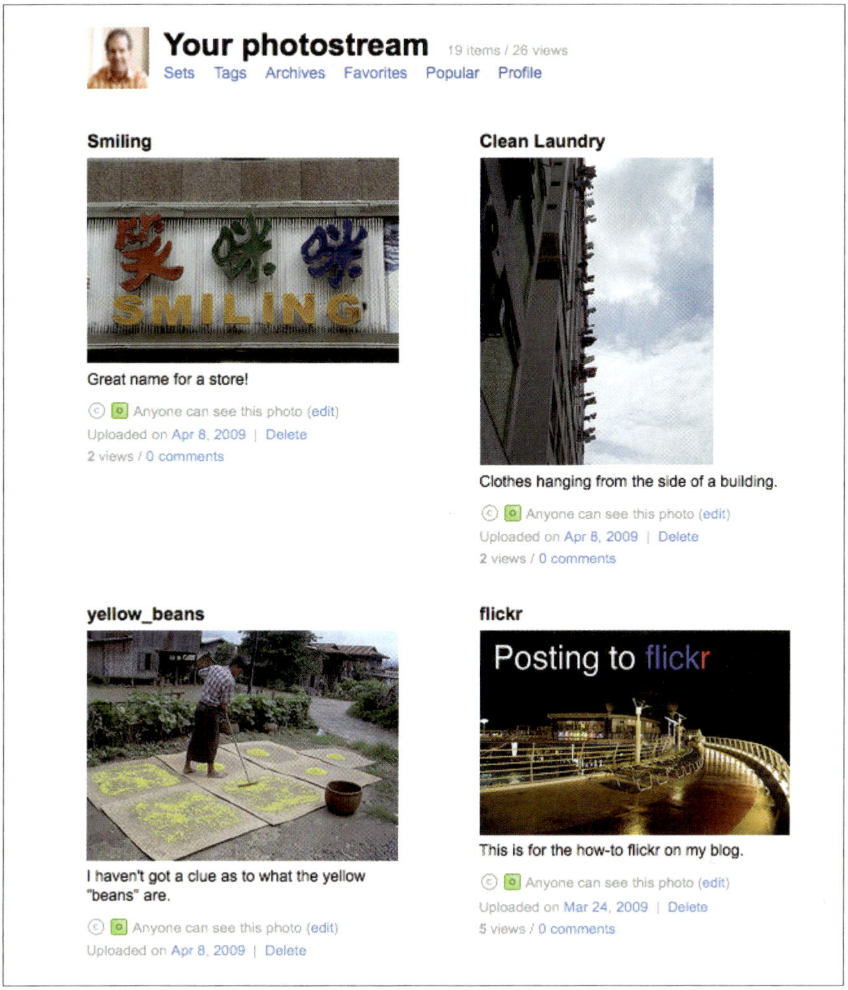

Figure 2.1 Flickr calls your uploaded photos a *photostream.*

When you click Organize (at the top of the window with Home, You, Contacts, Groups, and Explore—and the Search box, just under the Flickr logo), look at the tabs at the top of the window (Batch, Organize, Sets, Groups, Map). Each of these choices helps you manage your files. For example, if you have created a set already, you will find it by clicking on the tab for Sets.

To share photos, you can add friends and join groups. Adding friends to Flickr is easy. You can find people you know by typing their name into the People Search (Contacts > People Search on your homepage). You can invite friends by filling out email forms (Contacts > Invite Your Friends). You'll get a history of your friends pending and accepted (Contacts > Invite History). You can even extend your hand to make friends by leaving comments on other people's photos.

To find photos you like, search by tag words. The Search box is at the top-right part of the window on every Flickr page. Try typing in the word "retro," and hundreds of thousands of images will come up that people have tagged with that name. For more about tagging your photos, see the upcoming "Tagging Your Photos" sidebar.

Joining a group on Flickr is a cinch, too. You can search for groups just like you do people and photos. Just choose Groups > Search for a Group. You can reach out to your groups by joining and then posting photos to their pages. Simply click on Add Photos next to where it says Group Pool.

Finally, you can perform the same action on more than one photo by using Flickr's Batch system (Organize > All Your Content). To perform an action on a batch of photos, just click and drag from the bottom of the window into the batch processing area. There, you can edit titles, tags, and descriptions (Edit > Titles, Tags, and Descriptions), rotate (Edit > Rotate), and/or delete photos (Edit > Delete).

NOTE

Resize your photos before uploading to Flickr—you're only allotted a certain amount of upload space per month.

For photo sizes that Flickr accepts, see the "Storing Your Photos Online" section in Chapter 1. For editing options in Flickr, see the "Using Image Processing Programs to Tweak Your Photos" section in Chapter 1.

TAGGING YOUR PHOTOS

Tags—or keywords that you associate with a photo or a blog post—can help others to find and view your stuff. Most photo sharing sites and blogs will ask you to type in tags for a picture or post. Tags can be terms such as *architecture*, *President Obama*, *scandals*, *animals*, *bears*...well, just about any word or word string you can think of. For example, if you have uploaded a picture of a live turkey on a photo sharing site, you can type in words associated with the turkey, such as *turkey*, *live turkey*, *bird*, *Thanksgiving*, and so on. Flickr lets you provide up to 75 tags for any one picture you upload. Tags also can help your picture and/or blog post get picked up by Google. If you have a good picture of a turkey, there's a chance that when someone types "turkey" into Google, your picture will come up.

Sharing Using Picasa and Picasa Web Albums

In Chapter 1 we talked about managing your photos on your computer using Picasa. Google has another program—Picasa Web Albums—that lets you share your photos online. Once you're signed into Google, you can send your photos by email from Picasa or from Picasa Web Albums. The program works with both Picasa and iPhoto. In order to share photos online with Picasa Web Albums, you have to create a Google account. To do that, go to www.picasaweb.google.com. You'll see a place to register on the right side of the window, where there's a button to create an account.

I can remember my surprise the first time I opened Picasa Web Albums. As a member of Blogger (a blog-building site that you must register with Google to use), my images from my blog were already put into Picasa Web Albums without my being aware of it. More about blogging in Chapter 6, "Photo Blog Heaven."

The first thing you want to remember when using Picasa Web Albums is that clicking on the tab My Photos (see the top of the window shown in Figure 2.2) will take you to your albums that are online.

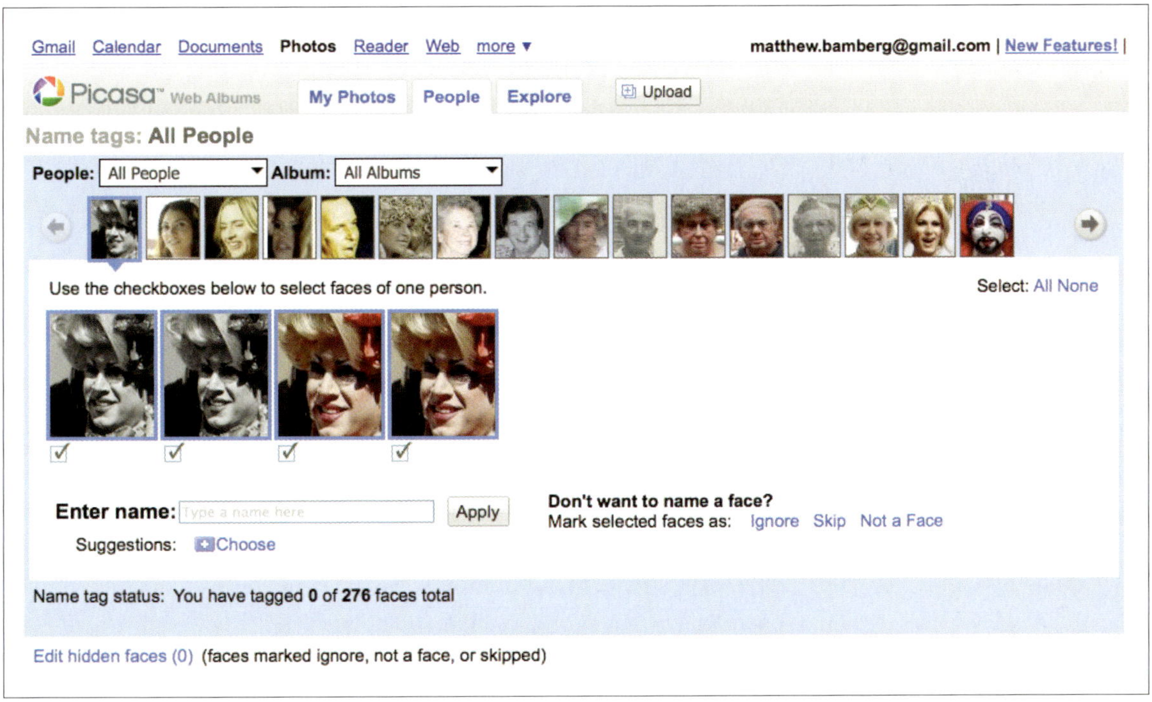

Figure 2.2 Picasa Web Albums can locate all the people in your pictures and show them to you so you can name them.

If you have pictures on your computer that you want to put into Picasa Web Albums, you can do it automatically from Picasa using the Sync to Web feature in the manner described in the "Managing Your Photos in Picasa" section in Chapter 1. If you want to do it manually, you must have Picasa installed on your computer. In that program, you click on the Upload button that appears at the bottom of the window after you open the program. The Upload to Web Albums window will appear, where you can select options from two drop-down menus.

On the Your Photos homepage are image links to all your albums. When you click on an album, you see the pictures that are in it; when you click on one of those pictures, you see the picture enlarged. You can perform actions on the page where the pictures in an album are displayed or where an individual picture is displayed. If you want to delete a Picasa Web Album, you click on the album on your homepage (you'll have all the pictures in the album shown) and choose Edit > Delete Album to get rid of all the pictures in it. To email a link to the pictures in the album to someone, you click on the button that says Share and fill in the email address that you want the link sent to in the email that appears. To delete or send a picture, click on one of the pictures shown in the album. You'll get a window with the enlarged picture inside. Choose Edit > Delete to get rid of the picture. Choose Share to email the image.

To set up Picasa Web Albums' face-recognition technology and to share the people the technology finds, click on Settings. Scroll down to where it says Turn Name Tags On. Also, make sure the Hide Name Tags in My Public Albums by Default option is not checked. Then click on Save Settings. Now, if you click on the People tab on the homepage, Picasa will locate all the pictures of people in your albums. From there, you can name the people who are in the pictures and send those people emails of the pictures.

Posting and Sharing at Shutterfly

In terms of storing your photos, Shutterfly has got to be one of the best photo hosting sites around because there are no restrictions on the amount or size of the photos you upload. Shutterfly makes its money by selling calendars, cards, photo books, and other items that contain your pictures in their online store. First, you have to sign up at the site. It's easy—just enter your name, email address, and password, and then you confirm by an email that is sent to you. After you sign in, the site is neatly laid out with the main links running across the homepage of the site. Clicking on My Shutterfly will always bring you back to your homepage.

The first thing you probably want to do in Shutterfly is upload pictures. To do this, just click on My Pictures. If you have all the photos you want to upload in one folder on your computer, you can navigate to it after clicking on the Upload button. If you want all the files in a folder to be uploaded to Shutterfly, hold the Shift key and click on the first and then the last file to select them all. Figure 2.3 shows the Upload Pictures window.

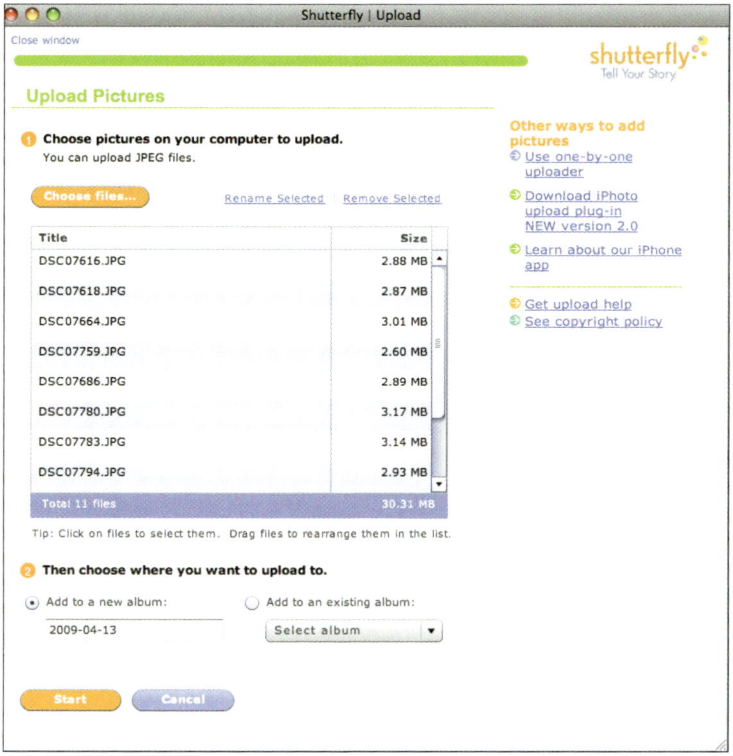

Figure 2.3 You can upload multiple files in Shutterfly.

When I tested Shutterfly, I found that it takes about five minutes to upload 30 MB worth of files. Not bad for 11 high-res photos!

After you upload, the album appears in the interactive window on the My Pictures page with the date it was uploaded. Double-click on the album, and you'll get all your pictures displayed in the interactive window (see Figure 2.4). You can move any of them around (or delete them) by moving your cursor over them and clicking on the downward-pointing arrow to the right of the filename. (A drop-down menu gives you an assortment of choices for what you want to do with the file/album/picture.) You can also move any of your pictures around by clicking and dragging them where you want (even into the folders in the left frame). Finally, if you click on the picture name, you can input info such as a description of the image.

To email pictures, just select the ones you want and click on the Share button. You get two options after clicking the Share button—Email These Pictures and Add to My Share Site. If you choose to email them, an email comes up for you to send them to whomever you want. If you choose Add to Share Site, you'll have to have one built (which Shutterfly lets you do). When you're finished emailing, you'll find that you can post the images to a number of social networking sites, blogger sites, and sites such as www.Digg.com and www.StumbleUpon.com.

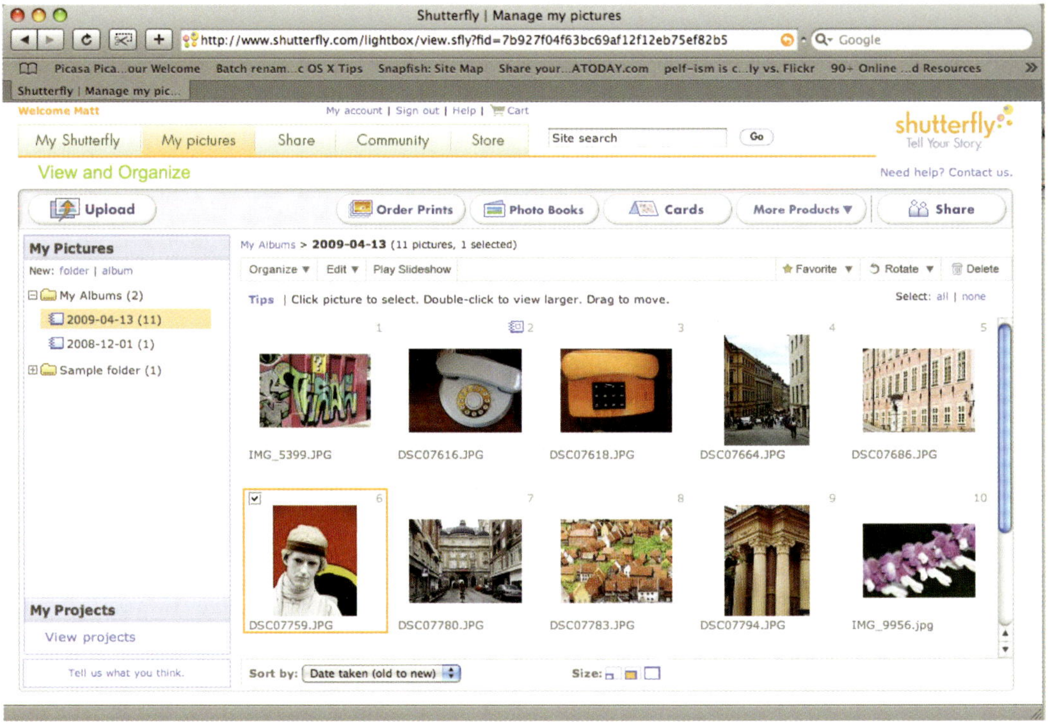

Figure 2.4 The View and Organize window of Shutterfly.

Posting and Sharing at Photobucket

You could call Photobucket the Hollywood of image hosting sites. The first things you might see when you get to the site are the latest pics of Hollywood stars and ads promoting their movies. It's easy to register, though—no need for email confirmation.

> **NOTE**
>
> After you register at Photobucket, you are taken through several windows of special offers. You must scroll down and click on the Skip button to remove the window.

One of the nicest things about Photobucket is that it gives you a URL for every photo (and for albums) you post, so you can copy the URL to other programs. It even gives you HTML code so you can put your picture into blog templates. (You'll learn more about blogs in Chapter 6.)

Also, on your Main Album page (My Albums tab), you have options to share your albums on Facebook, MySpace, and Blogger (among other sites). When you share an album, it will appear on the site as a slideshow. How cool is that?

To upload images, you just click on the Choose Files button, below where it says Upload Images & Video. There's a drop-down menu next to where it says Reduce To that lists sizes from tiny to 1 MB. Photobucket automatically changes the size of your file when uploading—as close as possible to the specs you provide. If you want to upload more than one image, hold down the Shift key to upload contiguous images; hold down the Command (Mac) or Ctrl (Windows) key for non-contiguous images.

NOTE

As soon as you click Select in the Upload navigation window from which you choose images, your files are uploaded. No ifs, ands, or buts about it.

Just in case if you were wondering where your pictures went, wonder no more. They're added at the bottom of the Main Album webpage window when the upload is complete.

After you upload, you'll get a window where you can type in titles, descriptions, and tags. You can do that right away or go back to it later by clicking the sliding cursor over Albums & Upload and clicking on Tags.

NOTE

The Main Album webpage is also referred to by your username and Main. Click on any of those linked words, and you'll be brought to the Main Album webpage. On most other sites, the Main Album would be called the homepage.

Every new album you create is listed and linked to the pictures inside it on the left side of the Main Album, under the heading Albums. (If you can't see it, click on the arrow next to the word to make the drop-down menu appear.) You can add new albums where it says Add a New Album on the left side of the window. You can see these options in the left side of the window shown in Figure 2.5.

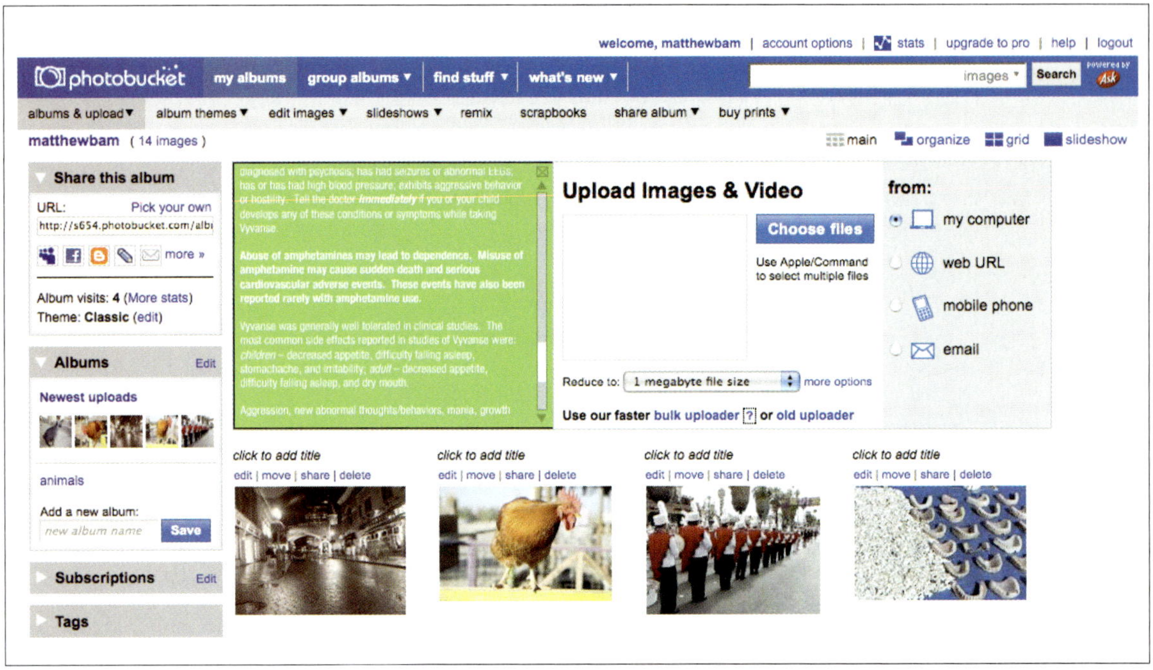

Figure 2.5 This is the Main Album webpage in Photobucket. It's also given your username and sometimes referred to as Main.

Photobucket also has an Album Organizer (to get there, click on the Albums & Upload drop-down menu in the top-right corner of the window and select Album Organizer), which is a pretty nifty package. It's shown in Figure 2.6. You can click and drag your pictures within the right frame to reorder them, or you can put them in different folders by clicking and dragging one or more from the left frame to a folder in the right frame. When you're in the Album Organizer, click on Main to get back to the Main Album.

Photobucket teams with FotoFlexer to provide some pretty sophisticated editing capabilities, which includes a tab for basic editing functions, such as Crop, Resize, and Adjust (saturation/brightness). More elaborate editing features include tabs for Effects, Decorate (Text and Draw are here), Animation, Beautify, Distort, Layers, and Geek.

Last but not least, you can share pictures or albums. As mentioned earlier, you can share your albums with social networking and blogging sites. You can also share your albums by email by clicking on the envelope button under Share this Album. To share a picture, you click on Share above where the Main Album shows the picture. Three tabs at the top of the next window give you a choice of where to send it. You can post to a social networking site or a blog, email it, or get the link code.

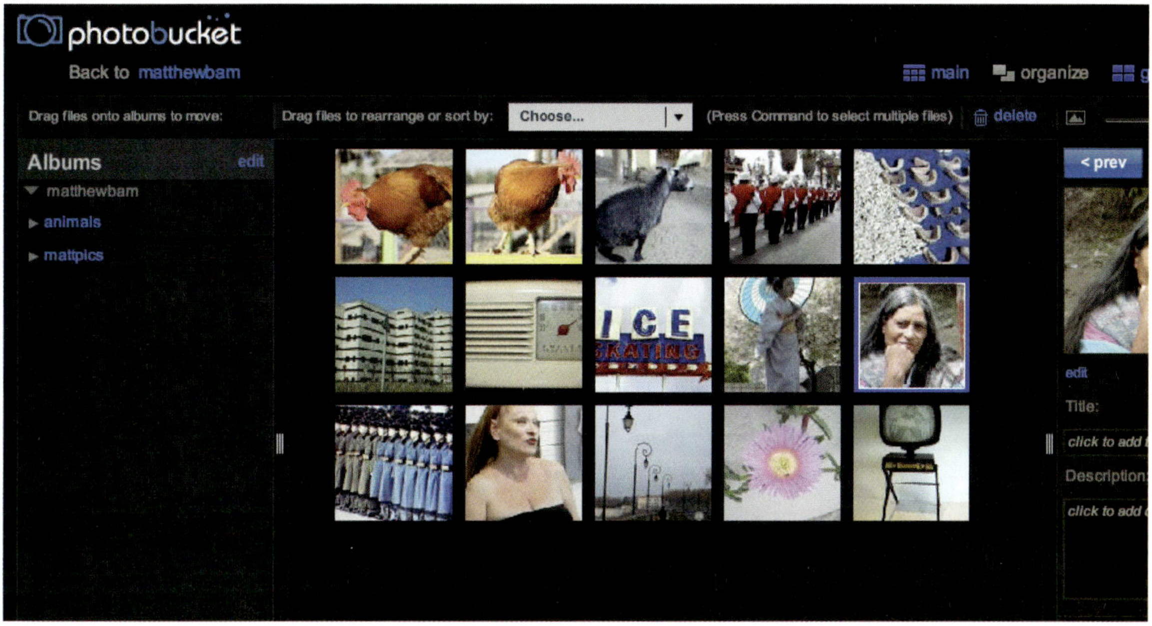

Figure 2.6 You can click and drag pictures to different albums using Photobucket.

Posting and Sharing at ImageShack

If you want a quick place to get a URL for your photo so you can embed the HTML in a program or send someone a link that connects to the picture, ImageShack is the place to go. It's the only image hosting site where you don't have to register in order to upload a photo. All you have to do to post a photo is go to their webpage (www.imageshack.com), click Browse, select the file from your computer in the navigation bar that comes up. Hold down the Shift key to upload contiguous images or the Command (Mac) or Ctrl (Windows) key for non-contiguous images. Click on Host It or Start Upload. You don't even have to put in your email address! After you click Start Upload, the image will upload, and ImageShack will come back with a URL for your image and different HTML codes to post a thumbnail to other websites and forums.

There are advantages to signing up for ImageShack. You can keep track of all the images you upload, and you can delete images. When you sign up for ImageShack, you'll have to check your email confirmation before you can log in. When you log in, you'll be taken directly to the same upload page as you would if you weren't a member. You'll just have your user name listed in the top right of the window. You upload in the same way as you would if you weren't a member. To see all of your images, click on your user name at the top of the upload page.

> **NOTE**
>
> One difference between ImageShack and other photo hosting sites is that it doesn't provide an interactive window to move your image files and folders around.

When you click on My Images on the top menu bar, you'll get to a page where you can perform actions on each of your images (see Figure 2.7). Next to each image is six buttons. The most important ones are the first three. The first one lets you share your photos. The second one lets you enlarge the image. The third one lets you delete it. When you click on the Share button, it takes you to a screen with the URL for sharing the link to your image, as well as other HTML codes you can use to post your image on forums, comments, and other places that use code.

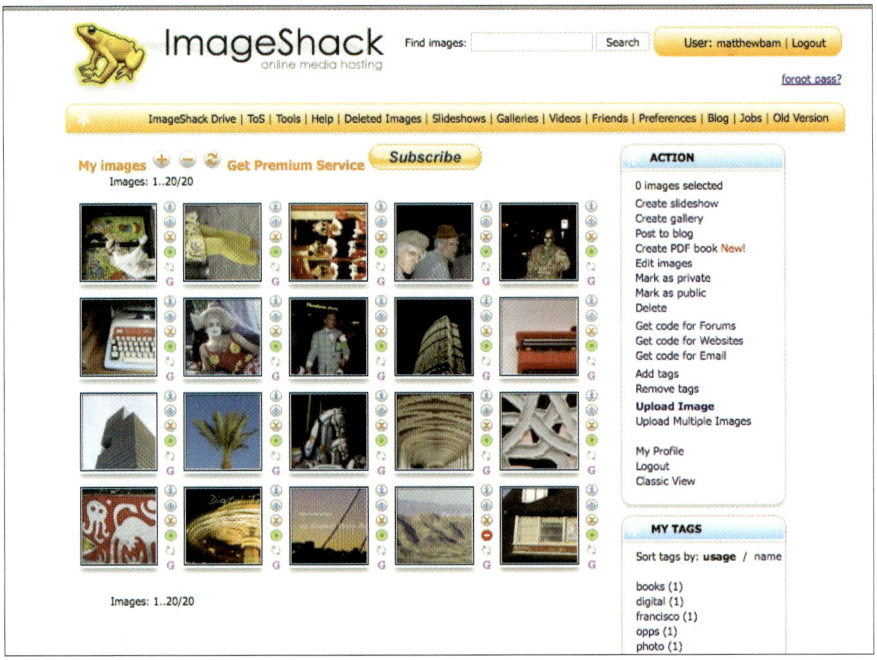

Figure 2.7 You have a lot of choices for what to do with your images on the My Images page.

> **NOTE**
>
> To delete multiple images, select some by clicking on each one and then click Delete in the Action links list to the right of your images.

NOTE

Images are not really deleted on ImageShack; they're still there. To see them, just click on Deleted Images in the top menu bar.

There are more sharing options when you click on the image on the My Images page. Select one or more images and click on Post to Blog on the right side of the page in the Action box. A window will come up. Click on QuickPost (the button that says Post to...). Then choose where you want your image to go from the icons posted in the next window. From there, you'll go from window to window clicking on various prompts (including login information for the site you're posting to) until your images appear on the blog or social networking site of your choice.

Finally, you can create a gallery of images by selecting some on the Action page (the page you get to after clicking on My Images). After you select the images you want to go into the gallery, click on Create Gallery under the Action heading. A prompt will come up stating how many images are selected to go into the gallery. Click on Proceed in that prompt. You'll see thumbnails of your images in the next window. Click on Click Here to Edit Your Gallery. In the next window, enter a title for your gallery and then click on Click to Save Changes. On the right side of the window, you'll get links to share this gallery with others. And, of course, you can share that gallery by proceeding with the prompts after clicking on the Share button.

Creating a MySpace Photo Album

MySpace is a social networking site popular with young people. If you're over 40, Facebook's a better bet. MySpace is a site that many junior high and high school students join, so parents should become familiar with it. Unlike Facebook, the other big social networking site, MySpace gives you a webpage which you can tweak with HTML codes any way you like (as long as you follow the Terms of Service).

MySpace has a click-and-drag module program for maintaining users' Profile pages. The program is called Profile 2.0, and it's the easiest way to deal with MySpace (if you don't want to get into hairy HTML coding to set up your MySpace page). You can see the different modules that make up a Profile page in Figure 2.8.

You have the option of putting a picture to identify yourself on MySpace. MySpace calls this your *default photo*. To insert or update this photo, go to Profile > Customize Profile. Move your cursor over your picture and click the Edit Basic Information icon. (It's a picture of a pencil and paper.) Scroll down to where it says Photos. You'll see the photos you have displayed there.

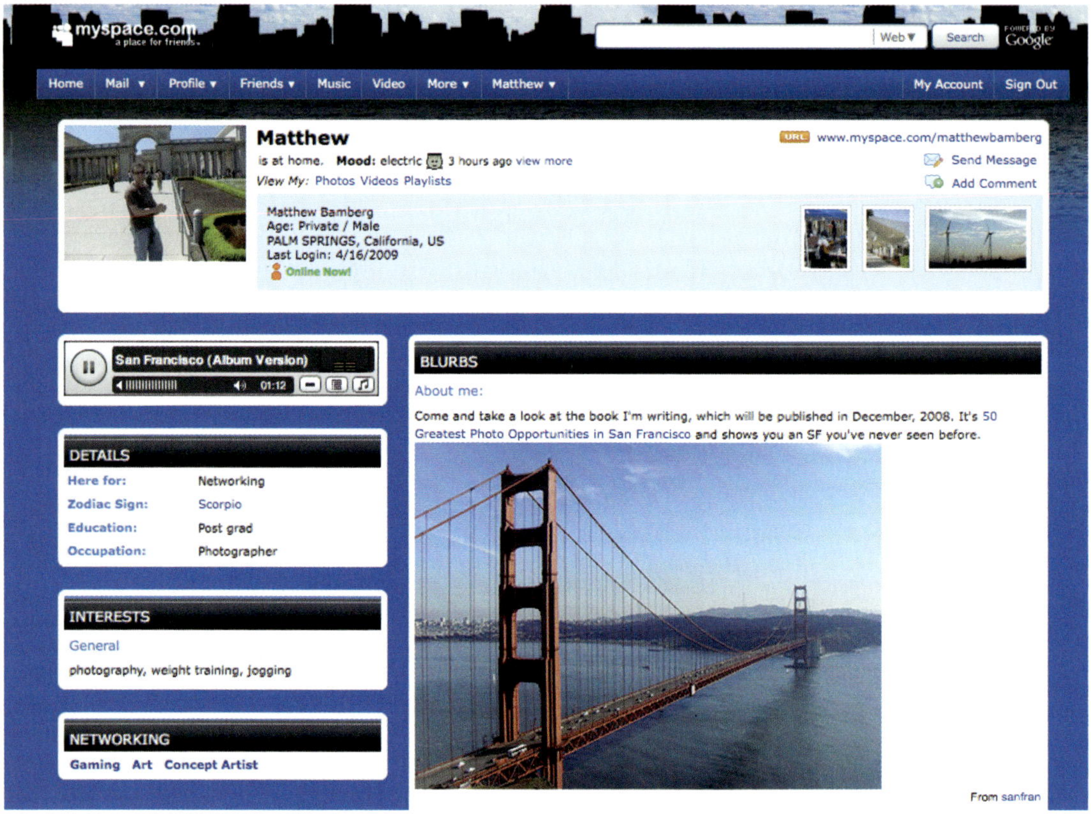

Figure 2.8 This is a profile page for MySpace.

The first one is the default photo. To change it, click on the Change Photo button under it. This will take you to your My Albums page. Click on an album. Your pictures will appear with empty circles under them. Just pick the image that you want as your photo and then click Done.

> **NOTE**
>
> MySpace is constantly changing. If you find that these directions are off a bit, MySpace has probably updated its photo management application.

You can upload photos on your homepage (the page MySpace takes you to when you sign on and when you click on Home in the menu bar at the top of the window of every MySpace page). Just click on where it says Upload under your default image, next to where it says Photos.

What MySpace does next is a lot of fun. First, at the top of the page, you have an opportunity to take a photo of yourself using your computer's webcam. Just follow the prompts. As far as uploading pictures, you're presented with a navigation toolbar on the left and an interactive place to choose your photos by their thumbnails on the right.

To select the photos you want to upload, just navigate to them on the left side of the window and select them on the right. You can choose to put them in an album you already have (using the drop-down menu at the bottom left of the page), or you can create a new one by typing a name for it in the space just to the left of the Upload button. Figure 2.9 shows what all this looks like.

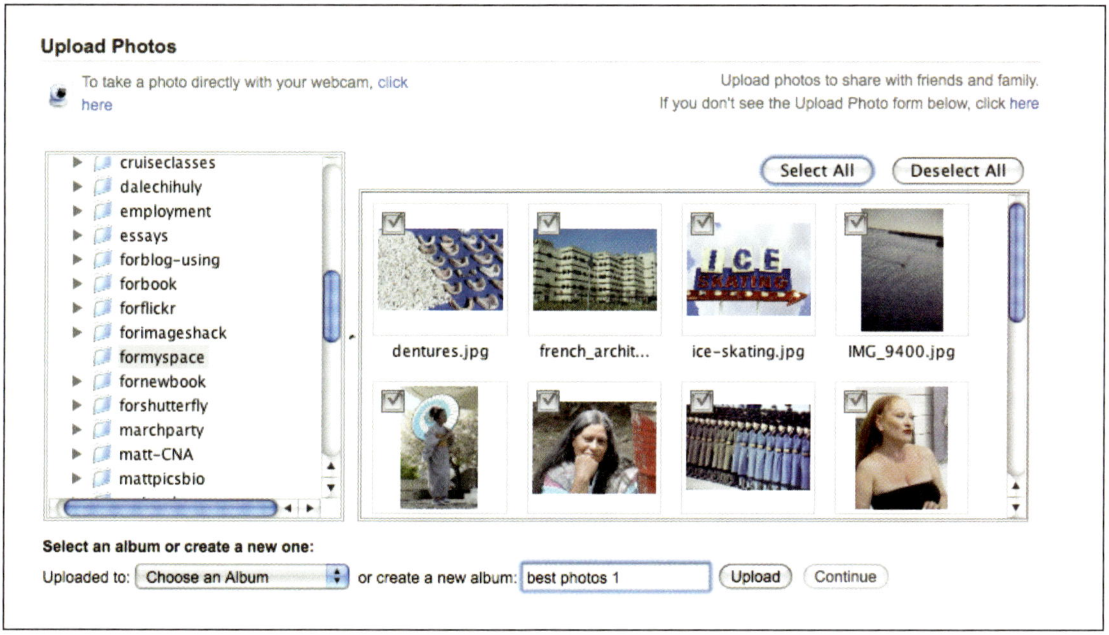

Figure 2.9 MySpace's interactive navigation to upload photos.

> **NOTE**
>
> MySpace limits photo sizes to less than 5 MB each.

When you're finished uploading photos, there's a place where you can add captions and tags to them. Tags here are different than what they were for other sites. In MySpace, you tag people in photos by which friends they are in the friends you have listed, so when you scroll over the picture of the person in the photo, it's identified with a pop-up of a person's name.

To view and share your photos, click on Profile > My Photos. After you click on an album, the photos in that album will show up. This is where you have the opportunity to send the album to faraway places. Just click on Click Here to Share This Album with Friends. To send an individual photo by email, click on the image you want, scroll down to below the image on the page that comes up, and click Email to a Friend. You can also click on Share, which lets you send the photo off to Facebook and other places such as www.Digg.com, which is a social content site where people vote your photo thumbs up or down—called *digging it.*

> **NOTE**
> Sites such as Digg and Shoutwire let you submit articles and photos, and people vote on whether or not they like them. The ones that get the most votes rise to the top of the heap.

Creating a Facebook Photo Album

Facebook is extremely popular. It's a place where adults (of late, it has become extremely popular with the over-50 set) can go back to their youth by reuniting with people they haven't seen in a long, long time.

When you sign up for Facebook, you're taken to a homepage. This is the page where you get information about what your friends are doing (after you get a couple of friends, that is). This is where you can see the most recent pictures your friends have taken.

If you don't join a group, you'll only see profiles and pictures of the people you've made friends with. Once you've joined and have a few friends, you'll get lots of news and images from your social group. By joining a photography group (type **photography** in the search space in the upper-right corner of the Facebook window), you can upload pictures that members of the photography group can see. (Some groups have more than 50,000 members.) To see the groups you've joined, navigate to Profile and then click on the Info tab.

To get to your Photos page on Facebook, navigate to Profile, then click on the Photos tab in the window that comes up. To upload photos to an album, click on Create a Photo Album on the right side of the Photos page. Facebook will ask you for the name of the album and the location of where the images were taken. It will also give you a drop-down menu of choices for how private you want the photos to be. Make your selection and then click Create Album. An interactive navigation menu will come up in the window, with your folders on the left and the images that are inside them on the right. You navigate to the folder you want and then choose from its contents on the right. Figure 2.10 shows an example. In the figure, you can see

I've named the album Matt Bamberg Photography, because it's a sample of my photography that I want people to see. It also says the max upload is 60 photos. So now I click on the Upload button. When the upload process is finished, you'll get a note that your photos have been uploaded.

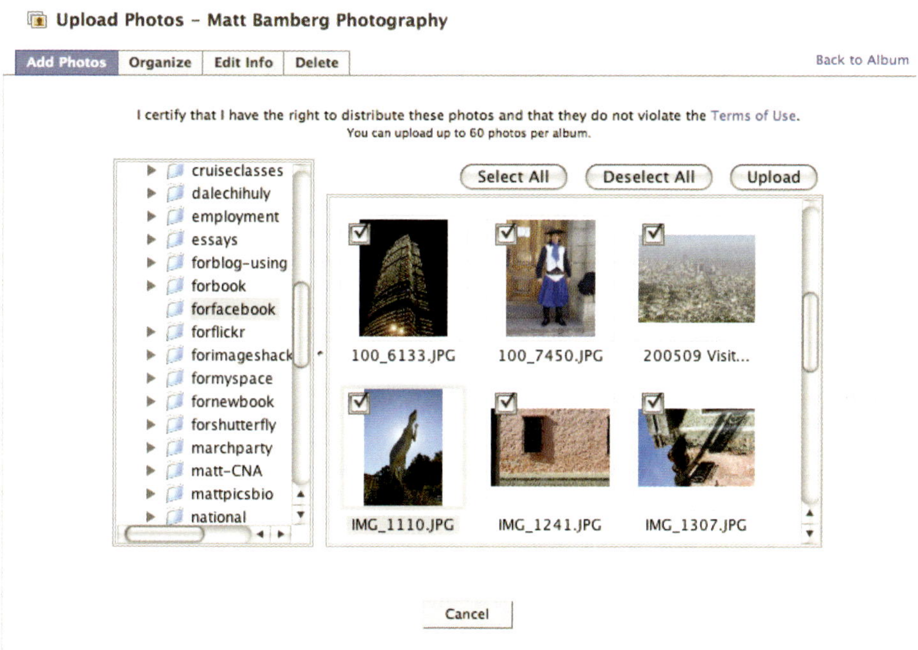

Figure 2.10 Interactive navigation to your computer in Facebook lets you click on a photo to upload.

In the next window your unpublished photos are displayed. Here you can provide tags for them, as you can on MySpace, selecting a person in an image by clicking on that person in the image and entering his or her name. You can also delete photos here. You'll always be able to come back to this—the Edit Photos page—by clicking on the first tab of the row at the top of the window. When you're ready to publish, click Publish Now. The other tabs across the top of the window let you add more photos (taking you back to the interactive navigation), organize your photos (which gives you an interactive window to click and drag your photos around), edit the name of your album, and delete the album.

The last thing that happens to your photos is automatic. They get shared on the homepages of all your friends. They'll also be posted on the wall of your Profile page. Your wall includes everything you've done, including your conversations with others. Figure 2.11 shows the announcement that I've posted new photos.

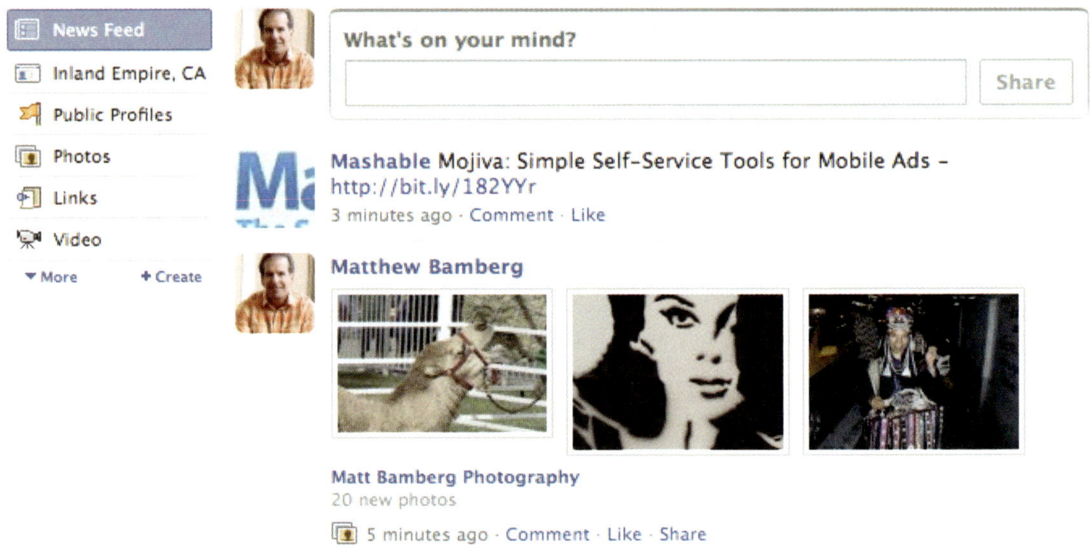

Figure 2.11 An announcement is made to your friends that photos have been posted.

Wait—there are a couple more things you can do with an individual photo by clicking on one in an album. In another window, the photo comes up enlarged, with a couple new options of what to do with it. Options are listed below the photo in the lower-right side of the window. Click on the Send button, and you can send this photo to your buddies by email. Click on the arrows, and you can rotate it. The rest of the options listed are ones you can also do when the photo is in an album (and were discussed earlier). Finally, there's your profile picture. To change it or add one, click on the picture on the homepage. (If you don't have one, click on the icon for it.) You'll have two choices on the left side of the new window that comes up—Upload a Picture or Take a Picture. When you click Upload a Picture, you'll be prompted to browse for your photo. Locate the photo and click Open, and voila—your image will be on the Facebook page.

> **NOTE**
>
> Note that, much like MySpace, Facebook is constantly changing and updating their interface. If the steps in this section don't work quite as explained, it's likely that Facebook has once again updated the application.

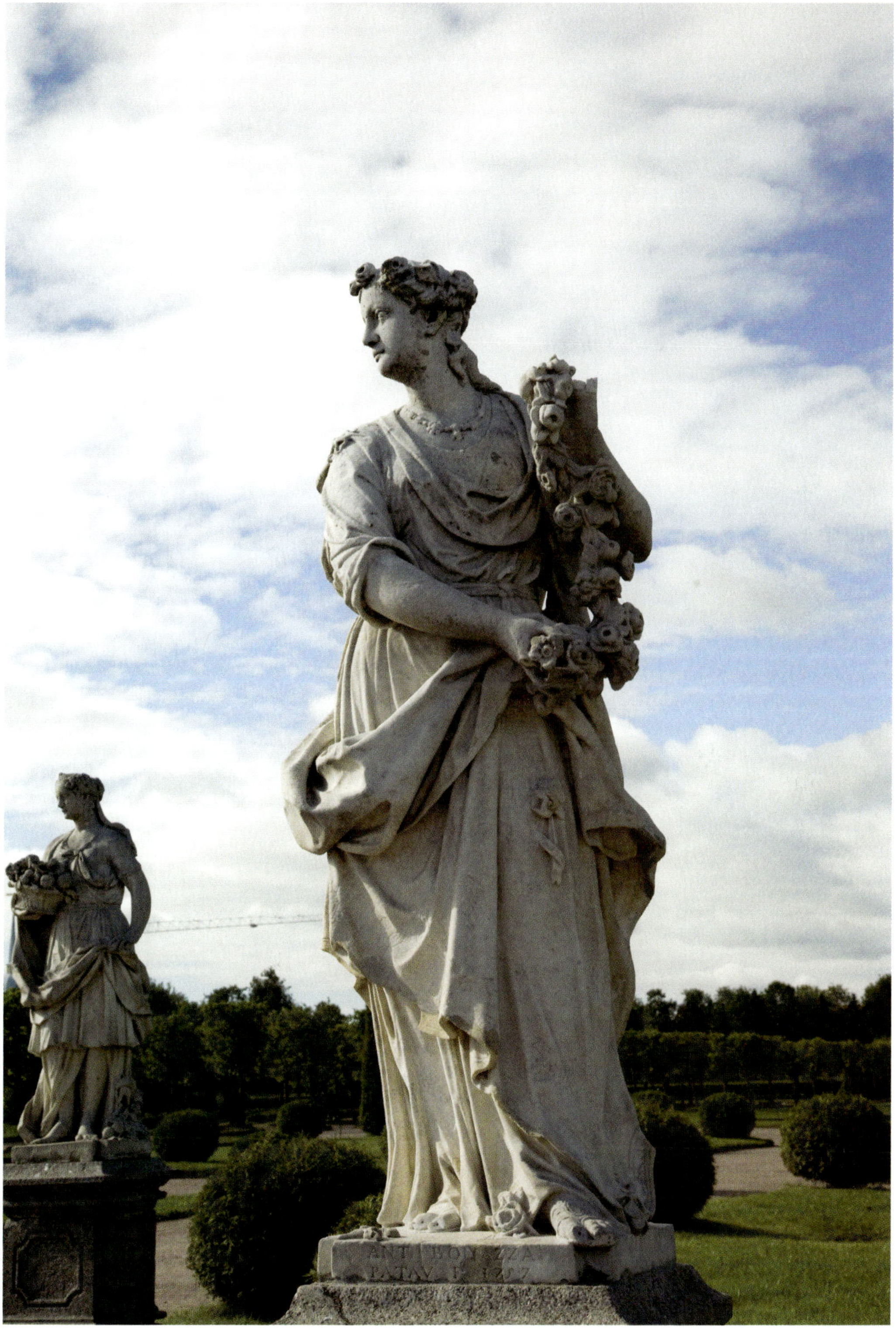

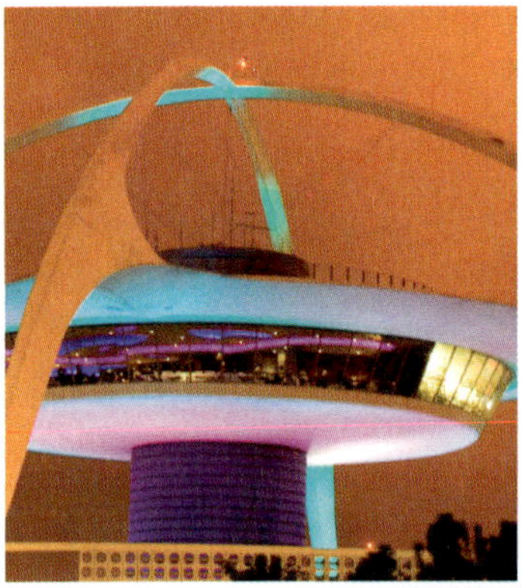

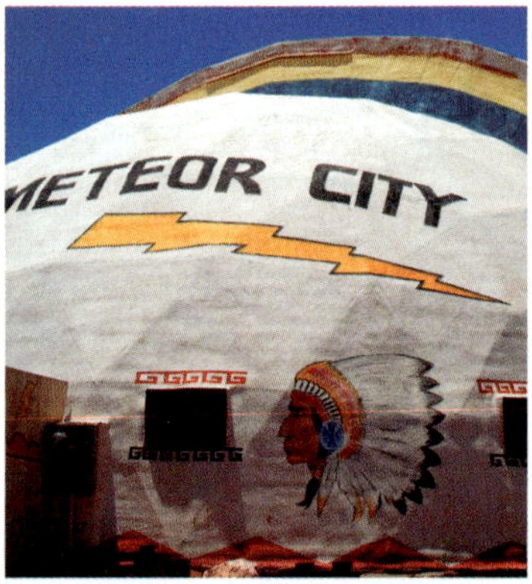
METEOR CITY

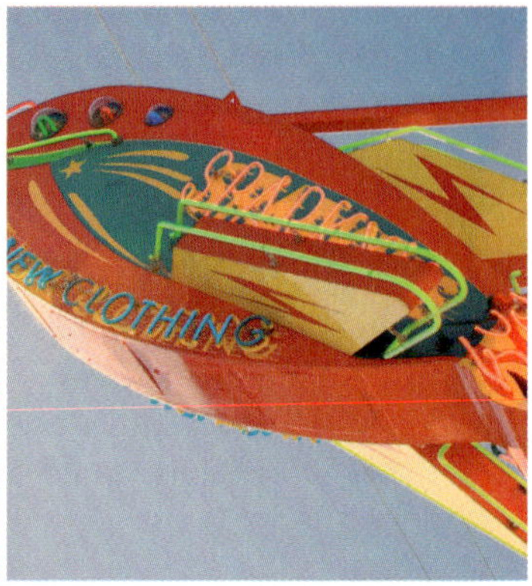
CLOTHING

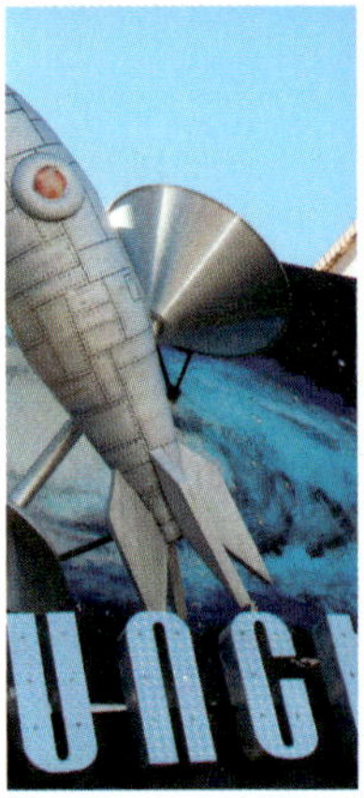

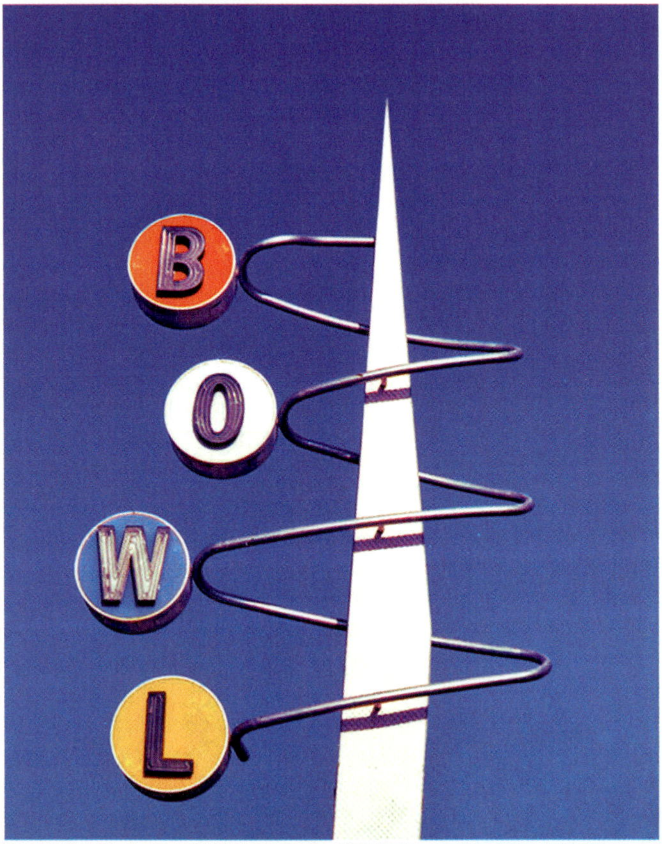
B
O
W
L

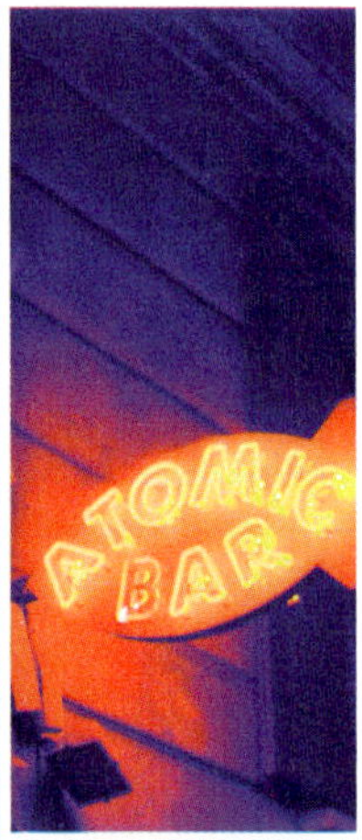
ATOMIC
BAR

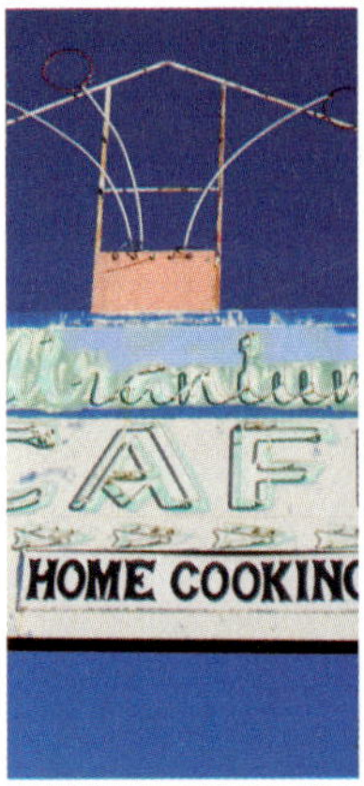
HOME

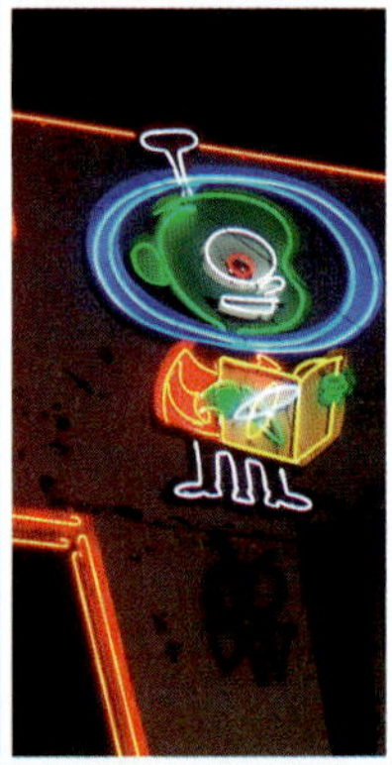

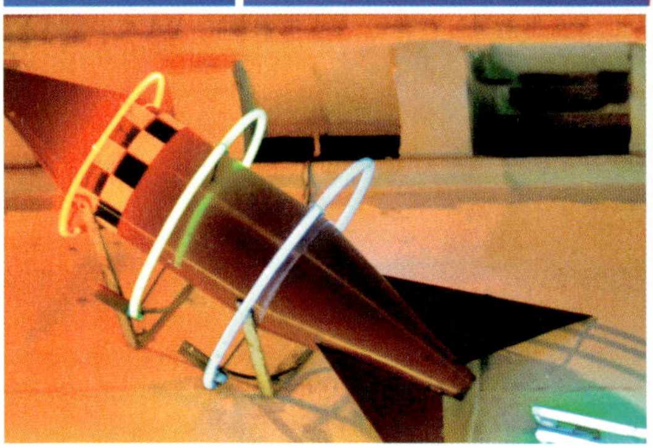

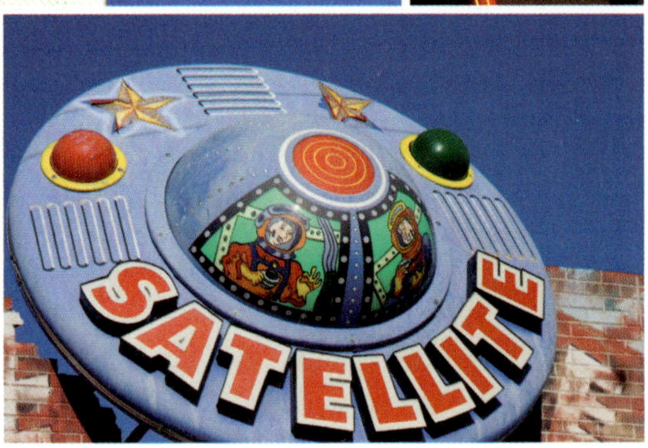
SATELLITE

CHAPTER 3

Sharing Your Photos with Family and Friends

As the popularity of digital photography spreads, more and more people are getting involved in sharing their photographs. Sharing photographs has become an essential part not only of online digital photo hosting and social networking sites, but also of more intimate settings, from social gatherings to family photo websites. Photography has also become a way to make new friends. You can enroll in an online photography class and work with others to improve your photography skills as you share the photographs you have and new ones that you shoot.

Hosting Photo Nights to Share Photo Slideshows

If you've just gotten back from a great trip, what could be more fun than hosting a slideshow of the pictures you took? It's the perfect after-vacation activity.

You have to think about two things for your show to run smoothly—choosing a slideshow program that you can easily use and knowing how to hook up your computer to your TV. You can make a slideshow in many programs. Some of them are free, such as Picasa. To make slideshows using some of these programs, go to Chapter 12, "Working with Slideshows."

When you make a slideshow, there are programs that have options to save the show as a movie file on a CD so you can burn copies for friends and family. Picasa is a good example of such a slideshow program because it's so easy to use. The program lets you play slideshows at the press of a button. It also has a Movie Maker you can use to save your slideshows and even a button that will create a movie and put it on YouTube for you. For specific directions on how to do this, go to Chapter 12.

CONNECTING YOUR COMPUTER TO YOUR TV

It's simple to connect an HDTV set to a PC. All you need is a VGA adapter, a 15-pin connector on both ends that you connect from your HDTV to your PC (see Figure 3.1). To get the picture on the HDTV screen, right-click on Graphics Options > Output to Monitor, and you're good to go.

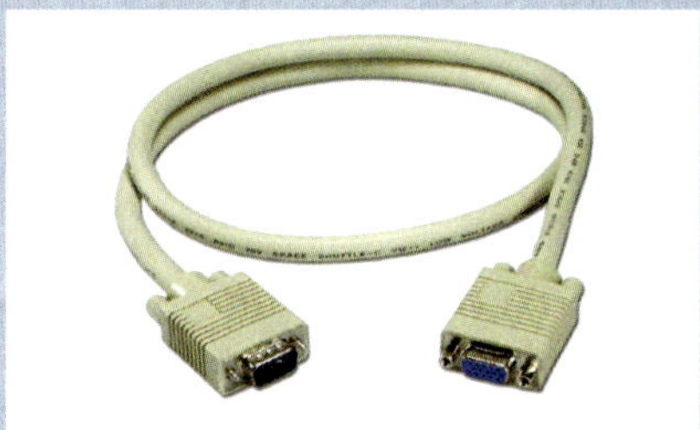

Figure 3.1 The VGA cable allows you to hook up your PC to a TV.

It's a slightly different story for a Mac. There have been times when I've gone to speak at a convention armed with my computer and a PowerPoint presentation, only to find that I needed an adapter in order to hook up my Mac to the TV. The cable that's made to connect a TV to a computer is made for PCs.

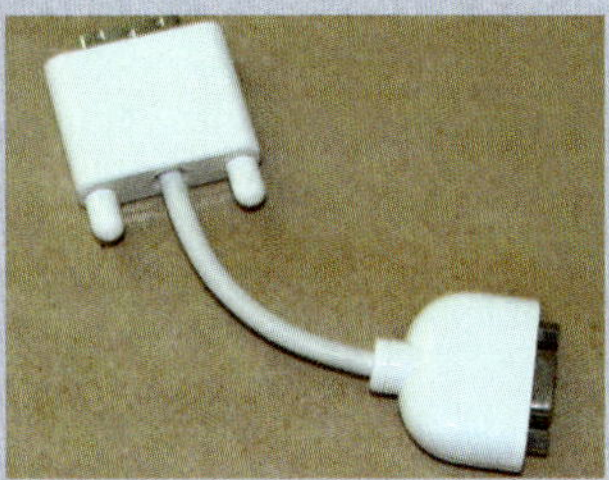

Figure 3.2 Use this adapter to connect a Mac to an HDTV set..

Sometimes it just feels like a PC-based world. I learned a lesson, though—I carry around a DVI-to-VGA adapter. While PCs have VGA ports, Macs have DVI or mini-DVI ports, depending on the model. The adapter (see Figure 3.2) is made to convert one end of a VGA cable to connect to the DVI or mini-DVI port on a Mac. Once you connect the DVI or mini-DVI end to your Mac and the VGA to the HDTV set, your Mac will automatically recognize what you're doing and change your screen to presentation mode so that you're good to go.

There are a couple of slideshow programs that aren't too expensive to buy that have many more options than Picasa. There's ProShow, which works with Windows, at www.photodex.com, and Slideshow for Macs at www.apimac.com/downloads. Both programs allow you to save slideshows as movie files so you can burn a CD/DVD and/or upload to YouTube. They also allow you to add music, transition effects, and text.

Joining a Photography Meetup Group

Have you heard of Meetup groups? There are Meetup groups all over the country, like the one shown in Figure 3.3. The purpose of these groups is to share similar interests with people in your community. There are groups for hiking, scrapbooking, and, yes, photography. At the time of this writing, there were 637 photography Meetup groups in 338 cities around the world. It's the way to get social in the new millennium.

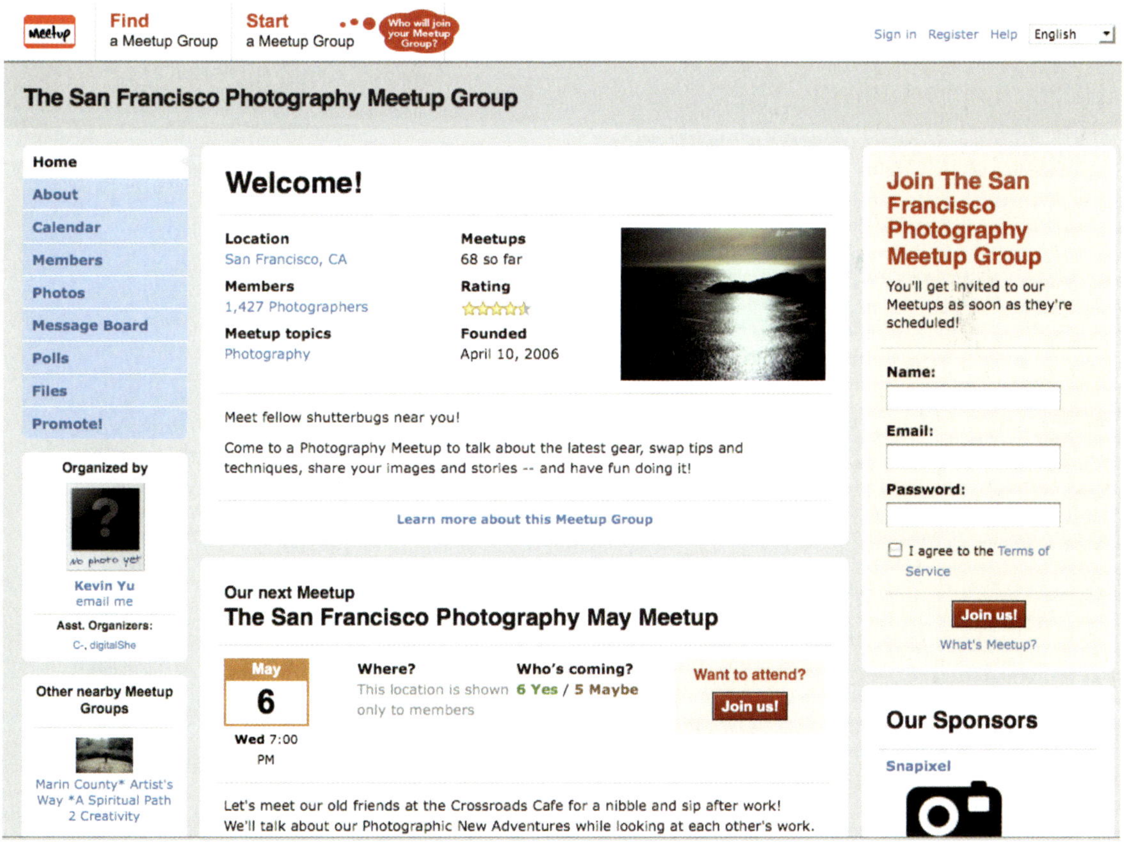

Figure 3.3 The San Francisco Photography Meetup group has more than 1,500 members.

Here's how it works: The person who starts a group, the organizer, pays a monthly fee to get the group started. He or she then makes a webpage describing the group. Next, the organizer names a date, time, and place where the group will meet and puts it up on the webpage for that group. The Meetup group site gives a list of suggested meeting places as one of the prompts included in the process of making the meeting announcement. When a person comes to the site (Google is very good at listing these sites at the top tier of sites that it chooses to list for a number of keywords related to photography), he or she can choose to register for the group and then make a decision as to whether he/she will attend the meeting. There are generally yes, no, and maybe choices for a "Will you be there?" prompt. Finally, the website keeps track and posts the number of people who RSVPed. Only people who are registered can sign up for the meetups. Registration is usually free.

At the meetings, participants share photos, go on shooting expeditions, and compare equipment. People with all different kinds of photography skills attend, from fashion photographers to those who shoot candidly. Finally, you don't have to be a pro to attend. There are plenty of beginners, too.

Taking an Online Photography Class

Another way to build an online community of photographers is to get together with others to learn about photography. You can take online photography classes where you are taught by some of the most skilled photographers in the industry. I think the two best schools (judging by the experience of the instructors) are BetterPhoto.com and the Perfect Picture School of Photography (www.ppsop.com). Many of the instructors are not only photographers; they are also photography book authors. Here's a summary of the two schools:

* **BetterPhoto.com.** BetterPhoto (see Figure 3.4) has more to offer than just classes; it offers four tiers of membership, which gives you opportunities to build your own galleries (for the Basic membership) and websites, with the ability to update quickly and easily for more elite levels of membership. There are also opportunities to sell your photos on the site.

  As far as courses are concerned, BetterPhoto offers four-week sessions once a month. Dozens of courses range from classes on learning Photoshop basics to classes that are camera model–specific (such as classes on the EOS Digital Rebels). They also offer eight-week courses once every two months. Those classes include broader topics, such as fine art flower photography and the business of photography.

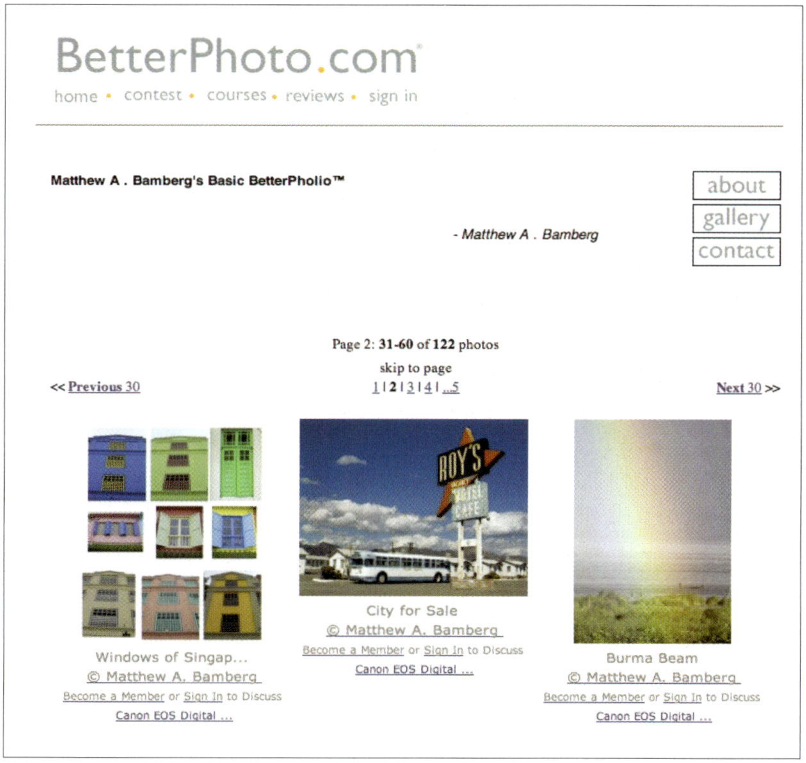

Figure 3.4 A BetterPhoto gallery.

- **Perfect Picture School of Photography.** Picture Perfect offers four-, six-, and eight-week classes with such course names as High Energy Fashion Photography, Documentary Photography, and All about Color. They also offer four- and six-week digital darkroom classes that use such programs as Photoshop and Elements, as well as teach how to create HDR (High Dynamic Range) photos.

Many of these classes have the instructors critique the photos you take or edit. For more about photo critiquing, see the sidebar below.

CRITIQUING A PHOTOGRAPH

If you've ever had someone tell you something you could do better in a photograph and you didn't exactly like it, take heart. Welcome to the wonderful world of photo critiquing. If you're going to take an online photography class, you'll get a slew of your photos critiqued by professionals. Sound intimidating? It's not, really. Having your photos critiqued can be really helpful.

There are four things you can do with a photo after it has been critiqued. If some minor corrections are warranted, you can make the changes you need in Photoshop. If the photo is just bad both compositionally and technically, you can toss it. But I know that can be really hard if you like the subject matter. For example, I have a photograph of women in the Caribbean walking with bags on top of their heads with no hands holding them up. It's a lousy photo—too soft and with too many harsh shadows and subjects that were just too far away from the lens to come out well. I haven't tossed that photo. What I did was crop it tightly, shrink it down, and put it on my blog on the Internet. The last thing you can do with a photo after it has been critiqued and evaluated poorly is to go out and reshoot.

While these are all possibilities for what you can do with critiqued photos, the most important part of being critiqued is to learn for the next time.

Consider critiquing the photo in Figure 3.5. You can evaluate it by its composition—meaning whether the photo invokes strong feelings—its technicalities, and, finally, things you like and don't like about the photo.

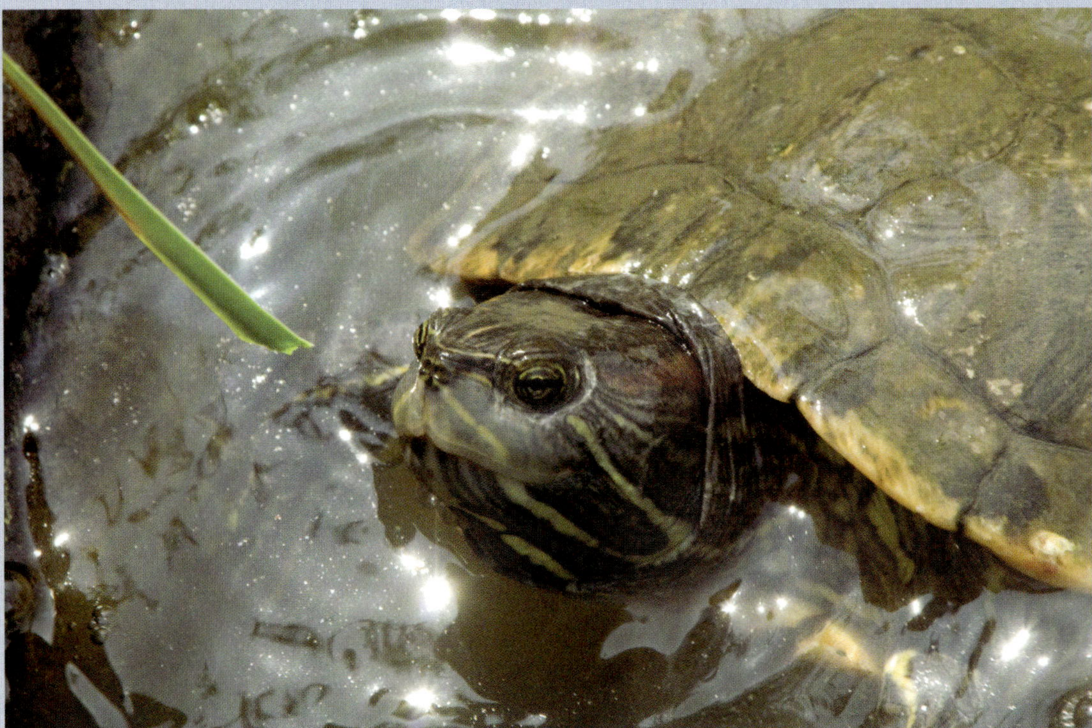

Figure 3.5 What's wrong with this photo?

Okay, I'll go ahead and critique it. Some might think that the muddy water takes away from the photo. It can be cleaned up by cropping out some of it. If you did that, you'd lose the grass, which adds to the image both by adding a contrasting color to the frame and in the interaction between the turtle and the blade of grass. That blade of grass looks as if it's in danger of being bitten, which is good thing. You wonder if the turtle will end up eating it. Technically, the photo needs some work. There are a few blown highlights (the sunspots on the water); some would say they like it, and others not. I like that the eyes of the animal are sharp. If you want one thing sharp in your subjects, it is best if it's the eyes. Finally, I don't like, again, the dirty look to the photo. I might want to clean it up a little in Photoshop by changing the color tones a bit.

Becoming a Member of the CityDailyPhoto.com Blog Group

If you're one to have an outing with your camera on a daily basis, then City Daily Photo could be the place for you. CityDailyPhoto.com is a place to register a blog that features a photo a day from any city around the world. There are just a couple of rules you have to abide by to register.

- You can only post one photo a day.
- The blog can be about only one city.
- The title of your blog has to include the city's name.
- All photo captions need to include English text.

There's a great benefit to signing up with the CityDailyPhoto.com website—your blog will instantly receive many more hits. (For blogs and hits, see Chapter 6, "Photo Blog Heaven.") Every day you post a picture, it's put up on the front page of the CityDailyPhoto.com website with a link to your blog. If you have an eye-catching picture, many people who are visiting the CityDailyPhoto.com website will click on the link to your blog. It didn't take me long to get more than 200 hits a day when I put up Palm Springs Daily Photo (see Figure 3.6).

Since you make a commitment to providing one photo a day from your city, you'll become an active photographer. You'll get in the habit of bringing your camera with you wherever you go and experimenting with different shooting techniques on a daily basis. You'll also have to get into the habit of downloading the photo onto your computer and then posting to your blog.

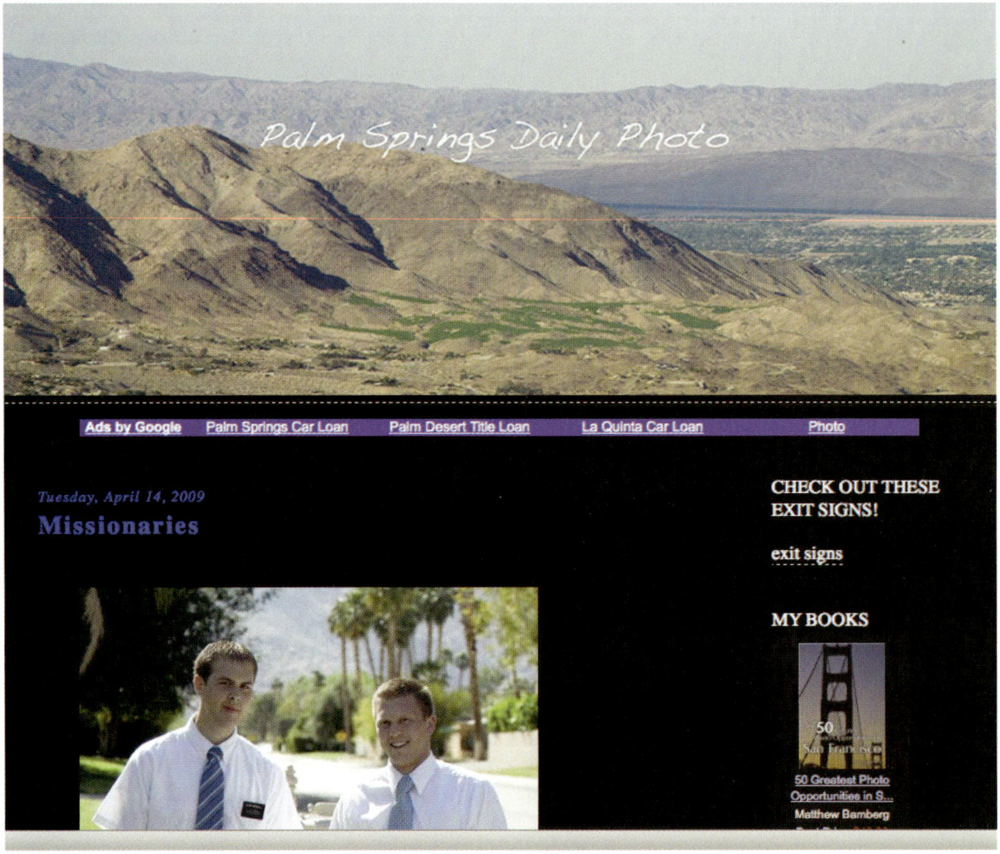

Figure 3.6 An example of a Daily Photo blog.

Making a Family Tree Website with Photos

TribalPages.com lets you build an incredible family tree website for free. All you do is sign up (no email confirmation required) and get started building your website right away. The sites are quite nice, too, with drop-down menu bars and a pleasant color scheme. In fact, the site's so good that I had to ask myself whether it will be around in the not-too-distant future. The answer to my question (an indirect answer) is on their first page. The site has more than 300,000 members, some of whom pay for premium status (which runs from $2 to $4/month), which I believe is a good omen for their future.

When you sign up for TribalPages.com, the site assigns you a URL on the order of yourname.tribalpages.com. My URL is bamberg.tribalpages.com.

To make the website (see Figure 3.7 for an example) or add to it, you log in and click Edit. In the next window, click on List of Names in the My Website category. From there, input *your name first.* After you're finished, you'll see the beginning of your family tree, with your name in the middle. To add photos, click on the camera next to your name and then click on Upload Photos. Click on Browse in the next window, navigate to the photo you want posted on the website, and then click on Upload. In the next window, click Done.

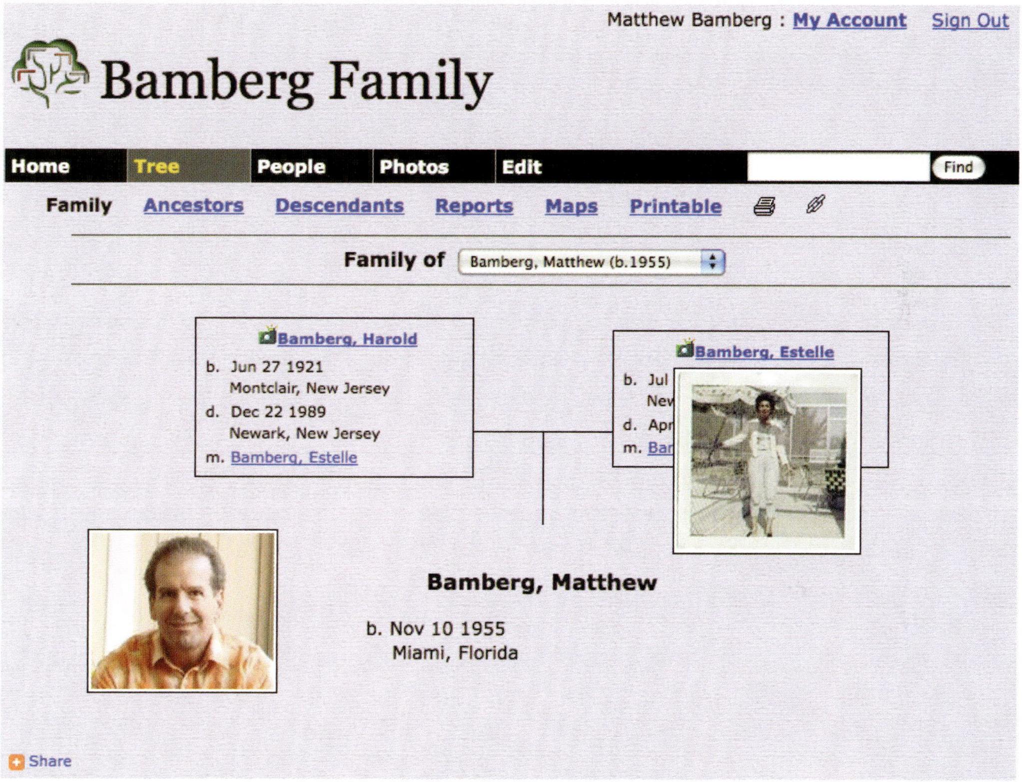

Figure 3.7 You can make your own family tree website at TribalPages.com.

> **NOTE**
>
> When you click on the name of person, he or she will appear first on the family tree.

When you've finished inputting a few names and images and you go to the URL of your webpage, you'll be pleasantly surprised to find the images in a slideshow on your site's homepage.

NOTE

One drawback of TribalPages.com is that when you go to your family's website, only the dead people show up. They don't show living people "for privacy reasons." You have to sign in to see them.

Finally, another one of the great aspects of this site is that you have the option to share the family tree at dozens of sites, including Facebook and Twitter.

Making a Photo Webpage

If you go to Weebly.com, you can make a photo webpage easily (see the sample in Figure 3.8) with a very user-friendly platform. You just use drag-and-drop commands on the site. After you sign up for Weebly and get into the website editing platform, you'll find under the Elements tab of the window a set of options that run across the top of the page—Paragraph with Title, Paragraph with Picture, Picture, Title, Paragraph, and other options. All you do is click and drag the option down into the interactive frame below the options. Once you click in the working box that is made after you've clicked and dragged down the option, a menu bar of new options associated with that box will come up. (For text, it's word processing options; for images, it's upload, border, position, and link.)

There's another set of options that are listed for Elements in the top-left corner of the window. If you want a gallery of pictures on a new Picture page (for a new page, click on the Pages tab), click on Multimedia and click and drag the Photo Gallery icon onto the frame under the Elements options. Click on Upload New Images at the top of the page in the menu bar that appears, and your images will be brought into the webpage. You can click and drag the images around and/or delete them by clicking on the red X in the right-hand corner of the image. You can change the columns and spacing between the photos using the drop-down numbers at the top of the frame.

Once you publish, you have the option to let friends and followers on Facebook and Twitter know you have a new website. Finally, you also have the option to import a Flickr photo slideshow of your Flickr photos.

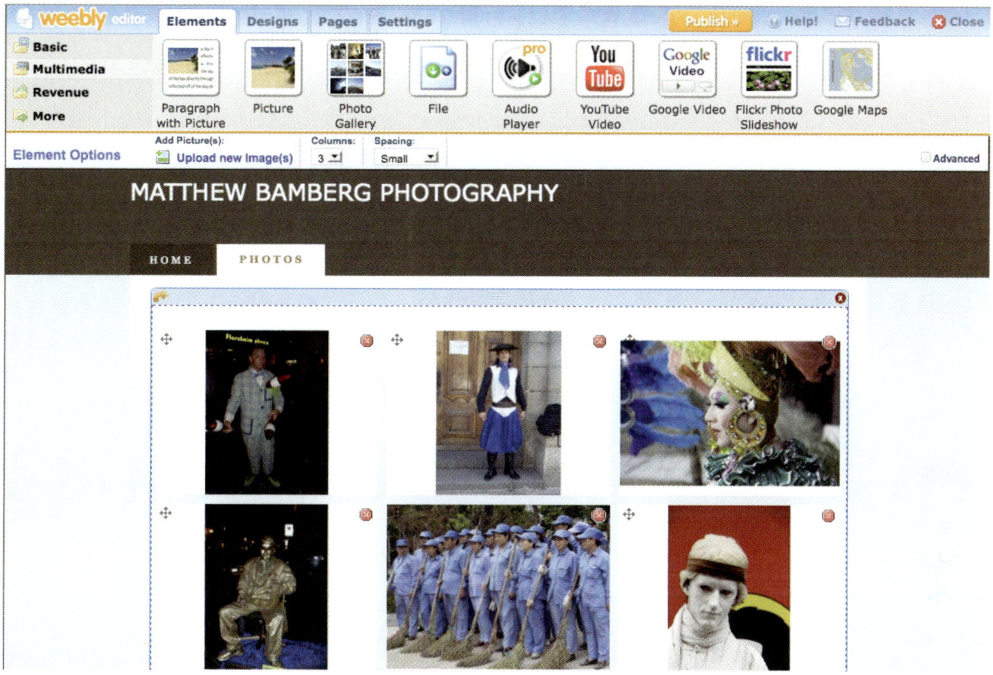

Figure 3.8 Making a photo website is a cinch on Weebly.

Making a Photo Collage

At some point in your online life, you'll probably want to make a photo collage to share with family and friends. These days, the quickest and easiest way to create a photo collage is to use Picasa (see Figure 3.9). You can use Photoshop or Elements to do this, but the process is complex with the use of many layers. Granted, if you know Photoshop or Elements, you have many more options for making a collage. You can feather images in Photoshop and Elements, for example, and you can't in Picasa. However, as mentioned, Picasa provides a quick and easy way to create a photo collage, so that's what I'll discuss in this section.

In Picasa, select Create Photo Collage under the folder that contains the pictures you want in the collage. You can also individually select the pictures that you want in the collage and select Create > Collage. Once you opt to create the collage, a new interactive window will come up, where you can click and drag, rotate, or resize any of your images after they are selected. Now you can start playing around with the images to create a collage.

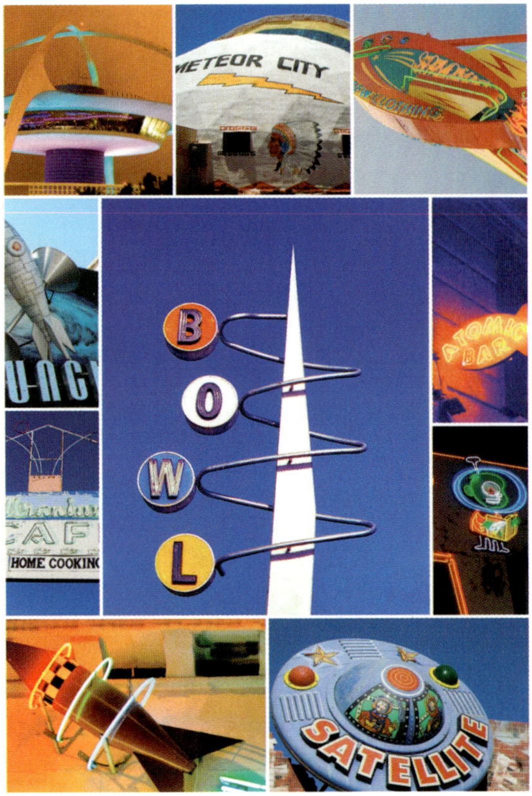

Figure 3.9 Photo collage made in Picasa.

> **NOTE**
>
> You'll notice three tabs at the top of the page: Library, Collage, and Import. You can toggle back and forth between any of the three tabs—a feature that is useful when you go to edit your pictures while you make your collage.

One more feature worth being aware of is the View and Edit button—the last of three buttons under the interactive window. If you select and click on an image after clicking on the View and Edit button, the Library Tab becomes the editing platform for your image. To get back to your collage after you edit, just click on the Collage tab at the top of the window.

At the top of the interactive window, there are four other important options: Select All, Select None, Remove, and Set as Background. The Set as Background option is really cool—it takes a selected picture and makes it the background of your collage.

Wait…there's more. The last thing to note is a set of options in the Settings frame to the left of the interactive window where you play around with your images. From top to bottom in this frame, you have the following set of options: a choice of options in a drop-down menu for organizing your collage, a choice of picture borders (when you choose an option other than Picture Pile, you'll get a Grid Spacer slider to work with), background options, a drop-down menu of page format options, a choice of landscape or portrait mode, shadow and caption choices, and options to get your collage created or reset the images. Figure 3.10 shows all the options when Picasa is set to Mosaic mode.

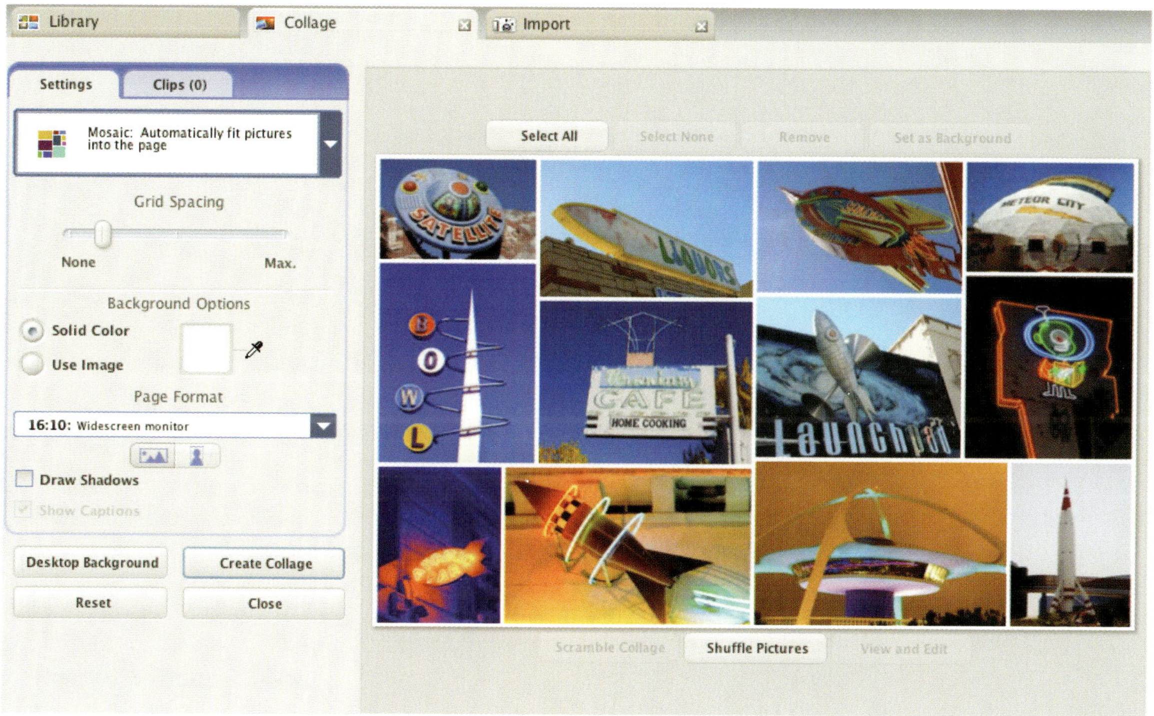

Figure 3.10 Mosaic option in Picasa's Collage Maker.

The last thing you do is click on Create Collage, one of four buttons at the bottom of the left frame of Picasa's window. Your image will be saved as a JPEG image in the Collages album of Picasa.

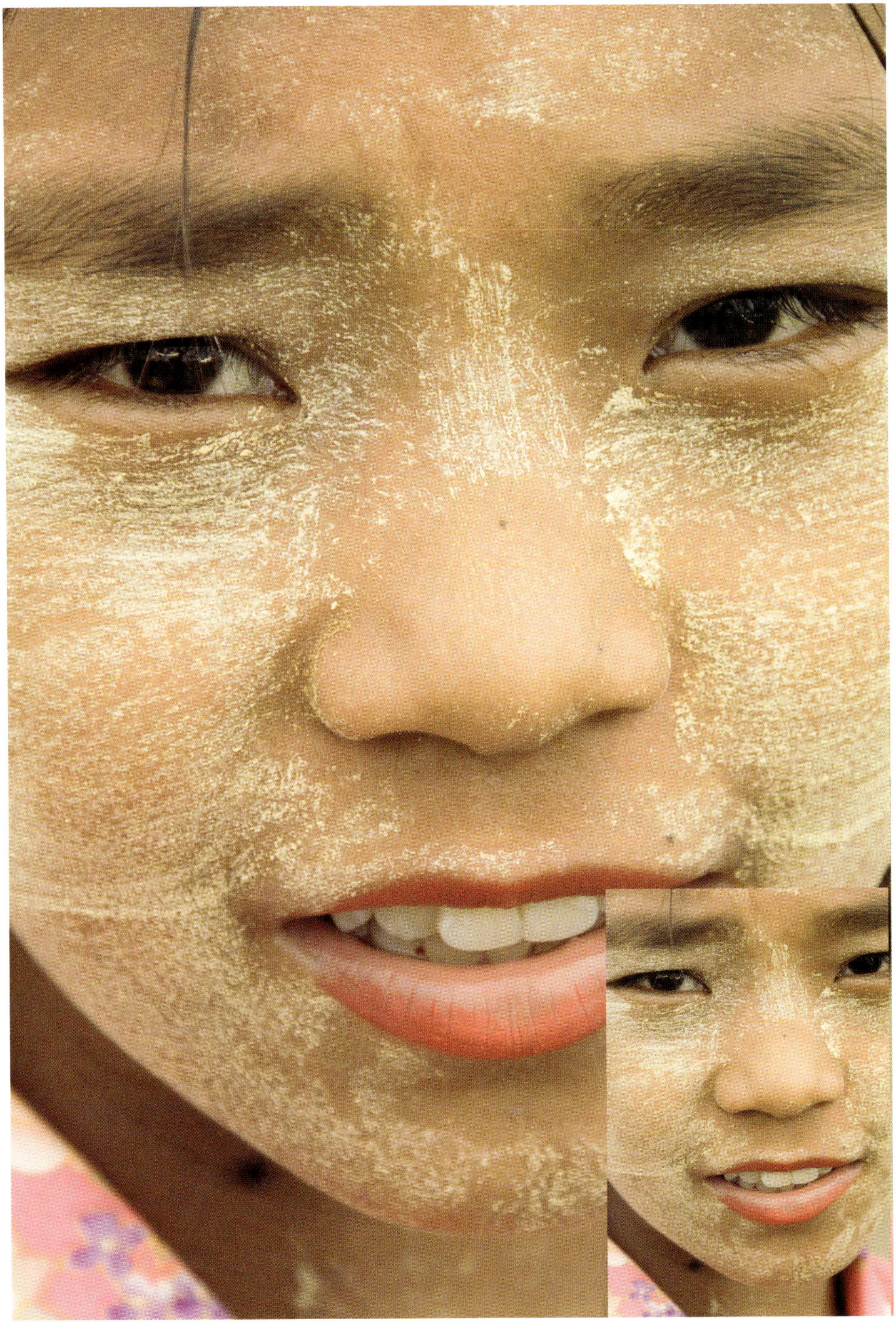

Chapter 4

Preparing Your Photos for Use

There's a good possibility that you have thousands of images on your computer (maybe even tens of thousands) and external hard drive(s), and you don't know where to start when it comes to using them. Rest assured, if you read this book, you'll be off to a good start toward putting your photos to good use. One of the first things you should do in terms of using your photos is to print some of the best ones. Prints give you a good idea of what your images really look like. With today's advanced printing technology, ink-jet prints that you make with your printer can last generations. There are a number of things you have to do in order to prepare your photos for printing. In this chapter you'll learn some of them, as well as the ins and outs of obtaining the best printer money can buy and of setting up for the printing process.

Printing Anywhere with a Portable Printer

Since Polaroid film (the film you put into a Polaroid camera that develops instantly after you take a picture) has all but bitten the dust, something had to give in terms of getting your images printed on demand.

It's not only the printer you'll want to consider if you're in the market for having your pictures printed quickly. The costs of paper and ink are surely going to be issues with respect to these machines. But if you have to have prints to hand out to your friends and family right away, with a portable printer, you know that your photos won't end up stored in your computer for who knows how long.

There are several portable printers on the market—some good and some bad. Here's the scoop.

Dell's Wasabi is a no-ink (called *Zink*) device that uses paper with dye crystals in it that Wasabi warms up to make a picture. The device weighs only eight ounces. Wasabi uses Bluetooth, which means it operates wirelessly. It takes 55 seconds to print a picture and can only hold 12 pieces of photo paper at a time.

The drawback to this device is that the pictures are only 2×3 inches. The paper (which comes with sticky backing) comes in packs of 24 and will cost you about 50 cents per piece. The nice thing about it is you don't have to buy ink. Polaroid makes a similar model that uses Zink technology called the *Pogo*.

Epson's PictureMate Dash (see Figure 4.1) can be carried around as you would a small lunchbox. It weighs a little more than five pounds. You can get a Bluetooth adapter to make the device work wirelessly. You can also purchase a rechargeable battery. The device is reasonably priced (about $150), and the paper and ink (about $40 for ink and the paper pack for 150 glossy photos) are rather reasonable, too.

HP's Photosmart 375 is a three-pounder that can read your digital camera's memory card to print photos. (You can also use the USB cable that comes with your camera.) There's a rechargeable battery you can get for the device. Supplies can be had for about $33 and include an HP 95 series cartridge and 100 sheets of borderless 4×6-inch glossy HP Premium Photo Paper.

Getting the Best Printer for the Price

The first thing to keep in mind if you're going to display prints in your photo albums or hang them on your walls is that inkjet printers are the best option for photography. You might think that ink smears and won't look good in a couple of years. Nothing is further from the truth. It's the paper and ink combination that, with today's technology, can create an archival (lasts more than a hundred years), smearless print.

You can get some pretty decent printers in the $200 to $300 range from a number of different companies. Mind you, these are not professional printers, but they don't do a bad job either, sometimes besting prints you get at Walmart.

One of the main differences between the two printers listed in this section and the pro printers is that the former print directly from a camera, something a pro wouldn't want to do because there is not enough control over what happens to the photo before it's printed. More about pro printers in the next section, "Printing with the Printer the Pros Use."

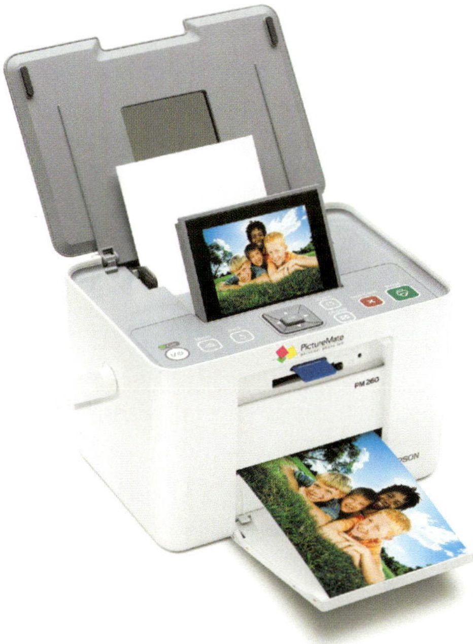

Figure 4.1 A PictureMate Dash printer from Epson.

Epson's Artisan 700 (see Figure 4.2) is an all-in-one printer that does it all: prints, copies, and scans photos.

You can connect this printer to your laptop or camera (if it is PictBridge enabled, a feature that many cameras have) with USB cable or Bluetooth. Or you can take out your camera's memory card and insert it into a matching memory card slot (each card can only fit into one-size slot) on the printer. You can even print from a USB flash drive. The printer lets you crop so that only part of your picture is printed. This printer is fast, printing a 4×6 image in about 10 seconds. The one drawback for this printer is the ink cost. It needs six different cartridges. At more than $12 a pop, that can get pretty pricey.

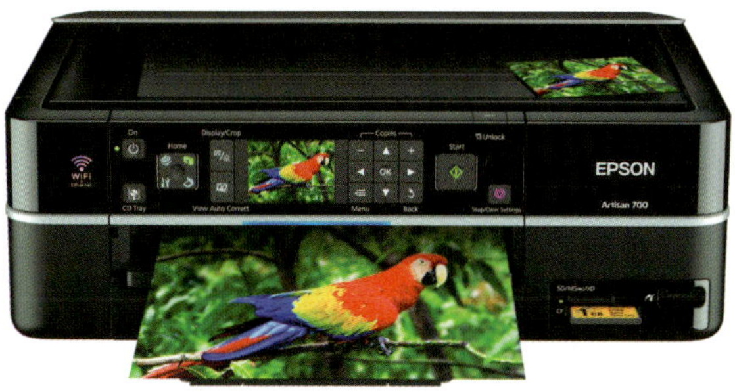

Figure 4.2 Epson's Artisan 700 makes archival prints.

With HP's Photosmart B8550, you can connect the printer to your camera (again, PictBridge enabled), and it has USB flash drive and memory card slots for direct printing from these devices. This printer has five ink cartridges, which you can get for $12 or so. The nice thing about the 8550 is that you can make extra-large prints (13×19 inches). The 8550 is a bit slower than the Artisan, though, printing a 4×6 photo in 18 seconds.

Printing with the Printer the Pros Use

To get pristine images like you see in a gallery, you'll have to use a pro printer with Photoshop, Photoshop Elements, or another professional image processing program. The two most popular manufacturers that make pro printers are Epson and Hewlett-Packard. Most professional photographers who print their own work use what is called a *workflow* in the image processing program. The workflow involves letting Photoshop (rather than the printer) determine the colors for the final print.

One of the first things you'll want to decide before you buy a pro printer is how big you want your photo. Pro printer selection is made by the width of the paper rolls the machine holds. (Machines also take single sheets.) Epson has professional models that hold 13 inches (Epson Stylus R2880), 17 inches (Epson Stylus Pro 3800, 4880), 24 inches (Epson Stylus Pro 7880, 7900), and 44 inches (Epson Stylus Pro 9880, 9900). Prices range from about $700 to $6,000. See Figure 4.3.

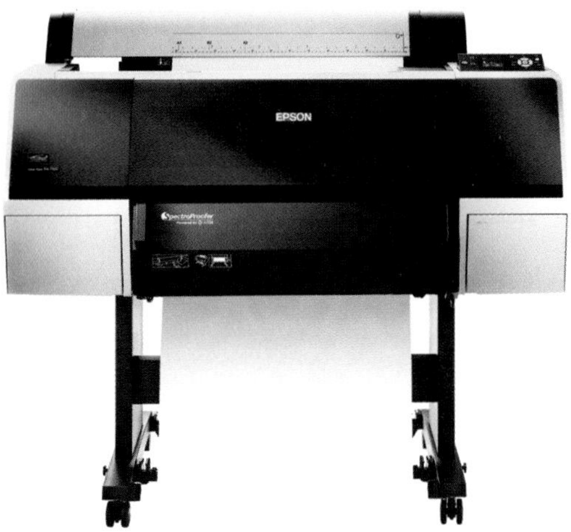

HP also has professional models that hold 13 inches (HP Photosmart Pro B8800, B9180), 24 inches (HP Designjet Z3200, Z3200ps 24-in), and 44 inches (HP Designjet Z3200, Z3200ps 44-in). Prices range from about $630 to $6,800.

Figure 4.3 The Epson Stylus Pro holds 24-inch-wide paper rolls.

Choosing the Right Paper for Making Prints

There is a wide array of papers from which to choose before you start printing your photos. The ones you choose will depend upon what you are going to do with your photograph. Most photographers would agree that archival acid-free paper is best for printing because the paper can last for several generations.

Photo paper varies from manufacturer to manufacturer, so you are best off using the paper the printer manufacturer recommends. I've seen many inconsistencies in printing when paper other than what the manufacturer recommends is used.

Epson, HP, Kodak, and Canon offer a variety of papers. The paper comes in rolls or in packages that contain single sheets. Generally, rolls are available for printers that are more than 13 inches wide.

In terms of printing for photography, Epson is the choice of many photographers who print on their own. One of the most common papers for professionals is Premium Glossy Photo paper, which comes in rolls and sheets. Photographers who sell high-end photographs sometimes print on textured fine art papers (made of 100-percent rag cotton) and/or velvet paper.

Just to get an idea of the range of papers you can use, the Epson R2880 can print on the following: plain paper, Epson Bright White Paper, Presentation Paper Matte, Premium Presentation Paper Matte, Premium Presentation Paper Matte Double-Sided, Ultra Premium Presentation Paper Matte, Photo Paper Glossy, Premium Photo Paper Glossy, Premium Photo Paper Semi-Gloss, Ultra Premium Photo Paper Luster, Exhibition Fiber Paper, Watercolor Paper Radiant White, Velvet Fine Art Paper, UltraSmooth Fine Art Paper, Premium Canvas Satin, Premium Canvas Matte, and PremierArt Matte Scrapbook Photo Paper.

Most photo paper manufacturers offer some type of canvas paper. You can create a painting-like photo using canvas (Epson offers a couple of different kinds) and an image that has been manipulated with a painting effects software program. Figure 4.4 shows a photograph printed on canvas. (Seascapes take well to this type of media.)

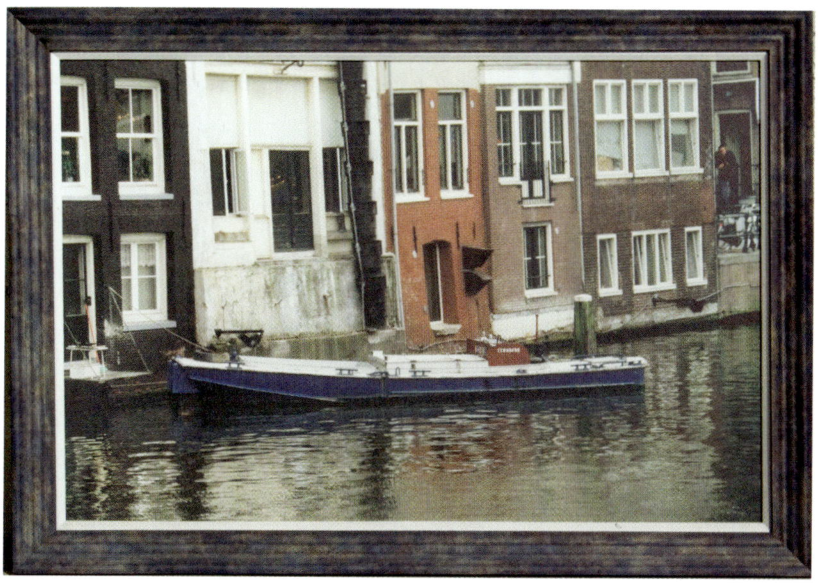

Figure 4.4 Photograph printed on canvas.

When you are printing on different types of paper, many printer driver profiles come without profiles for many papers. When they are missing profiles, you have to download the paper's profile from the manufacturer's website. (Epson's and HP's websites have profiles for all their papers.) Once you download the profiles, they are automatically installed to the place where they'll be read by your image processing program. The profiles help to make sure the colors that are printed on the paper match those on your computer screen. This process is a part of color management, which is discussed in the next section, "Learning Color Management for Great Color Photos."

Learning Color Management for Great Color Photos

To be sure, you don't have to use color management, a process where you set up an image processing program to carefully manage the color of your photo so what you see on your monitor matches what you print on paper. You can just let the printer decide on the colors. The print will look fairly decent, but not as good as if you tweak your photo in Photoshop and let that program determine the color.

Color management can be a very complex process. Entire books have been written about the subject. What you really need to know is how to set up Photoshop or Elements to print so that what you see on your monitor will be what you get on your paper.

The very first thing you do in your workflow in order to get a good print is to calibrate your monitor. You should calibrate your monitor once a month. PANTONE makes a Huey Pro for both Mac and Windows (for less than $100), and the system is a cinch to use. Just load the software and follow the prompts. During the process, you'll have to attach a sensor that has suction cups to your monitor. The process is really quite fun, and it does a great job at monitor calibration.

To make color management quick and easy, here are some suggestions for printing selections to be made in Photoshop CS 2, 3, and 4 for Windows and Mac. To get the best prints, print superfine photos at 1440 dpi at finest detail. See Figure 4.5 for a look at the Print dialog box in Photoshop.

For Windows:

1. Select North America Prepress 2 in the Edit > Color Setting dialog box.
2. Open and tweak the photo you want to print. If at any time your photo appears to change color during the workflow, re-tweak it to the best color you can see visually.
3. Click OK in the Embedded Profile Mismatch dialog box that comes up.
4. If the Missing Profile dialog box comes up, choose Assign Working RGB: Adobe RGB (1998).

5. Select your print settings in the Page Setup dialog box.
6. In the Print dialog box, click on More Options and select Color Management from the drop-down menu.
7. In the Print dialog box Options area, choose the option that lets Photoshop determine colors for color handling.
8. In the Print dialog box Options area, open the list and select the printer profile that matches the paper you're using. (If you're using an Epson printer and you need a profile for paper you're using in that printer, then go to Epson's site and download the profile for the paper you are using.)
9. In the Print dialog box Options area, choose Relative Colormetric and check Black Point Compensation.
10. Now, click the Print button in the Print dialog box and then click on Properties or Preferences. Choose your paper options in the drop-down menu and then click on Advanced.
11. In the next dialog box, choose your paper options again in the drop-down menu, choose ICM for Color Management and check Off (No Color Adjustment). Make sure the High Speed and Edge Smoothing options are not checked. Choose other options as needed (portrait, landscape, and so on).
12. Click on OK or Print to print.

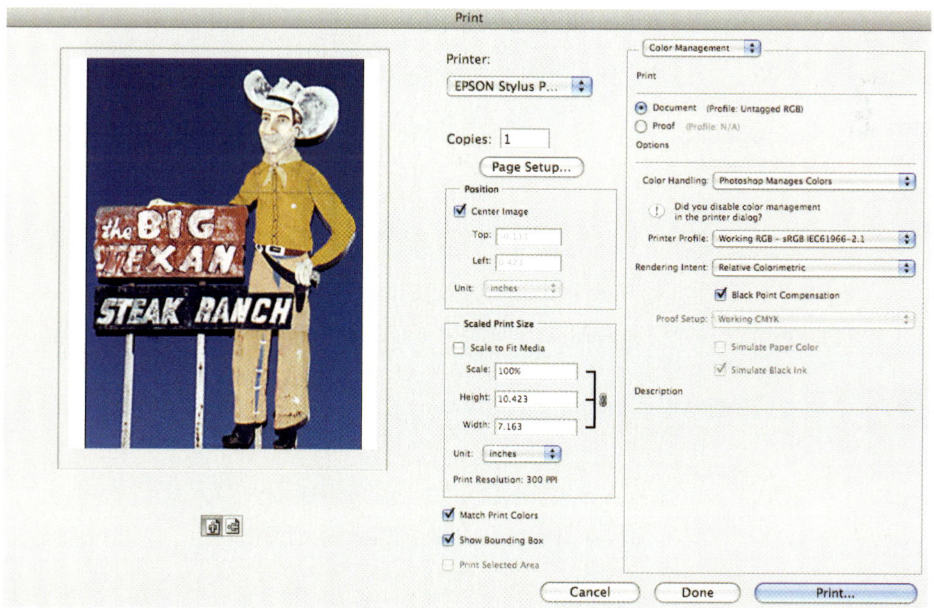

Figure 4.5 The Print dialog box in Photoshop has many options.

The Mac is much the same as the PC with slightly different options. The following list details the choices.

1. Open and tweak the photo you want to print. If at any time your photo appears to change color during the workflow, re-tweak it to the best color you can see visually.
2. In the Print dialog box (File > Print in Photoshop), select the printer you're using where it says Printer.
3. Check Match Print Colors in the check box and select Color Management from the drop-down menu.
4. Choose Document under where it says Print.
5. For Color Handling, choose Photoshop Manages Colors from the drop-down menu, select the ICC profile for the paper you are using where it says Printer Profile, and select Relative Colormetric for Rendering Intent. Finally, check Black Point Compensation.
6. Click on Page Setup from the Print window.
7. Locate and select your printer from the drop-down menu, select your paper size and orientation, and then click on OK and Print.
8. In the next Print dialog box that comes up, select Print Settings from the drop-down menu, below the one that says Presets.
9. Select your paper type from the drop-down menu, then select Color and click on where it says Advanced. Save your settings. Use them the next time you use the same paper as these settings are for. Change the settings for different papers.
10. Choose the print quality and speed you want.
11. Finally, click on Print.

> **NOTE**
>
> These steps vary according to your operating system and which version of Photoshop you are using. If you're having tech issues, it's highly recommended that you phone Photoshop technical support at 800-642-3623, Monday through Friday from 6 a.m. to 5 p.m. (Pacific time). They'll walk you through it step by step.

In both platforms you have the option of saving your settings so that you don't have to reset every time.

Printing in Black and White

When changing your photographs from color to black and white, the first thing you want to do is make sure that you have as much control of the gray tones as possible. There are several ways to get your photos from color to black and white in Photoshop and Photoshop Elements. More about those just ahead.

The next thing to think about is how to print in black and white. The workflow is basically the same as for color (see the preceding section). Epson printers have an Advanced Black and White feature, but that works only when the printer determines the colors, which isn't the best way to manage the gray tones. It's best to manage the gray tones just as you would the color tones.

Now, the real secret to getting a good black-and-white photograph in print is to get the image switched to black and white on your monitor. To change your photos from color to black and white in the Camera Raw dialog box of Photoshop or Elements, slide the Saturation slider to –100 in the Basic options. After that, you can tweak the various other basic options, such as Recovery, Fill Light, Blacks, Brightness, Contrast, and Clarity sliders. This is cool, but it's not the coolest feature of Raw. If you click on the HSL/Grayscale button (one of the buttons below the histogram) and check Convert to Grayscale, you'll have slew of sliders to tweak the grays. In fact, all the color sliders become tones-of-gray sliders for real control of your gray tones (see Figure 4.6).

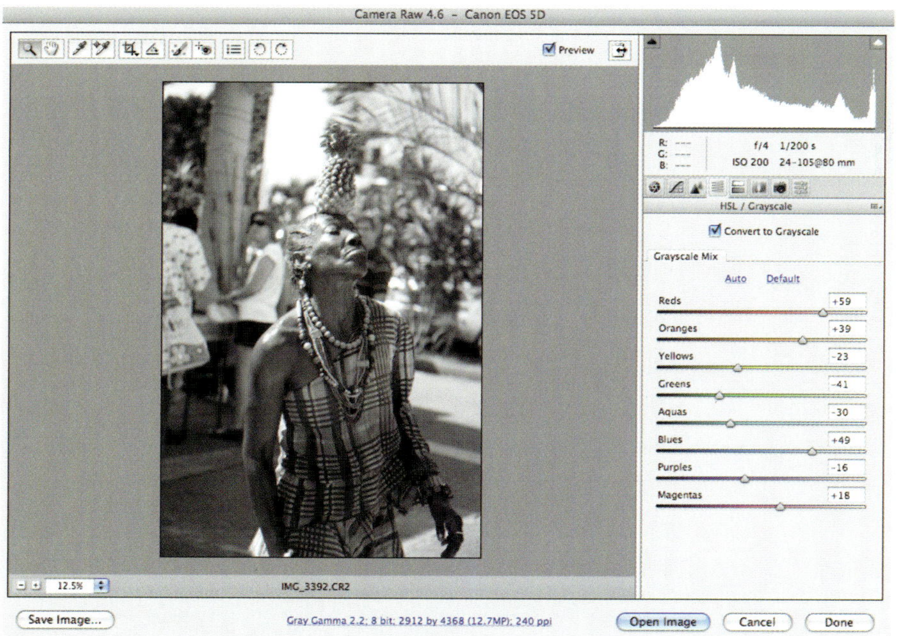

Figure 4.6 If you select Convert to Grayscale, the color sliders become sliders for gray shades in the Camera Raw dialog box of Photoshop/Elements.

You can convert JPEG files to black and white in the main program of Photoshop. The easiest way to do this is to navigate to Images > Adjustments > Black & White. Your image will come up in black and white along with a bunch of sliders with which to tweak it. (These work in the same way as the sliders in Camera Raw's Grayscale mode.)

Maintaining Your Printer

Normally you wouldn't think your printer has to be maintained, but it's a machine, and like all machines, you have to take care of it.

The easiest thing you can do to keep it in shape is keep the dust out by covering it. The next easiest thing you can do to maintain your printer is to go to the manufacturer's website and download the latest printer drivers for your model printer. This will make your printer run smoothly without any software glitches.

If you run the printer once a day, printing a picture rich in color, you'll have less of a chance of the print heads drying out.

One of the most important aspects of printing with inkjet printers (the type of printer used for most photography) is to make sure you use only the ink the manufacturer makes for your model printer.

NOTE

Don't ever refill your ink cartridges—that will not only make lousy prints, but it will destroy your printer.

It's not a bad idea to run a nozzle check and clean and align the print heads every month or so. To do this, follow the directions given in your printer manual.

If you don't use your printer for a long time, the cartridges get clogged and dry out. It can take hours to clean the print heads (you run the cleaning utility on them over and over again) before you'll be able to print normally again. It's worth doing this, though, especially if the ink cartridges are more than half full, because replacing all the ink cartridges in a good color printer is expensive.

NOTE

If you leave your printer on most of the time, the heads will be heated so that the ink is ready to go. Leaving your printer on works well if you use it frequently.

Outsourcing Your Printing

There are numerous options for ordering prints online. I've listed an assortment of services in Table 4.1. Each service is somewhat different in what products they offer, as well as the prices they charge for prints. In the table I've listed the price for 4×6 prints as well as the price for the largest photos they make. For more about enlargements, see the next section.

TABLE 4.1 PRINTING SERVICES

Service	Other Products	Types of Prints	Partners	Price for 4×6 print*	Largest Print Size (Inches)/ Cost*
PEphoto.com	Photo books, cards, calendars, canvasses, mountings, and lamination	Luster, glossy, metallic, mounted, laminated	PE ROES engine, downloadable software for upload	0.06	50×165: contact company for price (matte only); 30×40: $29.99 for first one, $10 for second
QOOP.com	Canvas prints, stickers, greeting cards, calendars, business cards, products that other site members make	Glossy, matte, canvas prints	Flickr	0.19	24×36: $26.99
Kodakgallery.com	Calendars, cards, frames, albums, photo books, and gifts	Glossy, matte	iPhoto	0.15	20×30: $18.99 (matte only)
PhotoWorks.com	Photo cards, gifts	Glossy, matte	Webshots, Flickr, Picasa	0.15	24×36: $34.95
Shutterfly.com	Photo books, cards, stationary	Glossy, matte, canvas	Picasa	0.15 (order 600 for 0.10 per print)	20×30: $22.99
Snapfish.com	Calendars, cards, frames, albums, photo books, and gifts	Glossy, matte	Picasa	0.09	20×30: $19.99

*Costs don't include shipping.

Many printing services require that you become a member of their site. As part of membership, they host your photos. For more about photo hosting, see the "Storing Your Photos Online" section in Chapter 1.

Print partners are a very important feature of ordering prints. Online print services team up with photo hosting sites for easy access to photos. For example, you can order the photos you have on Picasa from Snapfish.com. Picasa will forward your photos to Snapfish, Walgreens, Shutterfly, and PhotoWorks. To do this, go to your Picasa album (or photos), select Prints > Order Prints, go onto the next album (or photo), and repeat. When you're finished picking your photos to print, navigate to Print > View Prints. You'll be taken to a new window where you can forward the photos you've chosen to the print services company you want. Pretty cool.

Blowing Up Your Prints to Wall Size

If you're just itching to have one of your photos blown up big—really big—you can have it done by going to the web and ordering it (see Figure 4.7). Online digital imaging sites have software that lets you upload your photos to their servers so they can access them for enlargements. They can then enlarge and print your photo and send it to your snail-mail address.

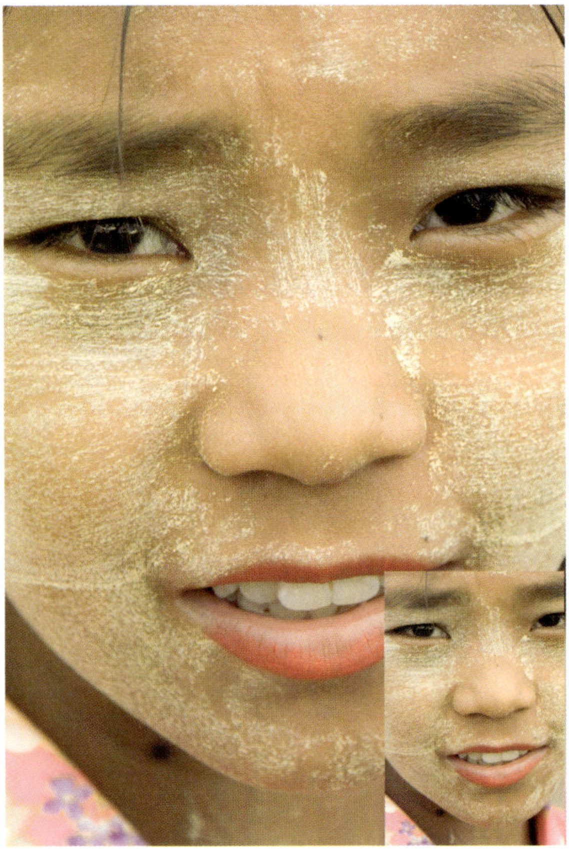

Figure 4.7 You can enlarge your photos using online digital imaging services.

NOTE

Remember that while it's nice to have an enlarged photo, you have to think about how you're going to mount and frame it after you get it enlarged and printed.

In Table 4.1, you can see that PEphoto.com blows up prints to sizes up to 50×165. Another site, EnlargePhotos.com, also offers photo enlarging and printing. Here's the scoop on some sites:

* **PEphoto.com.** You can even talk to these people about your project online at www.help.pephoto.com. A 40×60 print is $79.95 on glossy or matte paper. Shipping costs aren't included. They can mount photos up to 30×40 inches.
* **EnlargePhotos.com.** A 40×60 print, only available on semi-matte, will run you $108.50. Prints on Satin Canvas are also available; the largest they print on this paper is 32×48 inches. The largest print on photo paper is 34×51. Shipping costs aren't included.
* **Epostershop.com.** They can blow up your prints to custom sizes. Their recommendations for size are based upon what the resolution of the image is and how far people are from the image when viewing it. Blowing up an image to 36×54 costs $84.

Of course, enlarging a photo doesn't happen with just a snap of the fingers. There are many factors to consider about the photo before you print it. Those are described in the following sidebar.

BIG PHOTO MEANS BIG RESOLUTION

When you send out your photos for enlargement, it's best not to fool with them before you do it. If you resize or resample your photo in an image processing program (see the section in Chapter 1 called "Resizing Your Photos for Different Uses"), it's likely that you'll degrade its original quality. For example, if you increase the resolution of your photo to 300 dpi and enlarge it to the size you want it printed, Photoshop (or another image processing program) will rebuild the pixels. One thing is for sure, the rebuilt pixels won't provide the nice detail you had in the original photo. Many enlargement services use photo enlargement programs that are much better than Photoshop, so it's best to leave the enlargement up to them. There is a good one—Genuine Fractals GF PrintPro—that's fairly user-friendly if you absolutely have to do the enlargement yourself.

The photo that you upload should be one with a high resolution. Before you decide to enlarge a photo, look at it on your monitor at 100-percent magnification. (Type **100** into the bottom left of the window in which your photo is displayed in an image processing program.) If it looks soft or ragged, know that the inconsistencies will show up in the enlargement.

With today's high-megapixel cameras, enlargement has become a lot easier. It's not uncommon to get a photo enlarged to 42×64 inches if it's a decent picture taken with a dSLR camera of 8 pixels or more.

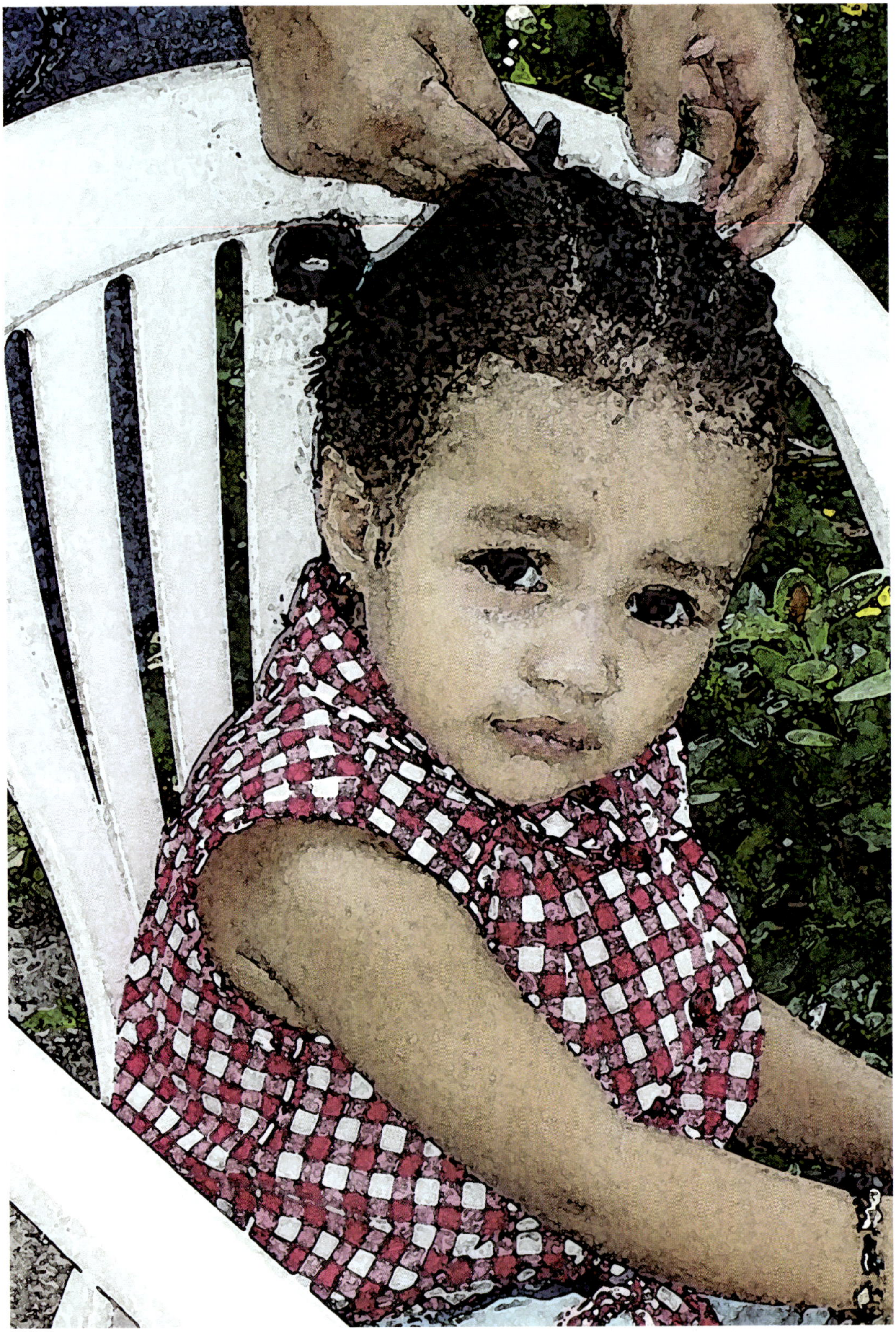

Chapter 5
Scrapbooking Bug Gotcha?

Scrapbooking and photography go hand in hand. Usually a scrapbooking page is made with a couple of photos. The photos used can be anything from a snapshot of the family to a compelling landscape photograph. It just depends on the photography experience of the scrapbooker. Many learn the two hobbies simultaneously. Some get so good at both that they are making money through online platforms, giving tips and advice about how to get better at both hobbies. A great example of this can be found at thepioneerwoman.com. She has an incredible grip on both hobbies (not to mention being a savvy writer)—so much so that her website gets millions of hits. In this chapter, I'll integrate the two hobbies so you can delve into both.

Photography and Paper Scrapbooking

Paper scrapbooking is one of America's favorite pasttimes. When you paper scrapbook, you can start out simple and work your way up to more complex projects. All you'll need to start are your photos (sorted by theme), a ruler, colored paper, acid-free adhesive (to prevent yellowing of images/tape with age), and stencils. To attach your images to the page, use tiny pieces of acid-free, double-stick tape.

Scrapbooks are either 12×12 inches or 8½×11 inches. If you want a quick and easy scrapbook, you may be overwhelmed by the choices when you get to the scrapbooking store or when you buy online. There are fancy cutters, adhesives, die-cutting systems, paper punches, rubber stamps, and other crafting tools. When shopping, stick with items that you know how to use. Remember, the goal for a scrapbook is to have many pages, so start out simple, and as you get the hang of it, try new tools. Stickers and other embellishments with your photos on a nice background sheet work fine. Figure 5.1 shows a scrapbook page I made in about an hour. It costs about $2 (for the stickers and paper) to make.

Here are some pointers about the page:

- **Tilt the pictures.** Notice how corresponding pictures in the bottom and top rows are tilted opposite from one another. I did that so there would be better balance on the page.
- **Build paper frames for your pictures.** However, this was not necessary on the old pictures I used because they were printed with frames.
- **Have at least a little bit of text on the page.** In the case of "Florida," one word is worth a thousand pictures. The word reminds people that the pictures were taken in Florida.
- **Use textured background paper of uniform color (which is usually less than $1 a sheet).** You don't want to have a cluttered background. Many papers have very busy backgrounds. To be sure, some like this and can get away with it if the foreground and background colors complement each other, but personally I don't care for it.
- **Don't overdo the stickers.** A couple on a page is enough.
- **Overlap images artfully.** Notice how the top and bottom rows of images overlap differently for additional balance in the page.

Finally, choose acid-free everything. You want the memories to last generations!

> **NOTE**
>
> Don't use too much tape to attach a photo to a scrapbook page. That way, you can take the picture off for another use without damaging it.

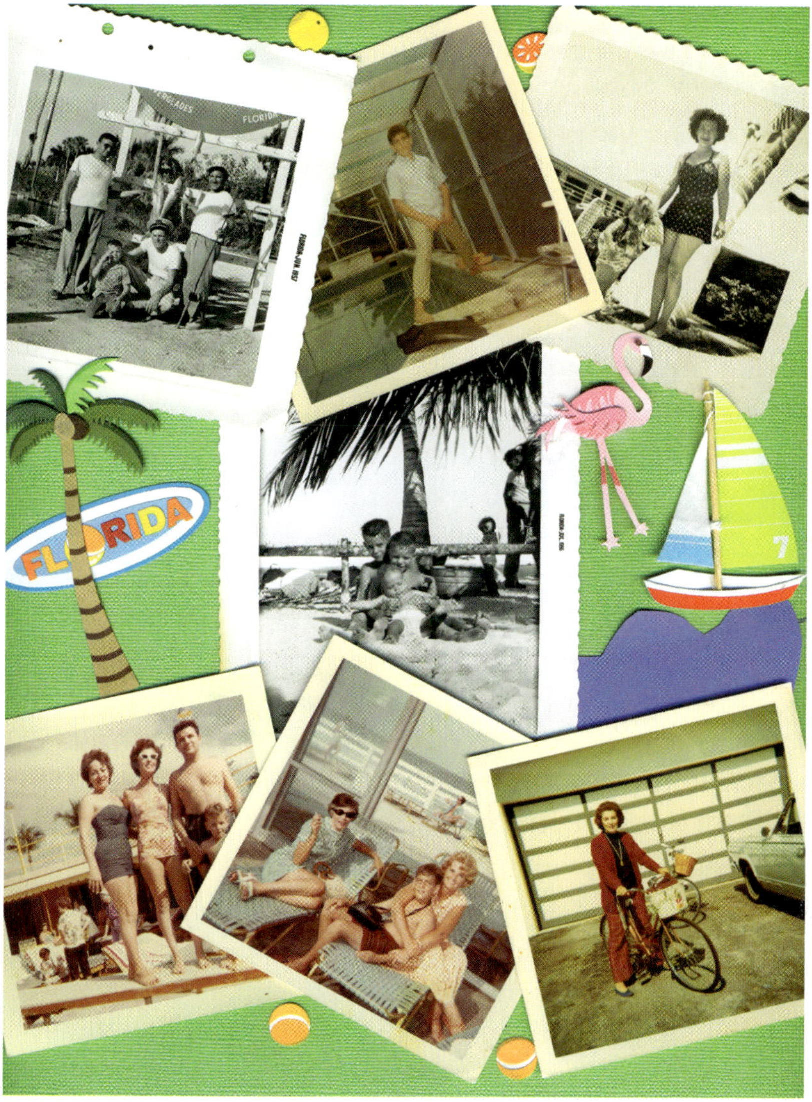

Figure 5.1 Scrapbooking old Florida photos.

Downloading Free Digital Kits for Your Photos

There are websites where you can get free digital scrapbooking kits, which include varied assortments of digital kits, embellishments, alphabets, and templates. Templates, or quick pages—the ones where you just slip in your picture—usually cost a nominal amount—a few dollars or so. If you're not sure what the words mean regarding the content of the digital kits, see the upcoming "Digital Scrapbooking Terms" sidebar.

NOTE

When you're inserting photos into a quick page, use a high-resolution photo and shrink it down (Edit > Free Transform and then click and drag the image until its size is changed) instead of using a low-resolution image and enlarging it. Your picture will be much sharper if you do the former.

- **ScrapbookScrapbook.com.** Their claim is that they have more than 3,000 printables. To find the freebies, go to www.scrapbookscrapbook.com/themes.html. Most are downloaded as easily printable PDF files.
- **DigiFree.** DigiFree (digifree.blogspot.com) scans blogs for free stuff for scrapbookers. Each day it lists blogs that are giving away stuff. If you scroll down the blog archive on the bottom left of the window, you'll find links to posts about past free stuff. Some posts lure you to their site, only to find out that you were looking at previews of available digital kits that cost money. The files are usually in Photoshop's PSD format or are zip files that can be unzipped with StuffIt or WinZip.
- **Scrapping with IkeaGoddess.** Scrapping with IkeaGoddess (ikeagoddess.blogspot.com) offers links to a batch of blogs, each offering free quick pages (templates). Once you get to one of these blogs and click Download for the template you like, you'll be taken to 4shared.com, a free file-sharing site. Don't worry about catching viruses—each download on this site has been checked for the pesky little buggers.
- **Scrapbook Flair.** Scrapbook Flair (www.scrapbookflair.com) has a wide selection of templates. Just go to their website and click on Templates under the Free Download heading, which is on the bottom left of the window. The templates are PTF files that are handled by free software the site puts out. Sorry Mac users, the program only works in Windows.
- **ShabbyPrincess.** ShabbyPrincess (shabbyprincess.com) has free kits. To get to them, click on Downloads in the upper-left part of the homepage. There are a dozen or so kits.
- **Digital Scrapbook Pages.** Digital Scrapbook Pages (digitalscrapbookpages.com/digitals) has inexpensive templates in PSD format. Navigate to Categories > Templates/Sketches. There are hundreds to choose from.

NOTE

On almost all digital scrapbooking sites, there are notes that kits are for personal use only. If you put up a scrapbook page that contains elements from a scrapbooking site, give that site credit in the post.

DIGITAL SCRAPBOOKING TERMS

You might find a few words in this scrapbooking chapter that are unfamiliar. In this sidebar, I'll familiarize you with some words that are used in digital scrapbooking.

- **Embellishments.** These are little things you can put all over a scrapbook page (much like stickers and other cutouts in hard-copy scrapbooks)—anything from frogs jumping to bright bows and ribbons. Embellishments usually match other elements of the page in style and color. See Figure 5.2.

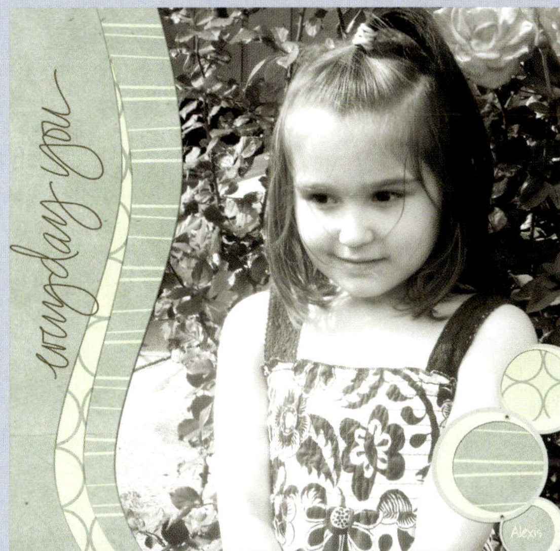

Figure 5.2 Embellishments are the extras you see in the lower-right corner of this scrapbook page. Page courtesy of Heather Landry.

- **PNG file.** Pronounced *ping*, this file is like a digital cutout. In part of these types of files, there are no pixels, and these parts turn out transparent after you insert them into a digital scrapbook page. An example of the contents would be a flower with a transparent background. For an example of a transparent background, see the "Getting Rid of Your Background" sidebar in Chapter 9, "Personal Accessories."

- **Digital kits.** These usually come as zip files, which, when downloaded on your computer, are usually automatically unzipped. Once the files are unzipped, you'll find a folder filled with digital scraps from alpha sets (letters and numbers) to papers (background textures).

- **Templates or quick pages.** These are premade scrapbook page files with layers embedded, into which you can add your photographs. They are usually in Photoshop's PSD format.

Trying Digital Scrapbooking

After you've got some of the free stuff (digital kits, alphabets, papers, and embellishments), go for the big kahuna—a digital scrapbook photo page. You can basically do the same thing with digital cutouts as you can with paper cutouts.

In order to construct a digital scrapbook, you have to either scan your prints or use the photos you have in your computer. You just have to be a bit tech-savvy.

You'll need a program with which to make a digital scrapbook. The best bet for your money is Photoshop Elements. You can also use Photoshop, Corel Paint Shop Pro, or Print Shop.

If you have Photoshop or Elements, you can pick and choose from the items in digital kits and put them on your scrapbook page. All you have to do is create a new layer (Layer > New > Layer) for each new item you add to your scrapbook page. Open the picture you want to add to your scrapbook page and then choose the Move tool (the first tool in the Tools palette in Photoshop) and move the picture from the open file to the scrapbook page. From there, you can resize or tilt the image by selecting it and navigating to Edit > Free Transform and then clicking and dragging the edges to make the image the size and orientation you want. To view the Layers palette to identify the layers you've made, navigate to Window > Layers.

The scrapbook page shown in Figure 5.3 contains scanned images, alphabets (the letters for Bryce and Mom), thumbnails of flags from Google images and a background from a digital kit. It contains the following layers:

Four embellishment layers (the clipart of the small flag images)

Frame around image of Bryce and Mom

Frame around image of Bryce

Picture of Bryce and Mom

Picture of Bryce

B

R

Y

C

E

&

M

O

M

Flag stripes

Background (flag stars)

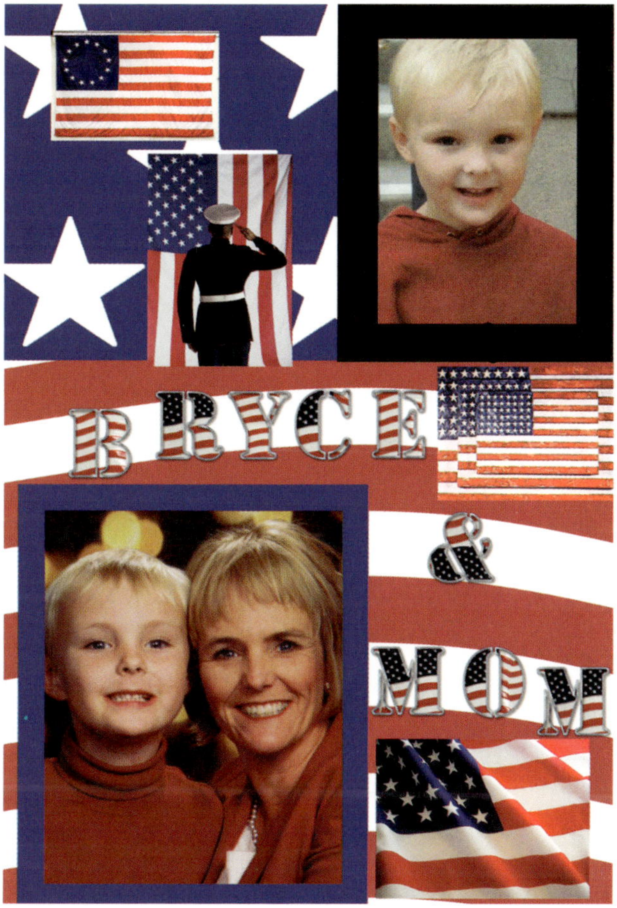

Figure 5.3 A simple layout for a patriotic-themed scrapbook page.

You can do tutorials for more sophisticated layouts using Photoshop or Photoshop Elements at the TheShabbyShoppe.com (www.theshabbyshoppe.com/tutorials/software_tutorials.asp).

Using Photoshop/Elements Filters to Make Art from Photos

Both Photoshop and Photoshop Elements have filters (such as Filter > Blur > Gaussian Blur) as individual commands and filters in a Filter Gallery (Filter > Filter Gallery) to work with in creating effects for your photos.

It's best to apply the filters to copies of the Background image layer (Layer > New > Layer via Copy) so you don't destroy the original. Use a copy of the image each time you add a filter—that way, you can click and drag a layer to the Trash in the Layers palette if you don't like it.

After you've added a copy of the background, use the Filter Gallery by navigating to Filter > Filter Gallery. A window that is divided into three parts will appear. On the right is a preview of your image, in the middle are filter icons, and on the left are sliders where you adjust the filter effects. Each time you click on a filter icon, your preview image changes. Each time you move one of the slider controls, it also changes. Each time you click on a new icon, your picture resets, and the filtering process starts all over.

So what filters look the coolest, giving you the best bang for your buck? That can be a matter of opinion, and it also depends on what kind of photograph you are changing. Some filters look great with landscapes, and others look good with portraits. Generally, I like to get my image to look like a painting. For this, here are two of many choices: Watercolor and Rough Pastels. Neither does much to your image the first time, even after you adjust the slider set of controls. Figure 5.4 shows a picture in which the Watercolor filter was applied several times.

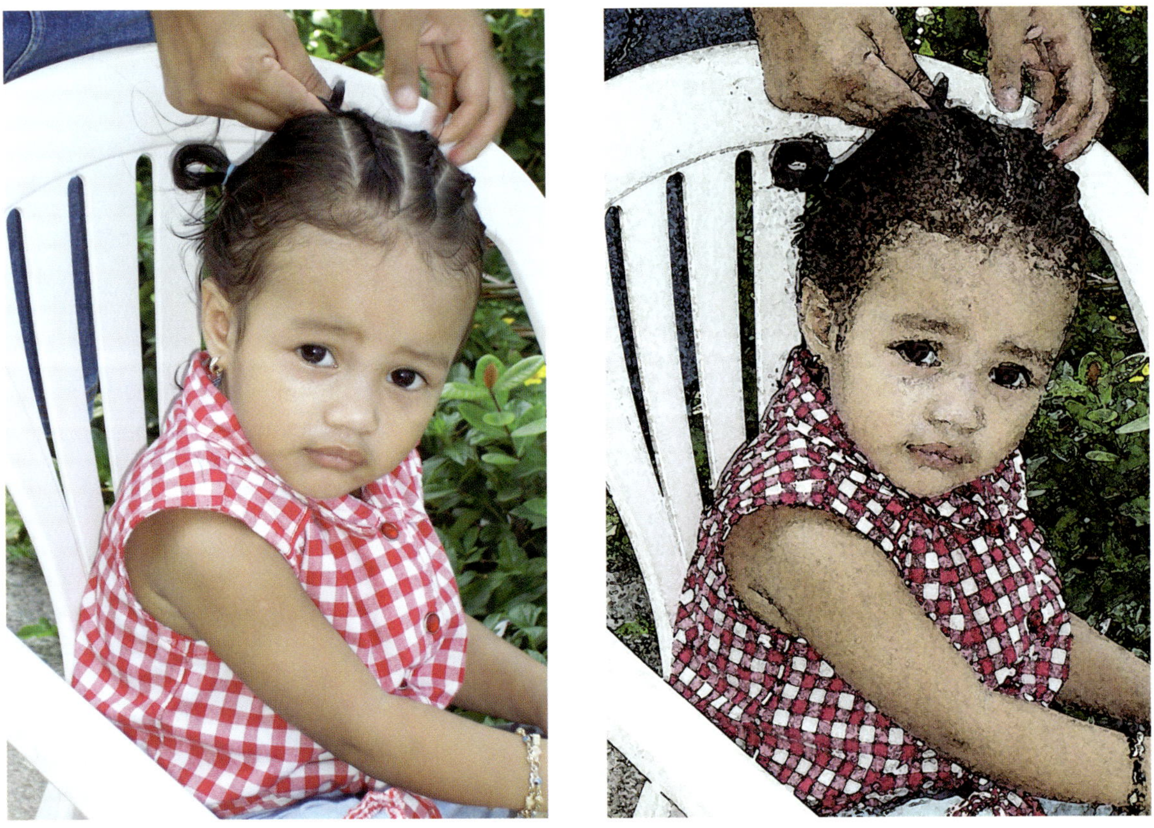

Figure 5.4 Before and after pics where the Watercolor filter was applied several times to get the effect.

NOTE

For some filters, such as Watercolor and Rough Pastels, you have to apply the filter several times.

To apply the same filter again or apply one filter on top of another, you have to close out the window by clicking OK. To apply the same filter again for more of the effect, navigate to Filter > Last Filter. To apply one filter over another, open the Filter Gallery again and choose the filter you want.

Finally, there are some filters, such as Poster Edges, that in one tweak will turn your image into what looks like a drawing. Watch out! You can start combining all kinds of filters and find that hours have passed without you really getting what you want.

Making a Theme for Your Scrapbook Page

Whether your scrapping is paper or digital, before you start, you can go through your photos and pick out the very best ones. Then you can pick a few themes and label folders for each theme, into which you can sort the photos. After that, you can shop for kits or quick pages by theme, and you'll already have photos selected for that theme.

As for themes, there are many. Consider holidays, birthdays, weddings, seasons, family reunions, trips, and other events for making a scrapbook page.

Good themes for kids are dinosaurs, space travel, fossils, Native Americans, the 50 states, your community, life downtown, your culture, your state, patriotism, scouting, and camping.

Around the house, consider themes of gardening, pets, swimming, cooking in the kitchen, and reading books (great for kids to see), as well as making pages for any hobbies in which you or your family might be engaged.

For travel, the sky is the limit (so to speak). Try putting pictures on a map to give a picture story of where you traveled. Print and include flags from the countries you visited with your images. Jot down mini-histories of monuments you've visited on luggage tags (white cardboard with string attached) to accompany pictures of them. Include funny quotes with pictures taken on a trip.

Finally, don't forget daytrips, such as to the local farmers' market or going fishing (see Figure 5.5). Or consider "a day in the life of…" pages.

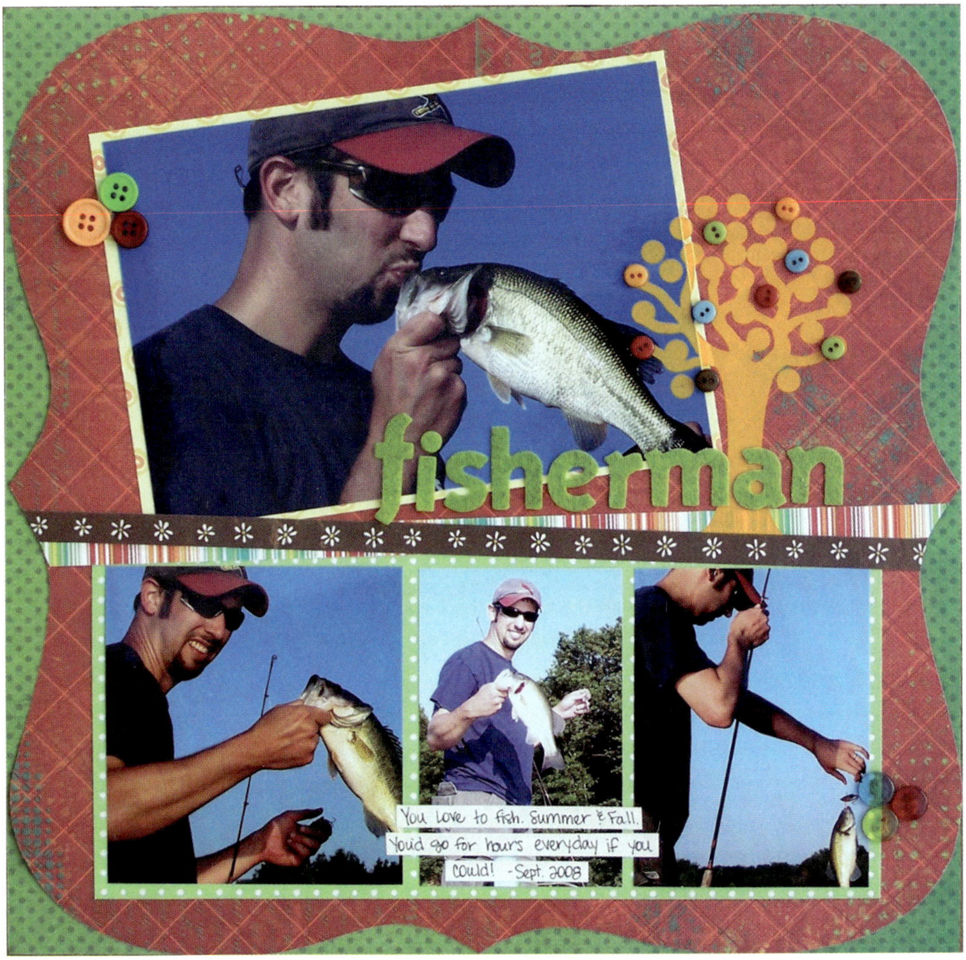

Figure 5.5 Fishing's a great theme for a scrapbook page. Page courtesy of Crystal Brothers.

Looking at What Other Scrappers Have Done

Don't reinvent the wheel; take a look at what other scrappers are doing. In any given minute at scrapbook.com, someone is uploading an image of his or her scrapbook page (see Figure 5.6). The scrapbook.com Gallery has hundreds of thousands of people's scrapbook pages. Themes such as the following grace the scrapbook pages on the webpages of this site: kids playing in the dirt, a trip to a volcano, being lost in the wilderness, being silly, puppy love, chewing gum, building sandcastles, sisters, candy, and encouragement. Titles such as Mr. Adorkable, Real Men Ride Scooters, When Grandma Was Young, My Addiction (diet soda), No Shirt… No Shoes…No Problem, My Monster (sweet kid, right?), and so on make pages containing everyday photos innovative and fun.

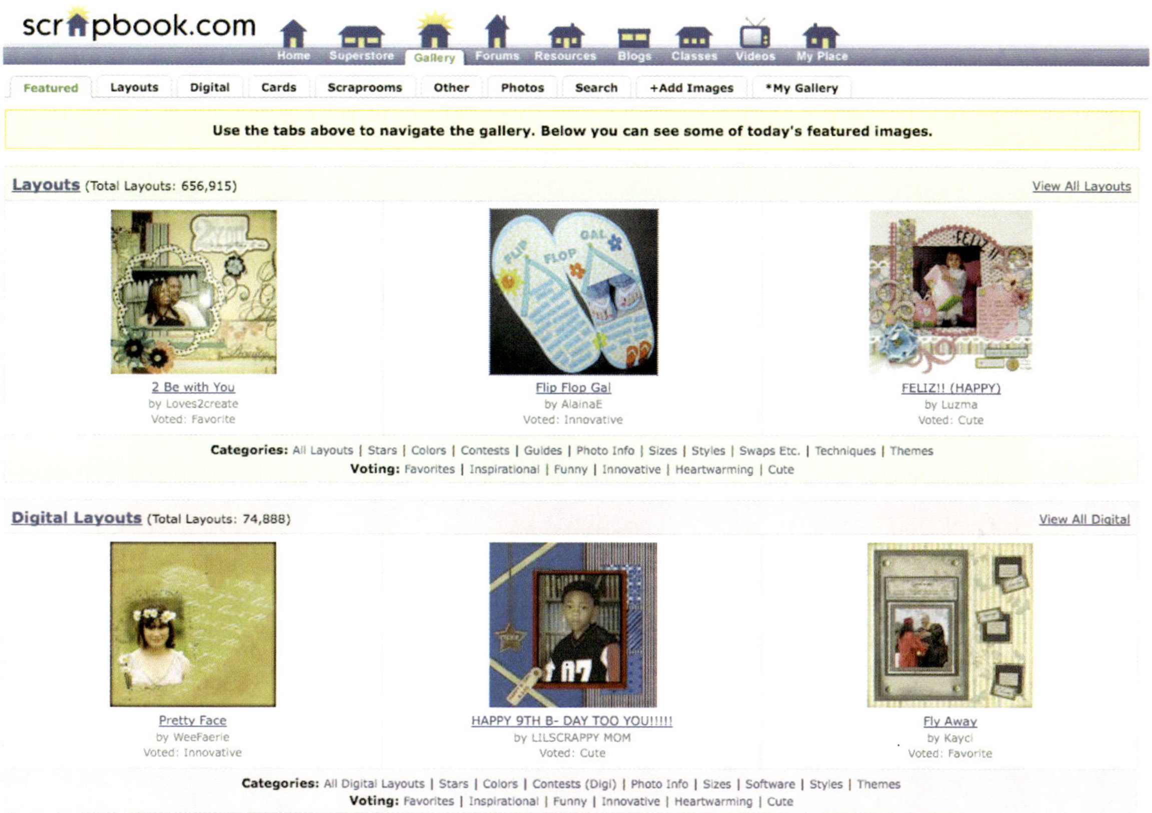

Figure 5.6 Many scrapbooking websites have galleries where users post scrapbook pages.

The scrapbook pages in the gallery are categorized by tabs. The first two—Layouts and Digital —are for viewing paper-made and digitally made scrapbook pages, respectively, in the View the Gallery frame. At the bottom of the View the Gallery frame are categories that apply to all tabs (Layouts, Digital, Cards, Scraprooms, Other Projects, Photos). On the homepage, they include Stars, Favorites, Inspirational, Funny, Innovative, Heartwarming, and Cute. If you click on Themes (click on All Layouts at the bottom of the View the Gallery frame, and in the next window, click on Themes—the last category underneath the tabs at the top of the page), you'll see some of the most popular as subcategories, each of which contains thousands of samples: Animals, Baby, Beach, Birthday, Book of Me, Children, Disney, Family, Floral, Food, Friends, Heirloom, Hobbies, Holidays, Inspirational, Love, Memorial, Military, Moods, Nature, Party, Religious, School, Seasons, Snow, Sports, Teens, Travel, Water, Wedding, and Western.

JOINING AND UPLOADING IMAGES AT SCRAPBOOK.COM

Anybody who's anybody in scrapbooking seems to be a member of scrapbook.com. Their photos grace their scrapbook pages, each one an original creation both beautiful and revealing. Members can upload their photography, too.

To join scrapbook.com, you just give an email address, login name, and password. When you click on My Gallery on the site's homepage, you're taken to a place to upload your images. Just click Browse and then navigate to the photo or photos you want to upload (up to 10 at a time), then click Upload. After the photo uploads, a prompt will ask you what type of photo it is—Layout (paper scrapbook page), Digital Layout (digital scrapbook page), Card, Scraproom (image of the room you scrap in), Other Project, or Photo. Then input boxes will appear, asking you for the Title, Description, and Keywords. There are also groups of categories that you can click, which turn into drop-down menus of subcategories that you can check so that your image shows up in the right place in the Gallery. Finally, you click Submit to place the image in the Gallery.

Organizing Your Scrapbook Album

There are many ways to organize your scrapbook. The way you organize it depends on what you're going to put in it. Your page organization depends on what kind of photos you are going to put in an album. The way you scrapbook old family photos will be different than the way you scrapbook current ones.

The easiest way to begin an organization scheme is to organize your scrapbook pages in the same way you've organized your photos on the computer. Each folder of images could actually make up an entire scrapbook. In Chapter 1 of this book, photos from a Caribbean cruise were organized into folders by port. Scrapbook pages can be organized in the same way—by port.

If the computer is not your guide to scrapbooking organization, you can always organize your scrapbook chronologically by year, highlighting the events of the year. If there are too many pages for one year, you can make seasonal books.

If you just have too many pages to fit in one book, sort your pages by theme and make a separate book for each theme (which you can then sort chronologically).

Another way you can organize your scrapbook pages is by the date you made them. If you do this, you'll see how your pages have gotten better (at least you hope) as time has passed.

If you have old photos you want to scrap, you can do it by decades—'60s, '70s, '80s—for a retro feel. You can also arrange pages by people. You can scrapbook only photos that have images of your mother (or yourself) to have a book about a person.

NOTE

Sometimes you'll find a great themed quick page for which you want to find a photo. If you have many pages where that is the case, there will be no rhyme or reason to your scrapbook pages. If this is the case, you probably can organize the scrapbook pages by the date you made them.

Finally, you can make books for life stages of your family, from your child's toddler years to your daughter's years playing soccer or other sports.

KINDS OF SCRAPBOOK ALBUMS

The best bet for an album for your digital scrapbook pages is a spiral-bound notebook (see Figure 5.7). The best are D-ring notebooks for a couple of reasons. It's easy to take out and put back pages. It isn't the greatest setup, though, for two-page spreads because of the large white space and chrome rings in the middle. If you're into making two-page spreads, post-bound albums are a good choice because they have minimal space between pages.

At scrapbook.com you can order albums at http://store.scrapbook.com/scrapbooks.html. You have choices of albums by size, type, color, and brand.

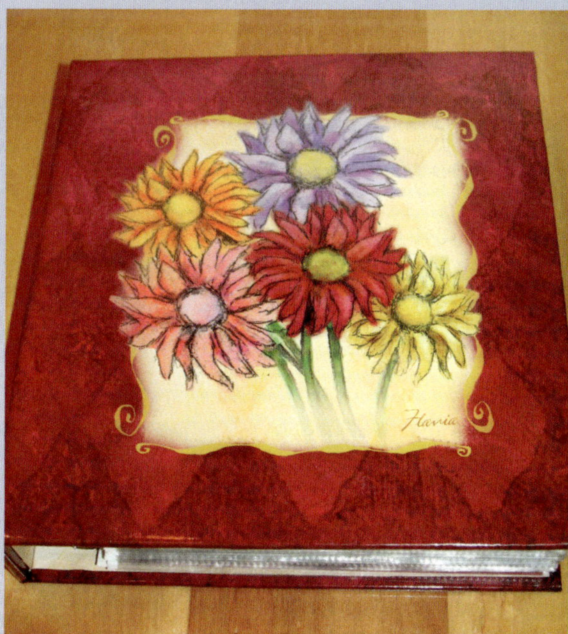

Figure 5.7 A spiral-bound album is a good choice for a scrapbook album.

NOTE

Along with your photos, you can include items such as invitations, concert and theater tickets, and postcards.

Paper Scrapbookers' Supplies Galore

So what's available to decorate your photos to the max (see Figure 5.8)? Here are just a few options to think about if you want to go all the way with your scrapbooking:

- **Alphabets.** Rub-on letters, letter stickers, download and print letters.
- **Background sheets.** Decorative sheets upon which you affix your scrapbook photos and embellishments.
- **Brads.** Two-pronged fasteners with decorations on the top.
- **Chalk.** Rub-on chalk and chalk pencils.
- **Chipboards.** Cardboard (anything from a cereal box inside to the back of a legal pad). You can also purchase chipboard with designs and a place for your photography drawn onto it, as well as chipboard alphabets.
- **Die cuts.** Designs that you cut and/or punch out from a cardboard page.
- **E-cuts.** Designs that you can color in Photoshop and then print out as many times as you want.
- **Embellishments.** Any extras on your scrapbook page—ribbons, buttons, brads (see above), stickers, and so on.
- **Page protectors.** Clear enclosures for scrapbook pages. (Archival is best to preserve pages.)
- **Photo corners.** Inserts that are placed on the four corners of the scrapbook page, into which you place your photos. (Archival is best to prevent damage to the photo.)
- **Paper punches.** Hole punches with which you can punch out shapes and designs or geometrical shapes (to make a frame on top of which you put your photo).
- **Ribbons.** Strips of decorative material from which you can make bows or that you can use to frame your photos.
- **Stamps.** Devices that come in different designs that you press on an inkpad and apply to paper.
- **Stickers.** Decorative material with adhesive on the back. (Use archival.)

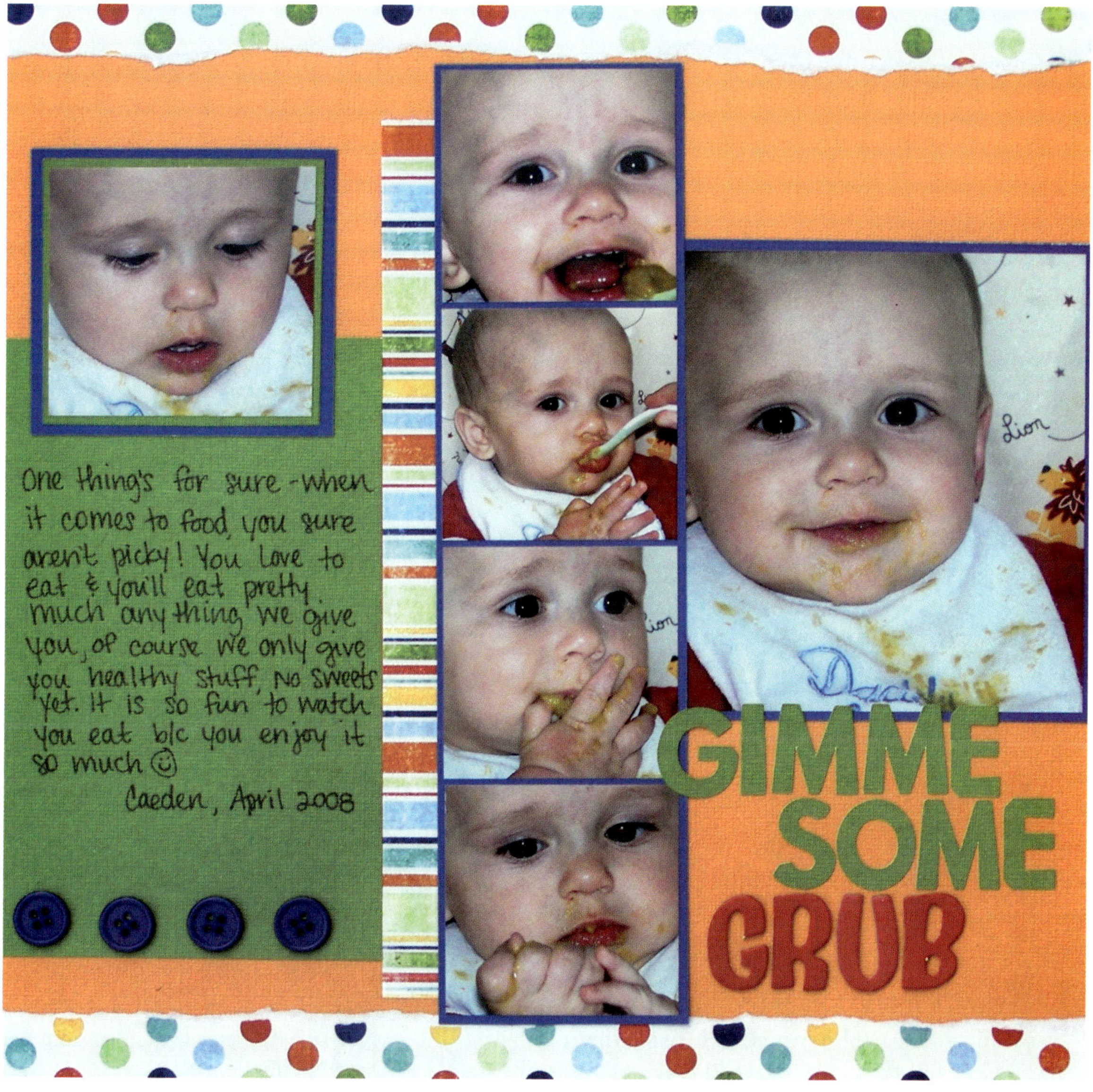

Figure 5.8 This page by Crystal Brothers has buttons, cardstock, patterned paper, chipboard letters, and die-cut letters.

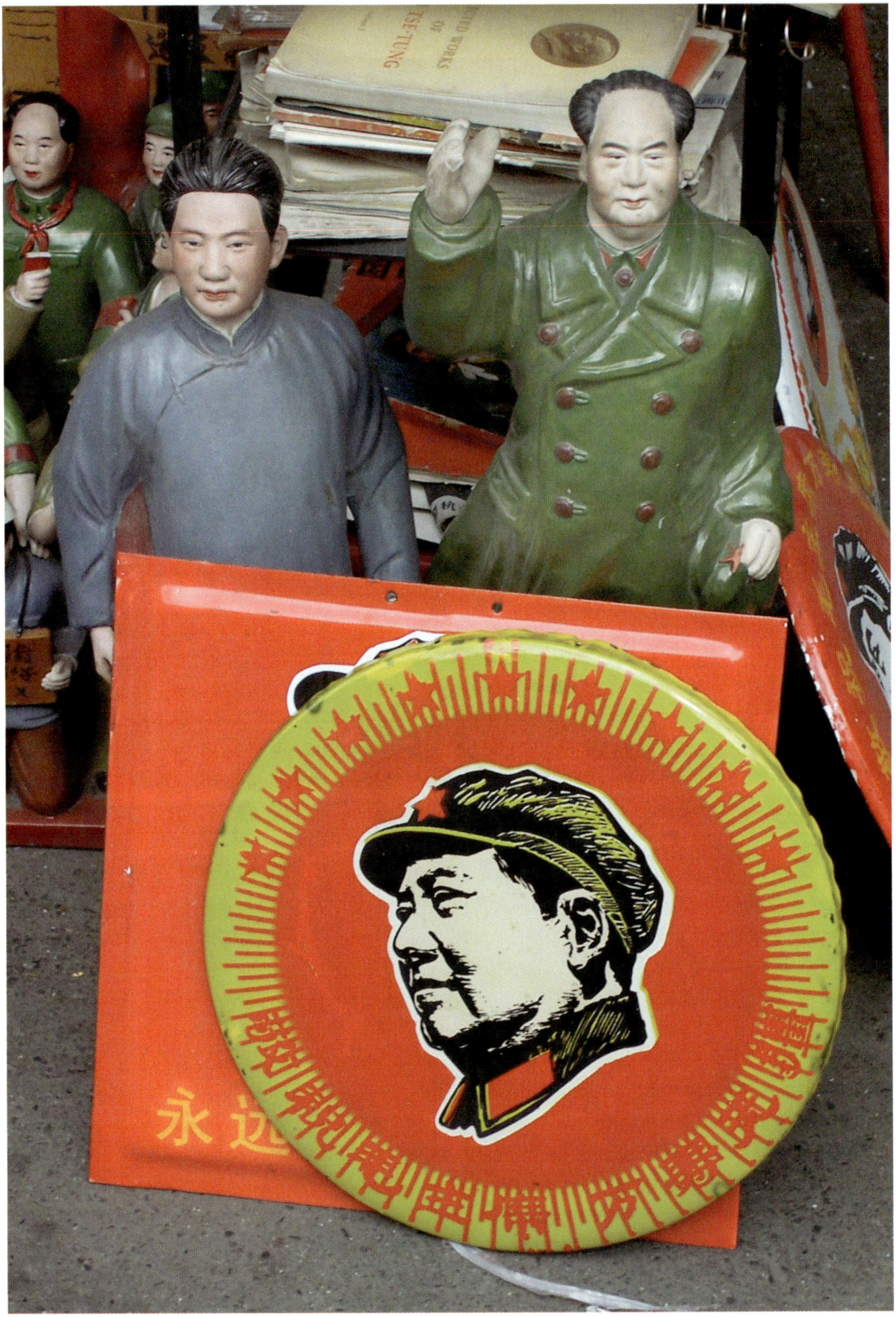
OF
TSE-TUNG
永远

Chapter 6

Photo Blog Heaven

You've probably heard about blogging—online journaling in which all kinds of people are engaged. Along with social networking, it's the thing to be doing on the Internet. And starting a blog has never been easier. A blog (short for *weblog*) started out as a personal diary online, but the size and scope of these online platforms has grown to include marketing, promotion, and selling of ideas, products, and services. Photography blogs are abundant on the web. Some are simple personal sites that illustrate travels and everyday affairs, and others are elaborate magazines, filled with articles and tips about photography and camera equipment. Blogs usually consist of entries or posts that include text information and photographs (though some include only one or the other). Today, blogs link to a number of different sites automatically (with the addition of HTML code to the blog template), so that many things a blogger does on a site are announced on his blog.

Starting a Photo Blog with Blogger

Blogger.com is a good hosting site for a couple of reasons. First, it's free. Second, you can make money off your site with Google ads and other third-party advertising companies, or you can choose to have no ads at all. (Blogger only offers free blog-hosting plans; other blog platforms have a choice of free and paying platforms.) Third and final is that Blogger allows you to upload as many photos as you want on any given day (unlike Fotolog.com, whose free plan only allows one photo a day). Figure 6.1 shows an avatar (illustrated heading) for my blog, Digital Traveler, and one post on Blogger.

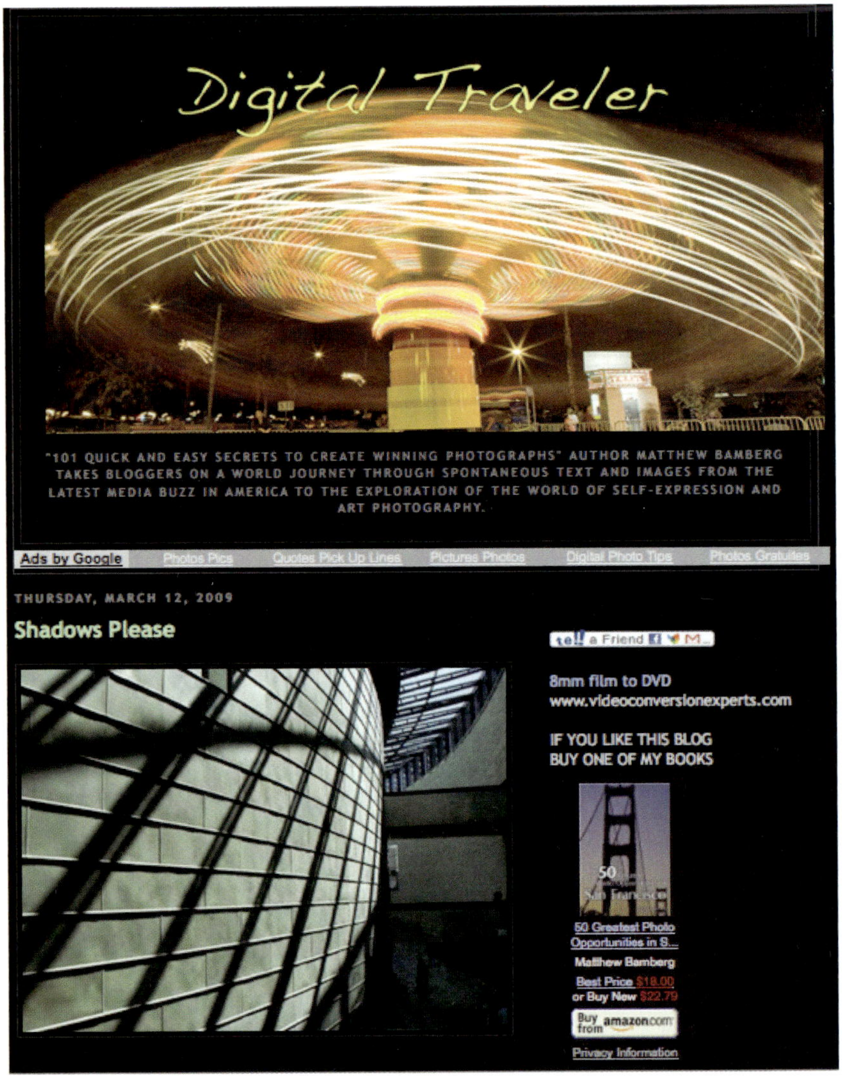

Figure 6.1 You can start a free blog with Blogger and other blog-hosting sites.

Because this is a quick and easy book, you want to create a quick and easy blog. At Blogger, all you have to do is follow these steps:

1. Click on Create a Blog at Blogger.com.
2. Create a Google account or sign in if you already have one.
3. The next page will be Name Your Blog. Type in the title of your blog. (There's a 29-character limit.)
4. Type in your blog address, which is in the format nameyoutypehere.blogspot.com and becomes the URL your blog will have after you publish it.
5. Check the URL availability. Someone may have taken the URL you want to create. If they have, Blogger will give you some optional choices to click on for a new URL.
6. Type in the word verification (a code, usually characters and/or numbers given to you, that you retype in a text box).
7. Click on the Continue button at the bottom right of the window.
8. Choose a template by scrolling through the bunch that appears and then clicking on one.
9. A page will appear, telling you that your blog has been created. Click on Start Blogging.

The next window that appears will look like a word processing document. As a matter of fact, it works like one, too. Move your cursor over each of the buttons, and a tag will appear, telling you what to do. Type in something and add a JPEG image and then click Publish Post.

Finally, you'll get a note in the next window giving you an option to View Blog. Go ahead and click on it. If you want to add another post, click on New Post in the top-right window.

The last thing to know about Blogger is that you can view and add HTML code in a blog's template. This comes in handy if you want to change the layout of your blog and/or add advertising content.

GUARDING YOUR PHOTOS

Take a look at the protester in Figure 6.2. Then think about these questions.

1. Who owns the photo?
2. Who can use the photo?
3. Does Blogger (Google) have any interest in this photo if you put it on their site?
4. What are the stipulations for use of this photo?
5. What would you have to do to protect the photo from others using it?

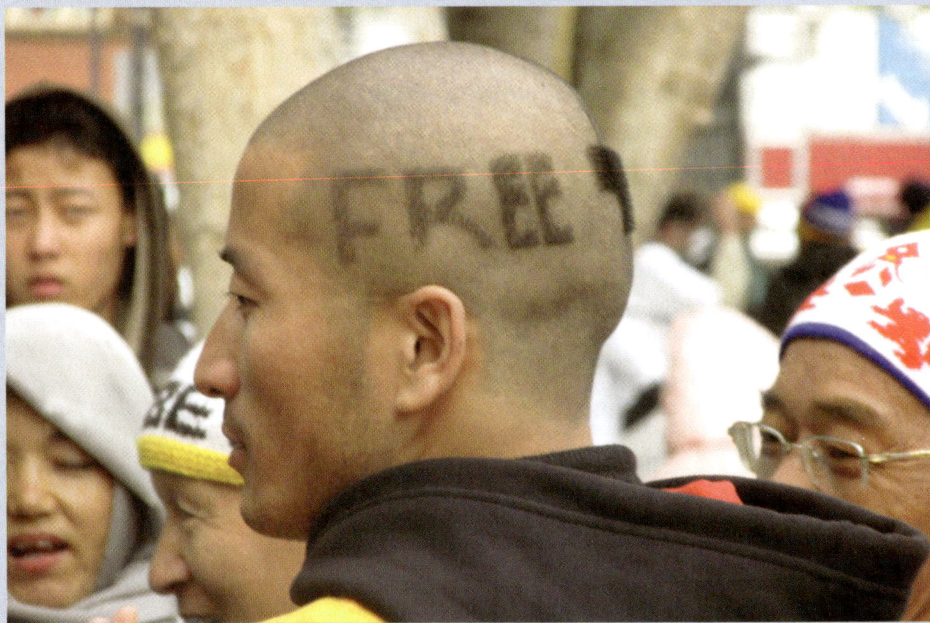

Figure 6.2 Picture of man at protest march.

As far as who owns your photos when you post them on a blog, the answer to that would be that you do, even if you don't state that the photo is copyrighted.

"All major nations follow the Berne Copyright Convention. For example, in the USA, almost everything created privately and originally after April 1, 1989 is copyrighted and protected whether it has a notice or not." This is known as the *Berne Copyright Convention*. Thanks to http://www.templetons.com/brad/copymyths.html for this information.

These questions I posed are some that come to mind when you post a photo on Blogger or Flickr. First, Yahoo!, the owner of Flickr, states that it "does not claim ownership of Content you submit or make available." Most social networking and blog hosting sites have this type of statement in their Terms of Service, so you don't have to worry about them taking your photos. If you get to a site where you are unsure, read the fine print—the Terms of Service. The same thing goes for someone using your photo for a print or an online publication. Don't sign something that gives them your rights to the photo, regardless of whether you get paid for it.

As for having other people take your photos, Flickr says it best: "Respect the copyright of others. This means don't steal photographs that other people have taken and pass them off as your own. (That's what favorites are for.)"

> This implies that you're free to link to others' photos, but you're not free to borrow them. If you want to use a photo, ask the owner for permission. I remember when an editor of a family magazine asked to use a picture I had taken of young Buddhist monks in a classroom. She had found the picture in my Better Photo gallery (which is public). I had to say no. It's not because I'm mean; it was because in the back of my mind I had plans for that photo. It ended up on the cover of my book, *101 Quick and Easy Secrets to Create Winning Photographs*.

Starting a Blog with Images and Text on WordPress

Another excellent alternative for bloggers is WordPress.com (see Figure 6.3), a free blog hosting service that has a bit more on its interface for making new blog posts than Blogger does. The most important difference between the two popular blog hosting sites is that you can make money with ads on Blogger, while you aren't permitted to on WordPress. Both blog platforms let you click and drag around widgets as part of organizing the layout of your blog. A widget can be anything from a display of your Flickr photos in the sidebar of your blog to monthly archive links of past blog posts.

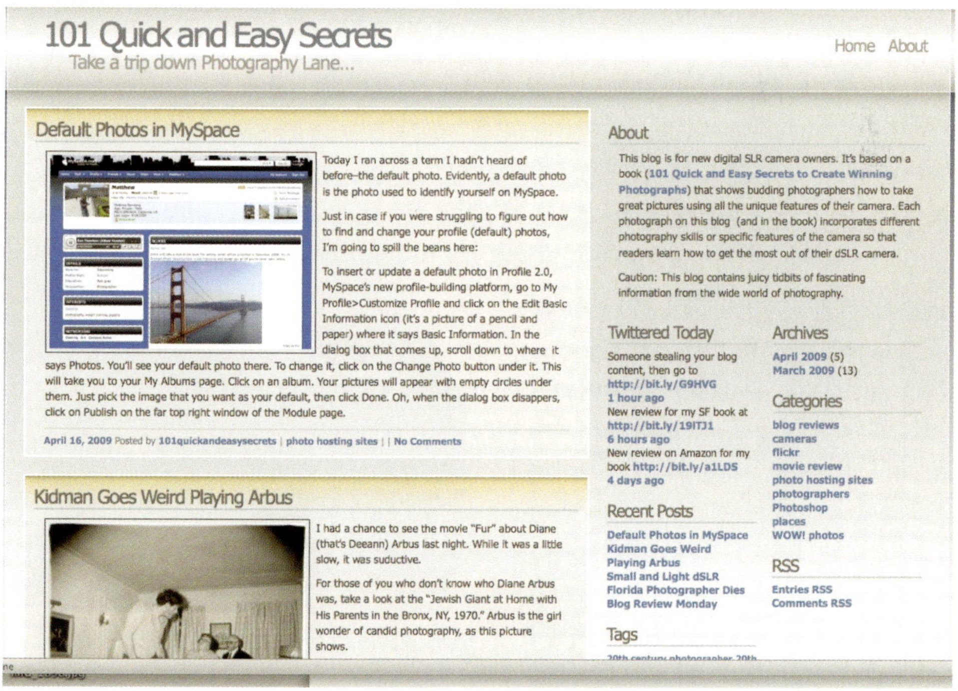

Figure 6.3 WordPress blogs can have a sleek three-column design.

To use WordPress, you have to register for the site, an easy process where you create a username and a password.

> **NOTE**
>
> Be careful with your username, as it will become part of your URL. Your username cannot have any spaces. For example, my username is 101quickandeasysecrets, so my URL is 101quickandeasysecrets.wordpress.com.

Next, you'll have to check your email to verify your account. After you verify, you'll be asked to log in. You'll then be taken to a Dashboard, where you submit a post. Again, like Blogger, it works like a word processing program, except that there are a few more bells and whistles on the page.

To create a new post, click on New Post at the very top of the window, where it's shaded gray. You'll be taken to a window that looks like a word processor. Type in a title and some content (perhaps write about the photo). Next, you upload your photo by clicking on the Upload Image button—one of a series of buttons next to where it says Upload/Insert. (It will say Add an Image when you move your cursor over the correct button.) A navigation window will come up. Click on Select Files and navigate to a JPEG image you want from your computer. A new drop-down box of information will come down with a thumbnail of your image. Here, you can type in a title, caption, description, and URL you want viewers to go to when they click on the picture. Next, choose your photo's size. (I usually choose medium—any bigger than that, and the entire layout of the blog gets messed up.) Last in this window, click on Insert into Post.

The photo will show up where you've typed in your content. Your text will be wrapped around it. You can now publish the post by clicking on Publish on the right side of the window. If you want to see your blog, just click on Visit Site in the gray area at the top of the window.

Starting a Photo Blog with Images on Aminus3

Aminus3.com, a photographer-run blog hosting site, has been highly rated by many professional photographers and bloggers. While it's a one-photo-a-day site, its other features make up for the limitations on photo uploads.

The first thing you do to make a blog at Aminus3 is sign up. When you do, the site will ask you for a subdomain name (a name that will be used in your new site's URL, on the order of http://subdomain.aminus3.com) among other things (name, title of blog, and so on) to get started. After you create an account, an email verification will be sent to your email address.

> **NOTE**
>
> After you've registered with Animus3 and gone to the homepage to sign in, it's difficult to find where you sign in. You have to scroll to the bottom of the homepage and click on Sign In on the left side of the window, below where it says Account.

After you sign in, click on Check on Your Account Page. At the top part of the window that comes up, there will be a note that your site is pending activation. Don't worry about this—after you post a few photos, your site will be activated. Below the note, click on Upload New Images. You'll be taken to a page of prompts, not a page that looks like a word processor. Unlike WordPress and Blogger, you can't add links or stylize text with Aminus3. This site has an emphasis on the photo!

The first prompt asks you to browse to your image. Click on it and navigate to a JPEG image (Aminus3 recommends that the image be between 800 and 2,000 pixels) on your computer that you want to upload. Other prompts include Category, Tags, Image Caption, Title, Description, Feature, Portfolio (mark this Yes if your image is really good and it will be placed in your online portfolio), and Adult—the last three questions have Yes/No answers.

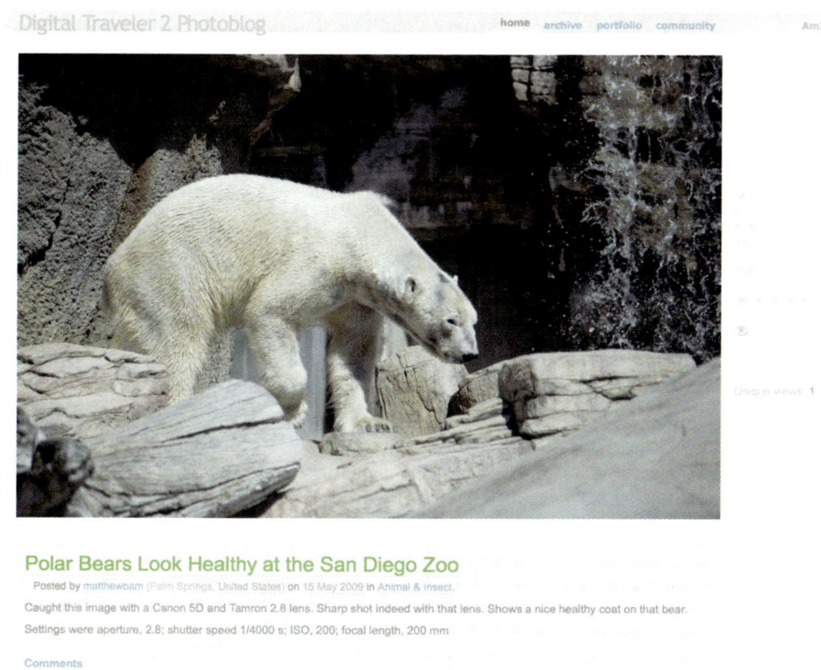

Figure 6.4 Aminus3 places your photo prominently in the post.

When you're finished providing all of the information, click on Save and View. You'll get something like you see in Figure 6.4, which shows that the design of the blog is quite nice with a very prominent image. Notice in the picture that there is a Portfolio tab—a place where you can put your best images, the ones you mark to be placed there when you make posts.

Finally, if you want to go back and edit the text, change some options in a post, or upload a new photo, you can go back to the prompts page by clicking on Img at the far top right of the window of your blog's homepage.

Getting Lots of People to View Your Photo Blog

There are a couple of ways that you can drive people to your photo blog. The following sections describe a few of the most up-to-date ways to do this.

Choosing the Correct Settings at Your Blog Hosting Site

Sites such as Blogger.com offer settings where you select publicizing options. For example, when you select Settings at Blogger, you have the option to set your blog to send pings (notices to the web that you've updated your blog each time you've published a blog post), post pages (make each post its own webpage), and turn on your site feed (people can subscribe to this, permitting parts of your blog to show up on their websites, such as other people's Google and Yahoo! homepages).

Claiming Your Blog at Technorati and other Blog Listing Sites

You can claim your blog on Technorati to get it listed in their search engine. To do so, you have to register first. (Don't worry; it's free.) From there, you just type in your URL on the Claim Your Blog page. After Technorati approves your claim, you'll be asked to input a description of your blog (have one ready that is free from grammatical errors and other errors of the English language) and tags (keywords) by which you can identify what content you have in the blog. For example, good tags for a photography blog with lots of candid shots would be "candid photography." For more about keywords, see the "Tagging Your Photos" sidebar in Chapter 2.

Other blog listing sites and/or search engines include BlogBurst, Blogged, BlogExplosion, Blogarama, and Popdex. Most are free. Why not let each know about your blog so you'll have the potential for hordes of visitors?

Submitting Your Blog URL to Google

You can also let Google know that you have a blog by submitting its URL to www.google.com/addurl.html.

Including Short Descriptions of Your Images within Your Posts

If you are uploading an image of a kid playing baseball, make sure you include a caption for the photo that says the photo is a kid playing baseball. If you do, Google Images might pick it up when people search for images of "kid playing baseball." It also doesn't hurt to name the file by what's in the picture. A good name for a photo of a kid playing baseball would be kid_playing_baseball, for example.

> **NOTE**
>
> Never leave spaces between words in filenames. Other people might not be able to view the files if you do. Many servers don't read blank spaces in filenames or URLs.

Composing a Photo Essay for Your Blog

If you're blogging at WordPress or Blogger, there's plenty of space for text and images together. Essay-blog.com describes a photo essay as "an essay that summarizes what the writer observes in a specific image." I couldn't have said it better myself. But there's more…

After writing nearly 1,000 blog posts over the past five years, I've come to the conclusion that there are two different types of photo essays. One type begins with an essay that is accompanied by a photo, in which case the essay is written first. Another type is an essay written about a photo, in which case the photo is taken first. When writing blog posts, you'll have photo essays that begin with a picture you've taken, as well as ones where you'll write text and come up with a photo to match after you've written a post.

Here are a couple of things you can do with a photo to create a photo essay from it:

- Describe a photo in detail in terms of the story or history it tells.
- Write about how you captured an image—say, for example, from a precarious vantage point (atop a steep cliff with a stiff breeze at your back).
- Write about how you achieved the effects that viewers see in an image. (This most likely will involve camera settings.)
- Write a fictional story about what's in a photo.
- Create a photo essay about all the places you visited on any given day on a trip.

You probably have figured out that the photo is taken before the writing happens with the photo essays listed here.

When you're thinking about doing the writing first, there are many ideas you can come up with. You can be imaginative, coming up with a photo relating to the writing after the fact.

- Write a short story (or poem) about a person and take one or more pictures of that person.
- Write about a place you enjoy visiting and then take a picture of that place.
- Write about a dream you have had and then find a photo that resembles that dream.
- Write about how to do something you're good at and then take a photo of each step of the process.
- Write a story for a web article site and find a picture that will go with it.

Now for the important part—an example of what a photo essay looks like. The following sidebar, "Mao and Shanghai Retro," shows a sample blog post—one that takes into account the history behind a photograph. Figure 6.5 is an image I've posted on my blog, "Digital Traveler," as part of a photo essay.

MAO AND SHANGHAI RETRO

All one has to do in Shanghai for some great shots based on the popular Mao era of the middle of the last century is hop in a cab (they're cheap) and go to the Dongtai Lu Antique Market. Just in case you were wondering who Mao is, he was the dictator who in 1949 declared the birth of the People's Republic of China. Several years ago, *Time* magazine reported that even though Mao was "beyond redemption," the Chinese still sell his image everywhere, especially in Dongtai Lu. The guy is ubiquitous in trinkets in dozens of market stalls, as you can see in Figure 6.5. However horrible he was, the propaganda that was spread was colorful and simple—just the kind of 20th century art many of us here in America have been craving of late. While our culture knows little about Mao's message (it wasn't pretty), we do recognize his hand waving and stoic posture that seem to amuse. See for yourself...

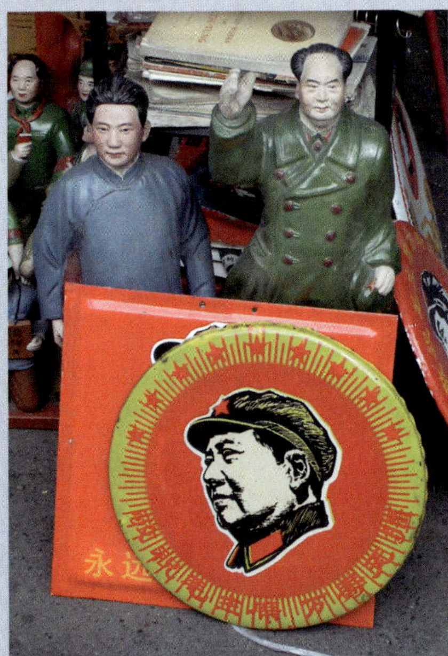

Figure 6.5 A photo as part of a blog post with a historical bent.

Choosing Photos That Tell a Story for Your Blog

When you look at the picture of the Elvis impersonator in Figure 6.6, an immediate story comes to your mind. It's the story of an iconic musician who died tragically and has been brought back to life time and time again through the impersonators who mimic his every move.

My point here is that if you catch an image of something like an Elvis impersonator, you have myriad story opportunities to tell in a blog post. Most people know the Elvis story, and most don't mind reading about it again, especially if you tell little tidbits about the man from things you know or have read on the Internet. For example, just by typing "Elvis facts" into Google, I found out that Elvis was a black belt in karate, made 31 movies, and won three Grammys for his gospel recordings.

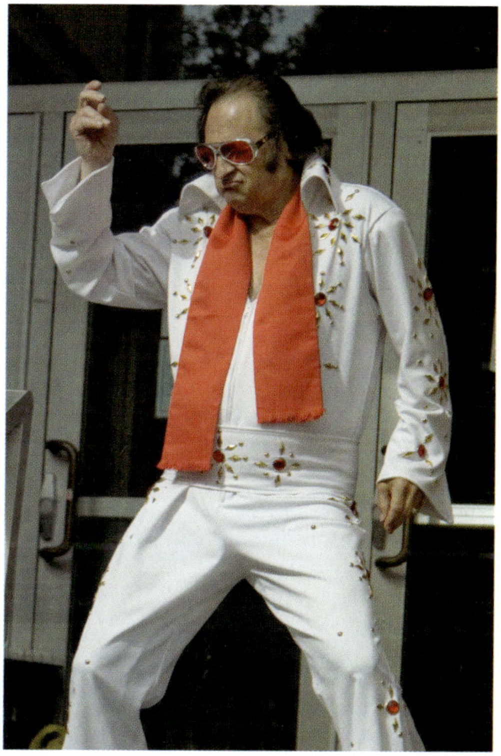

Figure 6.6 Everyone loves Elvis.

You can stretch the Elvis story like a Gumby doll, adding your own feelings about the musician, panning him, worshipping him, and/or parodying him. The sky's the limit with this guy. You can even critique the impersonator you have photographed.

Of course, Elvis is just one example. There are other stories that can be caught in a shot or two. When you associate a photo with a story, you're within the realm of photojournalism. You can find and save photos to tell stories by attending concerts, public meetings, demonstrations, community events, fairs, carnivals, fiestas, holiday celebrations, marathons, and/or baseball and football games. When you're at these events, look for the photo ops that will capture people's eyes and that will help describe a story about the event. Another way you can tell a story is to have your camera with you at all times and catch news as it happens. For example, if you see something on fire, photograph it.

Once you collect these photographs, make a folder called BlogPostPhotos. Put the photos that tell stories in this folder for blog posts you can use in the future. That way, when you come up short on an idea for your blog, you can look through your BlogPostPhotos folder and use a photo from there to write your post.

Discussing Camera Settings for Your Photos on Your Blog

Experiment with different camera settings and tell the world about it. There aren't very many photographers who don't take an interest in what settings were used to shoot a compelling shot. Today, finding out what settings you used for each shot has never been easier—not only with dSLR cameras, but with point-and-shoot models, too.

Figures 6.7 through 6.10 show four different pictures under a variety of circumstances, each requiring skill and knowledge of camera settings. In a blog post, you can write about any picture, focusing on the settings and making a caption for the photo you are writing about that states the camera settings used to take the picture. You can write about what mode you like to shoot in. (I prefer aperture priority mode.) You can also bring up what ISO speeds are best for different kinds of light. For more about aperture, ISO speeds, and other camera settings, see the "Camera Settings in a Snap" sidebar.

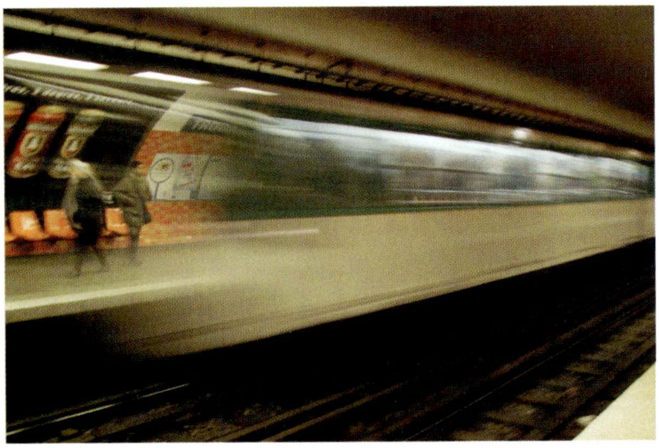

Figure 6.7 0.4 sec at f/2.8; ISO 100; focal length 36mm.

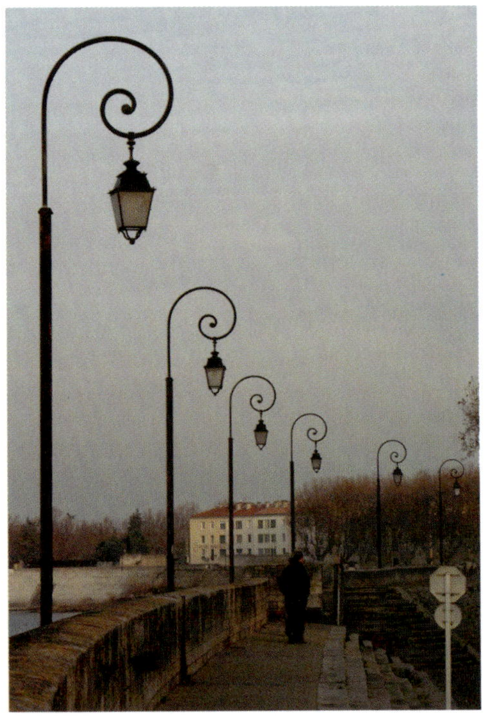

Figure 6.8 1/400 sec at f/11; ISO 400; focal length 110mm.

CAMERA SETTINGS IN A SNAP

Here's the skinny about the camera settings you need to know about in order to understand what your camera has done to take a picture.

- **Shutter speed.** Fast shutter speeds (1/1000 second) freeze action. Slower shutter speeds will blur action (see Figure 6.7).
- **Aperture.** You can control in front of and behind your subject by setting the aperture (the diameter of the lens opening). If you set the aperture wide (f/2.8–f/4), you'll get a soft background behind your subject. If you set it narrow (f/11–f/22), the entire frame will be sharp, as shown in Figure 6.8.
- **ISO speed.** This setting is a measure of how sensitive your sensor is to light. Most of the time, you set your camera to a high ISO speed (ISO 1000 and above, making the sensor very sensitive to light) when you're shooting at night without a tripod. Figure 6.10 shows a shot taken when the camera was set to a high ISO speed.

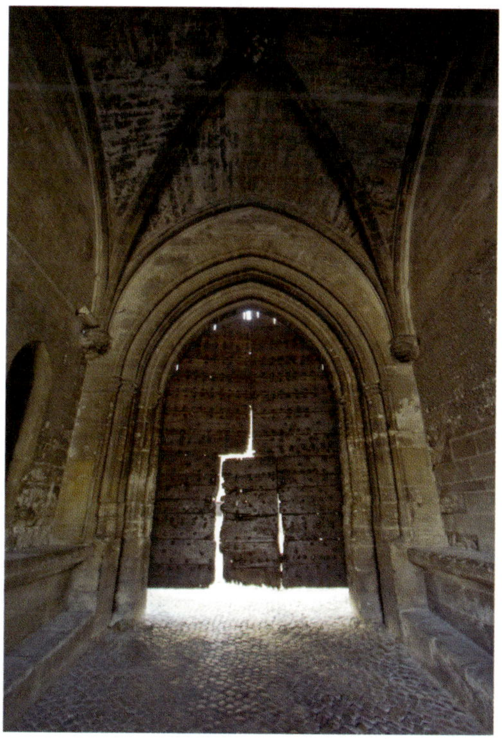

Figure 6.9 1/6 sec at f/4.5; ISO 200; focal length 60mm.

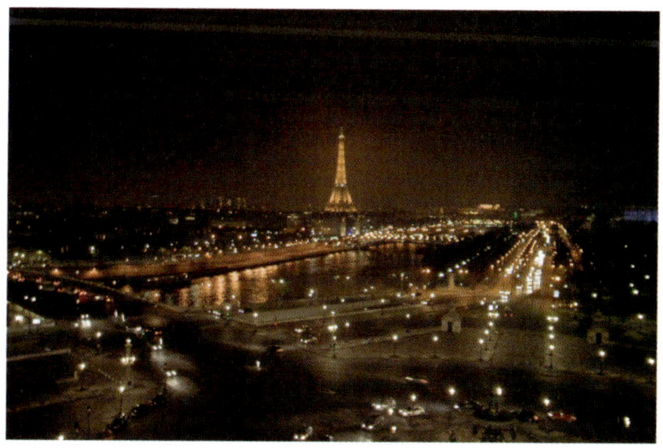

Figure 6.10 1/13 sec at f/4.5; ISO 1600; focal length 32mm.

Posting Retro Family Photos on Your Blog

Rolling back the clock is easy when you have a blog. You can post photos and write about any time period you want.

Images of the 20th century almost always please. There's one blog—Old Picture of the Day at old-photos.blogspot.com—where all they post are old photos.

If you have hundreds of old photos, you don't want to pick just any photo or even a photo that's a family portrait (unless it was taken near the turn of the last century—a time when the people would be posing outside in their Sunday best). You want to go for retro. Study your photos for:

- **Style.** When sorting through your photo collection, look for people in swimsuits by the pool (I've seen random pictures of these sell for big bucks), people posing in stylized clothing (for the 1960s, bell-bottom slacks and wide headbands, for example), and/or people engaged in an activity (such as talking on a Princess phone). For street scenes, look for what are now vintage autos in traffic and neon signs, as well as flamboyant architecture (think Tomorrowland).
- **Film type.** Some of the best shots you'll find in your photo collection are sepia-toned and black-and-white photos. Don't forget the cardboard ones from the turn of the last century. You'll also have fun posting the exaggerated colors of Kodak's Kodachrome prints. The pictures that popped out of Polaroid Instamatic cameras are fun to post, too!

Of course, when you post an old photo (family or otherwise), you're going to want to write about when and where it was shot. In Figure 6.11, a picture of my mother, I know from my family's history that the photo was taken in Miami Beach. (Perhaps the diving board is a giveaway.) My guess of the time period can be calculated by approximating how old she was in that shot (say, 20 to 30) and adding that to her birth year, which was 1926. That would make it a picture taken between 1946 and 1956.

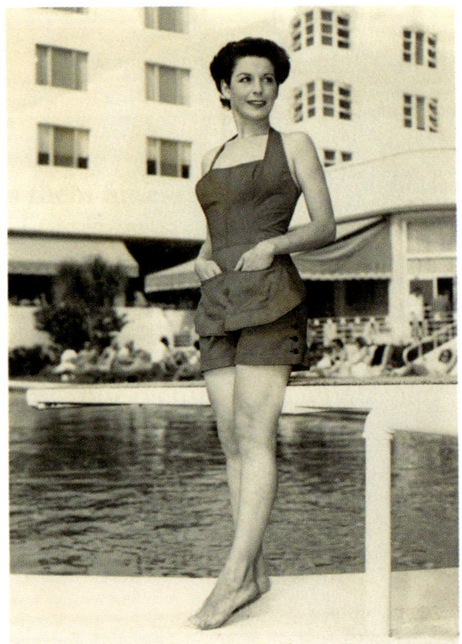

Figure 6.11 Images from the middle of the last century are great for blog posts.

SCANNERS: WHAT TYPE SHOULD I USE?

Since you are going to resize your photo for the Internet, you don't need a high-end scanner. You can get a good scanner, such as the Canon CanoScan 8800F (often rated #1 for scanners at amazon.com), for about $200. The nice thing about scanners is that you can set them to scan at 72 dpi, the optimal resolution for photos uploaded to the Internet. (If you plan to edit your photos, though, don't scan at 72 dpi, but at 300 dpi. Then fix the photos, then resize in Photoshop/Elements at 72 dpi. To save, navigate to File > Save for Web and Devices.) Most scanners will scan negatives and positives (slides), too. While today's scanner does a great job of scanning, the differences in price are determined by how fast the scanner is. Sometimes the cheap scanners are very slow.

If you want to archive your prints and negatives on your computer, you should scan at a higher resolution (300 dpi), so in case you *do* want to print them, you can. After you scan at a high resolution, you can resize in an image processing program to upload to the Internet. (See the "Resizing Your Photos for Different Uses" section in Chapter 1.)

Posting Your Photos While You Are on a Trip

When you commit to making a blog, it's best to make it an everyday thing. The more you post, the more hits you'll get. When it's time for vacation or travel, that's not the time to stop posting on your blog. As a matter of fact, it's one of the best times to post, because you can get new and different pictures to illustrate what it's like to be where you're at (see Figure 6.12).

I've blogged from everywhere. I've blogged from the big cites of Paris, Shanghai, Quito, and New York to the small towns in the far reaches of Montana and New Mexico. When I blog, I carry good equipment—my laptop, Canon 5D camera, and connections.

You can get access to the Internet via your laptop almost anywhere in the world. From there, you can access Blogger and post your pictures just as you would at home.

It doesn't have to be this cumbersome, though. You can moblog (mobile blog), which is described in the next section.

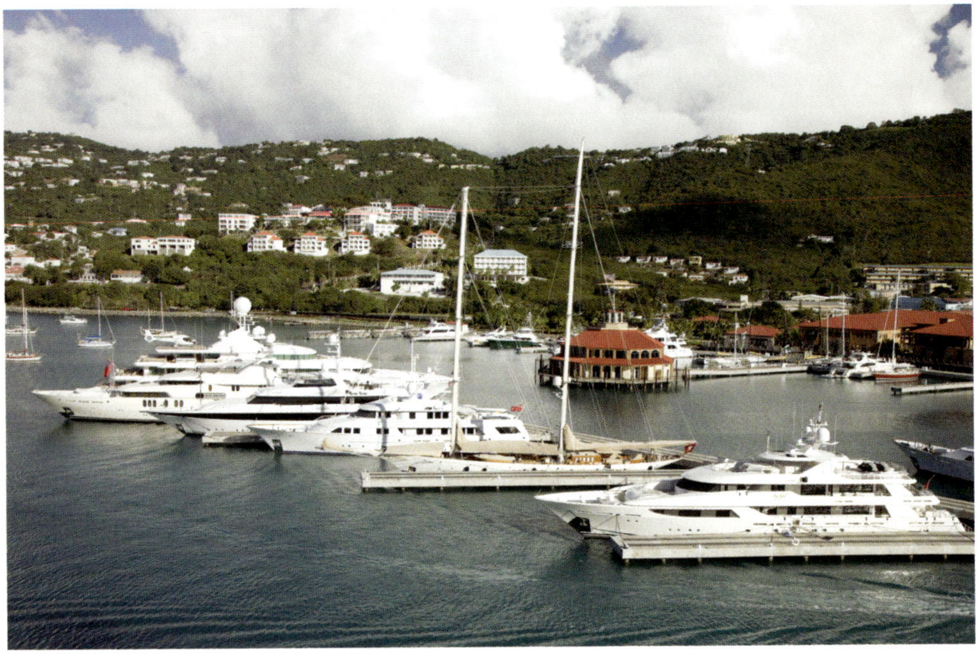

Figure 6.12 Fancy yachts in St. Thomas, Virgin Islands.

POSTING BY EMAIL

On Blogger.com, you can post text and images to your blog by email. This means that you can send an email (or picture message) with text and images to your blog hosting site from your cell phone, which in turn posts it automatically on your blog. To get started, you log in to your Google account via Blogger.com, which will bring you to your Dashboard (where you manage all of your blogs). For the blog to which you want to send a message, click on the envelope by its name. An Email Posting window (see Figure 6.13) will pop up where you create an email address to which you send your post. Next, go to your email account (say, Gmail or your cell phone's email address, for example) and embed or attach a picture to the email (picture mail) with some text under it. Send the email to the email address you created on Blogger. When you send via a cell phone, the entire message is posted, including the To, From, and Subject information.

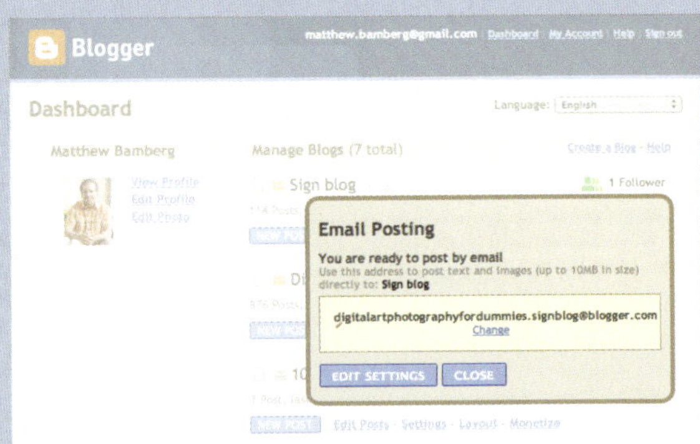

Figure 6.13 Blogger has an email address that you can send a blog post to for publication on your blog.

Building a Moblog

A moblog is a blog on your cell phone. You can post to a blog with a cell phone from anywhere in the world if you have a cell phone with text or media messaging.

To send a picture to your blog, send the image as an email via MMS (multimedia message) to go@blogger.com. To do this on an iPhone, for example, open the image you want to send, click on Send Photo, choose to email the photo, and then input go@blogger.com into the To field. Finally, click Send.

Blogger will then send you a message back with a claim token and a mobile blog URL. Next, go to go.blogger.com (see Figure 6.14), enter in your claim token, verify your registration by typing the distorted characters given into the text box below them, and click Continue. (If you do this on your computer, you can configure an existing blog to a mobile blog. To do this, see the "Configuring Your Blog to a Mobile Blog" sidebar.) From there, you can see the image on your blog if you already have one, or you can create a mobile blog by naming it, giving it a URL, clicking Continue, and then choosing a template and clicking Done.

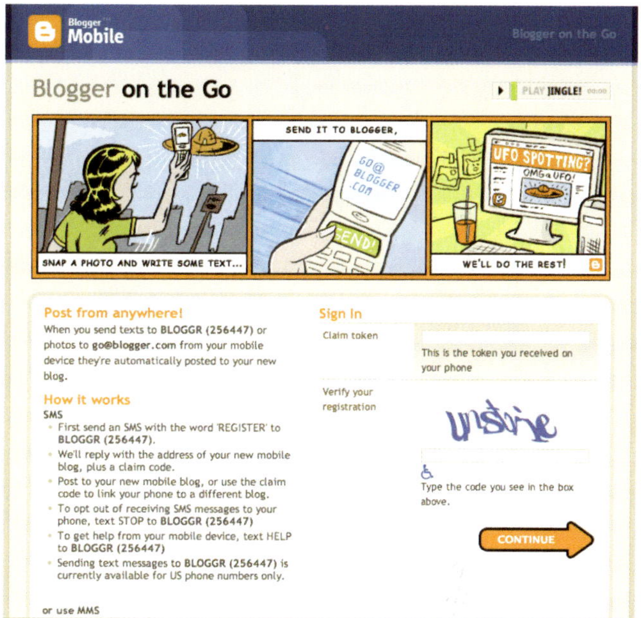

Figure 6.14 You can create a blog from a cell phone.

> **CONFIGURING YOUR BLOG TO A MOBILE BLOG**
>
> Now that you've read the "Building a Moblog" section, you know that you get a claim token when you email go@blogger.com from your cell phone. To post to a blog you've already created on a computer, type in the claim token at go.blogger.com on your computer. You then can register your blog. Use the same email address to register as you do to sign into Google. The system will then recognize your other blogs and display them in a window on your computer. Click on the one you want the mobile posts to go to in the Claim Mobile Blog window. Your mobile posts will then be forwarded to the blog you already have.

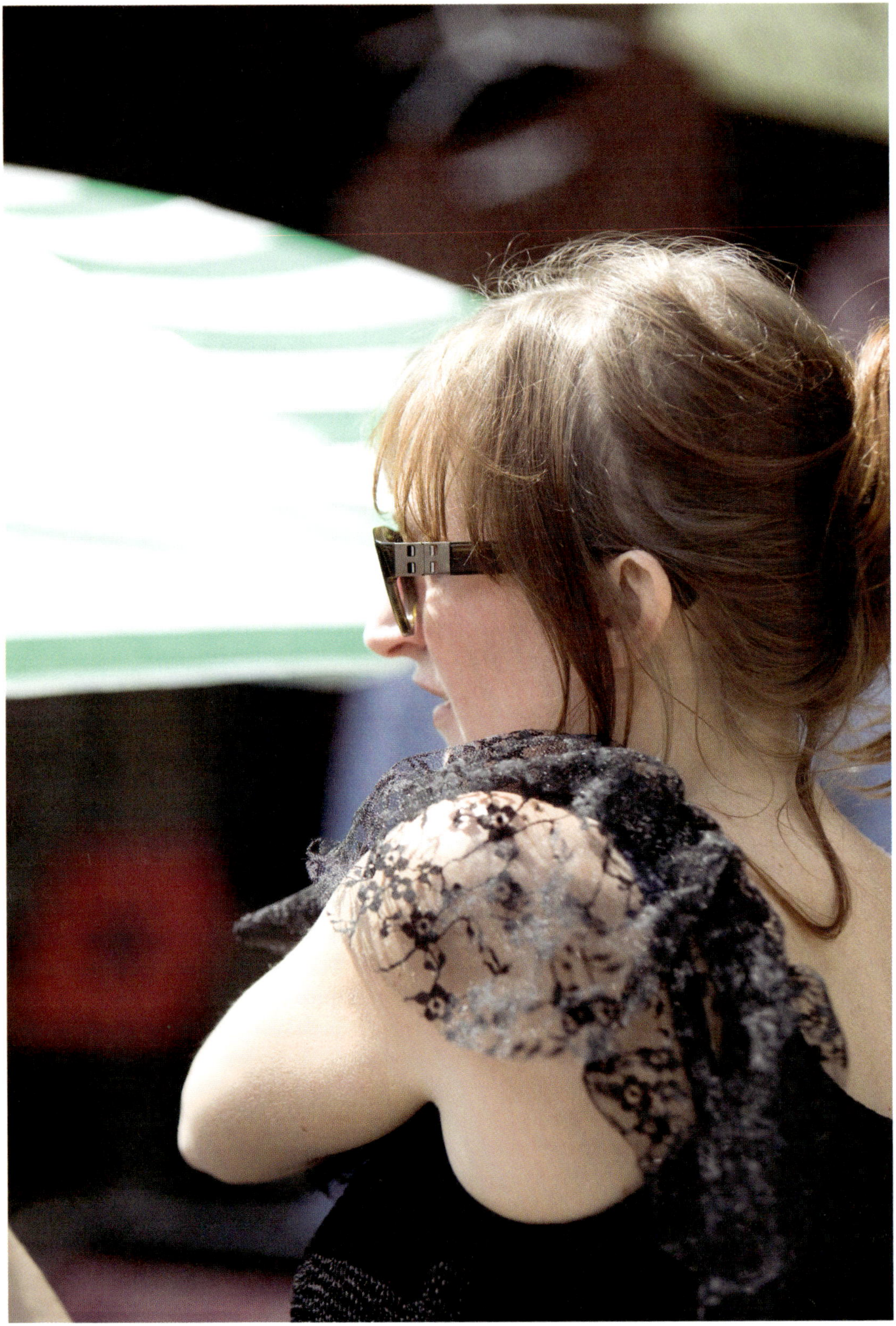

CHAPTER 7

As Pretty as a Picture Frame

How you present your picture is almost as important as the picture itself. There are all kinds of things you can do with your pictures in terms of framing and matting. What you do with your picture is dependent on where you are going to put it. If you are going to put a picture in an online gallery, you can make a photo frame for it either online or with Photoshop/Elements. If you're going to put it in an on-the-ground gallery or shop, you can order frames and mats online at reasonable prices. You can recycle frames by picking them up at garage sales or thrift stores and refurbish them to make them look brand new. Finally, you can put hundreds of pictures in a digital photo frame and have people looking at it for extended periods of time.

Putting Your Photos in a Digital Picture Frame

The latest fad to hit the walls and shelves of homes is digital picture frames. They run anywhere from $50 to $1,000, depending on the features they have. See Figure 7.1 for one example.

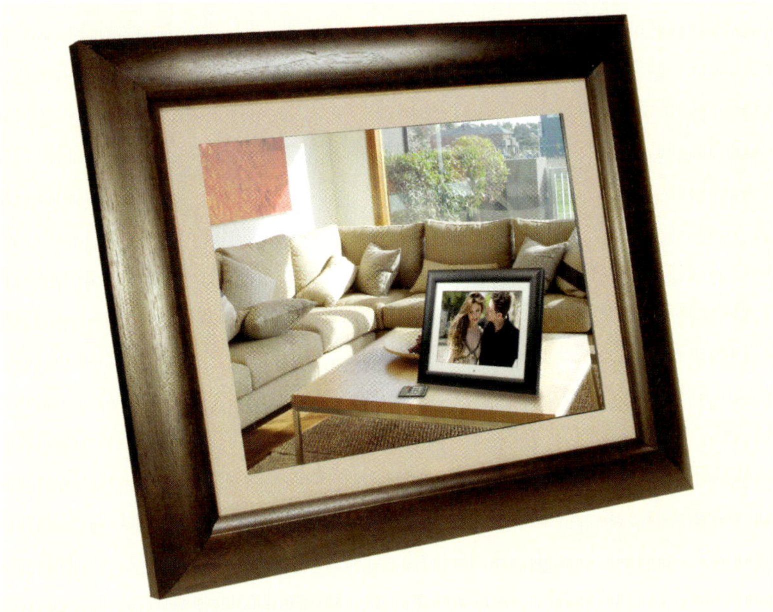

Figure 7.1 A Smartparts digital picture frame.

There are many brands to choose from, among which there are many models. The most important thing to look for is picture quality. Some brands produce fuzzy images; others produce sharp detail. When you buy a digital picture frame, make sure its resolution for showing your images is adequate. Anything less than 800×600 for an 8-inch frame or 1024×768 for a 10-inch one is too low.

Different frames read various types of memory cards, such as CompactFlash, SD, MMC, xD, and Memory Stick. Some digital picture frames have internal memories, onto which you can copy the pictures you want. On some frames, the pictures copy automatically into folders, which you can later update—moving and/or deleting both folders and pictures. Most frames give you options for slideshow speed, transition effects, and slideshow order.

Models vary widely. The basic Westinghouse 8-inch DPF-0802 800×600 plays video (no music) files and has a collage option, as well as makes slideshows from your images. The Synaps 15-inch 1024×768 has a remote control and an MP3 player and plays video and music files, as well as makes slideshows from your images.

PhotoVu digital picture frames support Mac products through the wireless capability of their frames. With the wireless connection, you can use your computer to arrange your photos and to connect with MobileMe (a platform that configures all your devices so that they are in sync). You can easily feature on your unit the photos you have in iPhoto (for more information about iPhoto, see Chapter 1) as well as photos from RSS feeds and from Google Picasa.

Kodak, HP, Sony, and others all offer digital picture frames. Bestcovery.com rated the Kodak EasyShare 10-inch W1020 number one in digital picture frames. This reasonably priced frame (about $200) offers WiFi and access to Flickr and Kodak photo galleries. It also has a power-saving mode (it shuts down at times you set) and supports MP3 files and video.

Framing Your Photo Using a Frame Purchased on the Internet

Photography is a unique medium in that the frames you choose for your work will be simpler than those for other visual art. Finding a frame for your *giclée* print (digital print) is as simple as choosing the frame you want from any number of picture-frame vending sites.

First, I'd go with a readymade frame. They come with all the pieces so you don't have to scratch your head to figure out how to put them together.

Sizes can be confusing when you're framing an image. If you have an 8×10 image, you probably want an 11×14 frame. You'll get a mat that is 11×14 with an opening of 7.5×9.5 so that a little of it overlaps the photograph. (For more about mats, see the next idea for using your photos.) The 11×14 size here refers to the size of the opening in the frame. The actual frame can be bigger when you include the dimensions of the molding.

There are many options for ordering frames online. Here, I've chosen to concentrate on sites that specialize in frames for photographs (see Figure 7.2).

FrameDestination.com offers frames specifically for fine art photography. You can choose from readymade frames or kits. I don't recommend the kits because they are too time consuming to put together. Basic black readymade frames range from $12.70 for an 8×12 frame to $25.70 for a 17×25 frame. They also have higher-end museum-quality Nielsen Bainbridge frames, which are a bit more expensive.

Pictureframes.com has archival metal picture frame complete presentations, which include a premium-quality metal frame, protective UV glass, archival-grade rag mat and mount board, and backing board with built-in hanging hardware. The price for an 11×14 frame presentation is $29.95. Wood (black) picture frames of that size run $35.95.

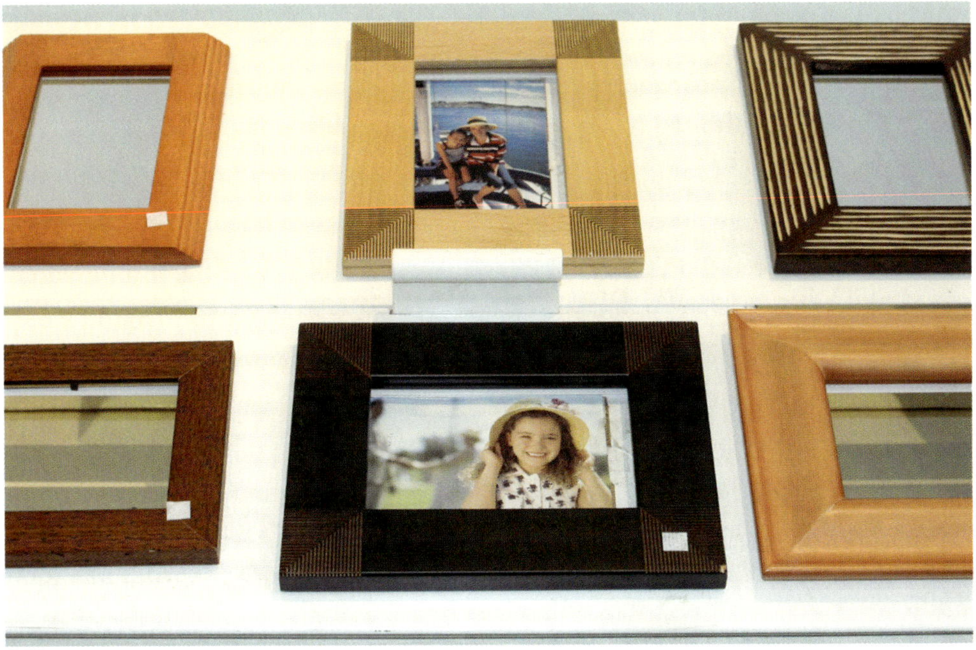

Figure 7.2 There is a wide variety of frames that you can order online.

> **NOTE**
>
> When you frame glass, you should clean it thoroughly with soap and water and rinse it well. Do not use Windex or other cleaners on glass, because you will get wipe marks on the surface of the glass. When you frame acrylic, you just need to wipe it down with a damp cloth.

Framing Using Acid-Free Mats

If you don't have your own mat cutter, the cheapest way to buy mats is precut. If you want your framed picture to last a lifetime, go with archival/conservation/acid-free mats, tape, and backing.

One thing's for sure: If you go to a frame shop and ask for a precut mat, it will be expensive—very expensive. To be sure, many frame shops sell precut mats, but they are often flimsy, not very thick, and only come in limited sizes. You're much better off buying mats on the Internet. There are real deals to be had.

NOTE

Photographs are usually enclosed in bright white mats. Using other colors will distract from the photography.

When you buy a mat, you need to have two measurements on hand—the outside dimensions of the mat, which are the measurements of the frame opening, and the inside opening, which is the area where you'll place the picture. The dimensions of the inside opening should be a bit smaller than the dimensions of the picture.

There are some sites that specialize in mats, most of which tend to be pricey. Two sites with a wide variety of acid-free mats at relatively reasonable prices are:

- MatShop.com offers every kind of mat you could possibly want at reasonable prices. You can order precut sizes of conservation mat board right off the Internet. An 11×14 single conservation mat costs $7.38, with a minimum purchase of five mats. Prices fall the more you buy. Thicker mats are also available at a bit higher price. Mats are priced according to outside dimensions. You choose the size of the opening.
- At MATcutter.com, there are no minimum purchase requirements (see Figure 7.3). An 11×14 mat with a 7½×9½ opening is $6.94. Prices fall the more you buy, but they don't fall as much as they do at MatShop.com.

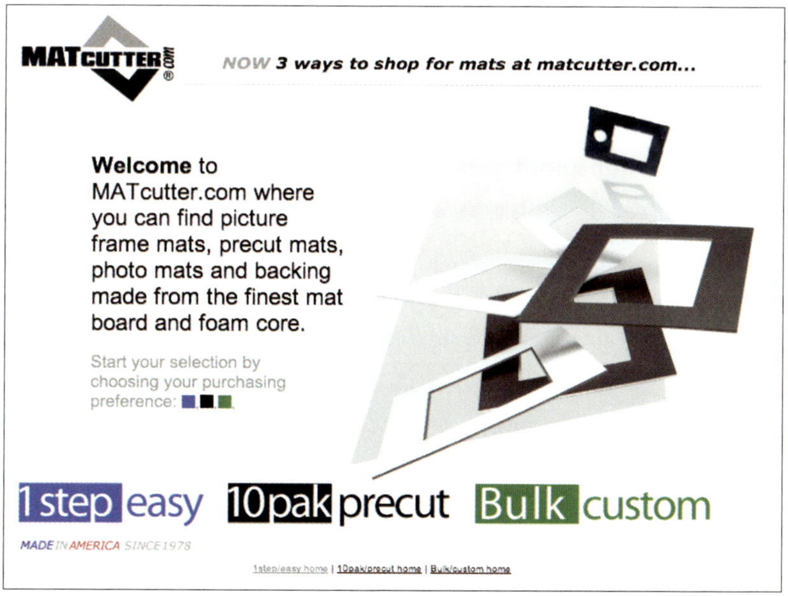

Figure 7.3 At MATcutter.com, you can buy mats in small quantities.

NOTE

If you're going to use conservation (archival, acid-free) materials, it's best to get UV-protected glazing (glass or acrylic).

For more about preserving photographic prints in a frame, you can view the Library of Congress website, which puts out a guide to preservation framing at www.loc.gov/preserv/care/mat.html.

Recycling Thrift-Store Frames for Your Photos

If you really want to get into the nitty gritty of shabby chic, you can buy used frames at thrift stores and refurbish them—a job any novice can do with a little sandpaper and spray paint. Once you refurbish the frames, you can buy some nice matting (see the preceding "Framing Using Acid-Free Mats" section) and have a brand-new framed photo at a quarter of the cost of what you would pay for a new frame.

It's a quick and easy process that I'll explain right here. You'll need some light-grade sandpaper and semi-gloss spray paint. If the frame is painted a dark color, also pick up some white spray primer.

1. Shop for some used frames. Buy only frames that are in good shape. Look out for any dents or other severe damage that would make a frame too difficult to refurbish. Grab the frame by two sides and pull up and down on it to make sure it's not going to fall apart.
2. Take apart the frame so that there is only wood to resurface. (You usually don't have to paint metal frames.)
3. Lightly sand the entire frame with sandpaper.
4. If the frame is painted a dark color, spray it with one or two coats of white primer. Make sure the can is at least a foot away from the surface you are spraying. Take a half-hour (at least) break between coats so one coat dries before you apply another.
5. Clean off the frame with a dry cloth to remove any debris from the sandpaper.
6. Spray paint the frame. Take a half-hour (at least) break between coats so one coat dries before you apply another. You may need up to five coats to completely cover the wood and/or paint on the frame.

I can tell you from experience that refurbishing a frame is almost as much fun as taking a photograph!

Framing Your Photo Online

LoonaPix.com, an online photo editing service, lets you create photo frames for your images online and save them to your desktop. While the resulting photo files aren't large (about 100 kb), they are good enough for Internet use.

To use one of the frames at LoonaPix to frame your photo, go to their site at LoonaPix.com and click on Make Photo Frames. Click Browse to navigate on your computer to the photo you want. After a few moments, you'll see your image on the left side of the window. Select from a frame category and then select a frame. You'll then see a sample of your image in the frame. Finally, click Save at the very bottom of the window.

Figure 7.4 shows a picture that was uploaded into LoonaPix, and Figure 7.5 shows a possible frame choice for the image. Before you save your image, you can scale how it fits into the frame using the slider on top of the framed photo, or you can click on the photo inside the frame to move it around.

You can choose to save your picture on the desktop. LoonaPix will also give your picture its own URL, and you have options to send the image you made off to MySpace, Facebook, Blogger, Friendster, and a host of other blogging and social networking sites.

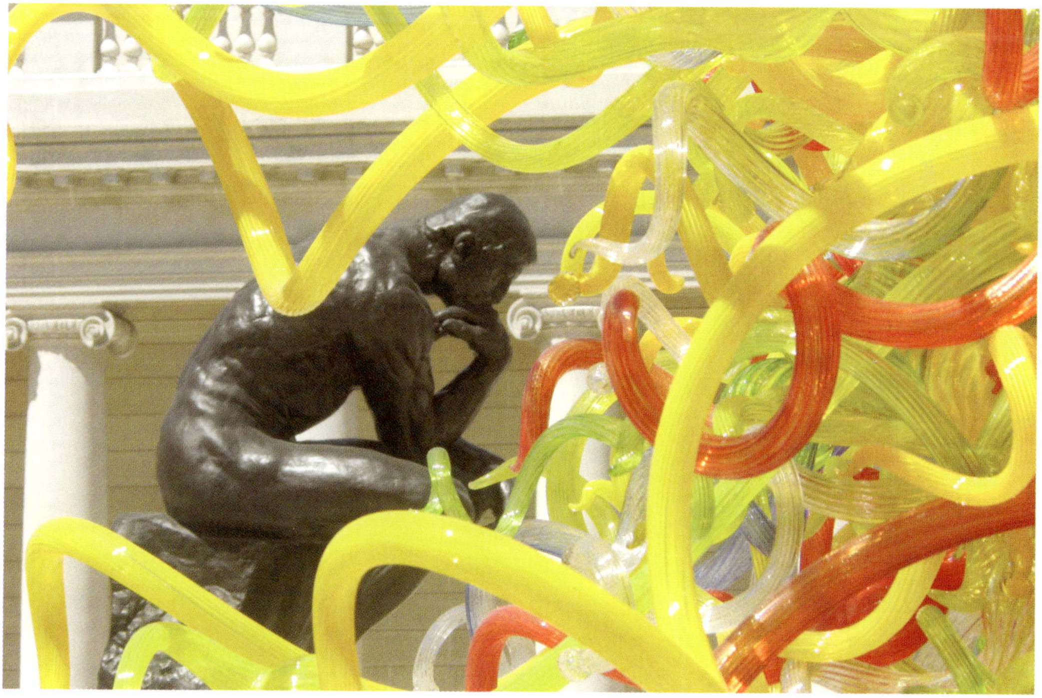

Figure 7.4 Picture uploaded into LoonaPix.

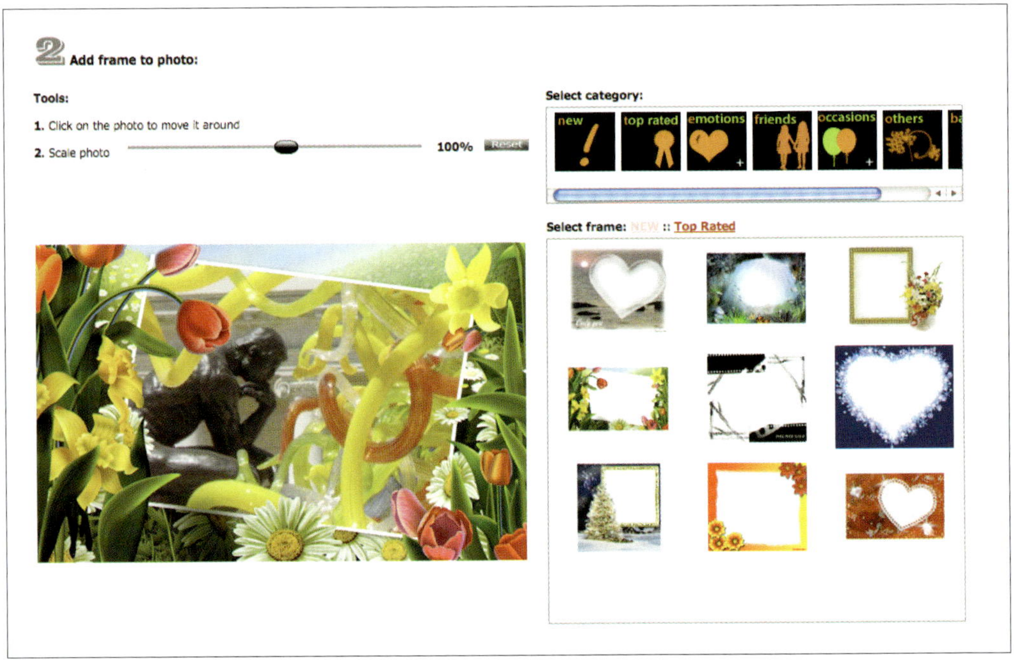

Figure 7.5 Step 2 in LoonaPix is to choose a frame.

LoonaPix also offers LoonaPic Effect and Face Effect options. One of the options for a LoonaPic Effect is to put your face on a hundred-dollar bill. What fun!

Making a Frame for Your Photo in Photoshop

Photoshop and Photoshop Elements have much to offer for framing a photograph. To be sure, it takes several steps to do it, but once you get the hang of it, the sky is the limit with the kinds of photo frames you can create. Here are the steps to make a basic photo frame in Photoshop. Before you begin, resize your photo to around 6×9 inches. (Refer to the "Resizing Your Photos for Different Uses" section in Chapter 1.)

1. Navigate to Image > Canvas Size.
2. For a 1-inch frame, add one inch to the height and width values. So, a 6×9 image would be a 7×10 canvas size. Choose white as the canvas extension color. (By checking the Relative box, you can enter any number you wish, without the hassle of addition. The program then adds whatever number you put in the Width and Height fields to the canvas size.)
3. Navigate to Layer > New Layer. (Name it Outer.)

4. Use the Rectangular Marquee tool and make a selection just inside the outer border of the canvas.
5. Choose Select > Inverse.
6. Navigate to Edit > Fill and choose black for the color.
7. Navigate to Layer > New Layer. (Name it Inner.)
8. Use the Rectangular Marquee tool and make a selection just outside the inner border of the canvas.
9. Navigate to Edit > Fill and choose black for the color.
10. Navigate to Select > Modify > Contract and type **4** for the value.
11. Navigate to Edit > Cut.
12. Go to the bottom of the Layers palette and click the Add a Layer Style button. Choose Drop Shadow from the drop-down menu.
13. Play with the Distance, Spread, Size, and Opacity sliders.

Voila! Your frame should look something like you see in Figure 7.6. You can change anything you want now—the colors with the Paint Bucket, the rectangle thickness with the Contract option (increase the value for a thicker rectangle around your frame), or the shading with the Drop Shadow option.

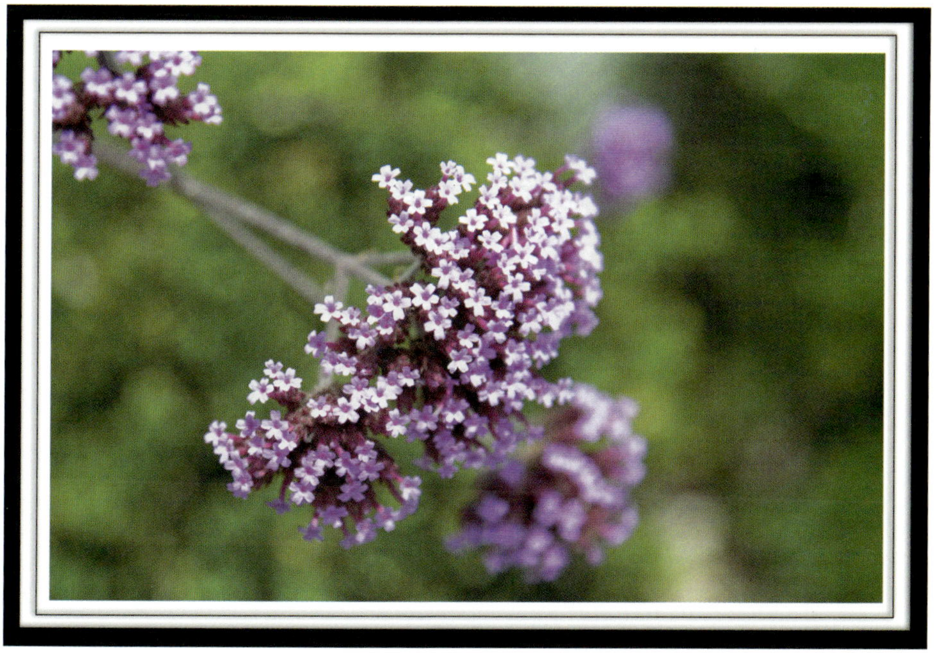

Figure 7.6 Make a frame in Photoshop.

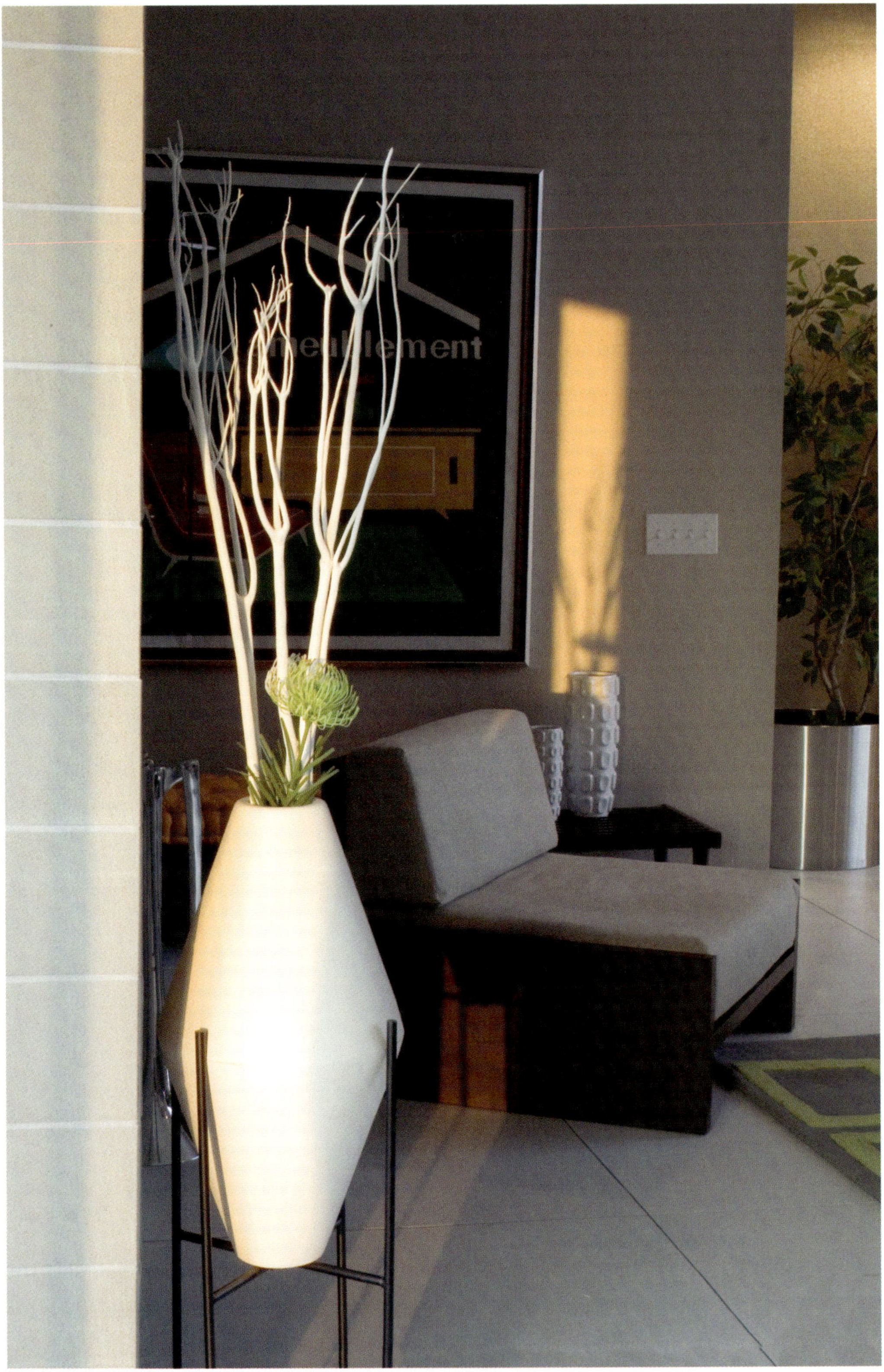

Chapter 8

Making Big Bucks Selling Your Photos (and Donating Them, Too)

Making some extra money with your photos might be easier than you think. Although doing so by, say, selling your photos to *National Geographic* is a tough proposition, selling them to microstock agencies isn't. If you've got a knack for taking sharp, interesting photographs of everyday situations, you'll have an easy time getting your photos approved for sale at any number of microstock agencies. There are other possibilities, too, for putting your work up for sale. After you have your photos printed and framed (which was discussed in earlier chapters of this book), your photos are ready to be put on the market. There are opportunities for selling the finished products at street fairs, on Craigslist, and in cafes. Once you have some experience in these venues, you can move on to art galleries and photo shows.

Selling Your Photos to Online Microstock Photography Agencies

Shipshape photos only, please! Microstock agencies don't accept just any image. An image has to meet their requirements.

If you're going to sell images at one of these agencies (see Table 8.1), note that:

- Agencies usually accept high-quality, high-resolution images, mostly JPGs.
- Most of the time, you have the option to submit your photos as exclusive (you'll only submit photos to one agency) or nonexclusive. In Table 8.1, the information is for nonexclusive use of your photos (which means you can sell at other sites).
- Agencies will not accept images that have logos/movie characters anywhere in the picture.
- Before submitting your image, view it at 100-percent size on your monitor. If it's not sharp at that size, it will be rejected.
- Using Photoshop or other image processing programs is fair game.
- Have a model release (you can download one at www.your-digital-photography.com/model-release-form.html) for all recognizable people in your image. BigStockPhoto accepts editorial-use photos—photos without a release—for street scenes, celebrities, news, and cultural events.
- Pay-per-shot varies because some people pay for photos on subscription plans. (They get a certain amount of photos per a time period at a set price.)
- Pay-per-shot usually depends on the size of the photo downloaded.
- Different sites have different requirements for you to be able to submit your images. Shutterstock is one of the strictest. You have to get 10 photos approved before they'll accept you. At Fotolia, there are no approvals needed to get started.
- All stock photo sites offer more commission for exclusive use of your photos.

In Table 8.1, I show figures for nonexclusive use of photos. Commissions increase at some photo agencies when the number of your photos downloaded reaches a threshold value.

Other stock agencies include StockXpert, 123RF, ImageVortex, Can Stock Photo, ShutterPoint, PhotoStockPlus, Crestock, SnapVillage, and Citizenside.

TABLE 8.1 NONEXCLUSIVE USE OF PHOTOS AT MICROSTOCK AGENCIES

Microstock Photo Agency	Pay-per-Shot	Royalty	Minimum Image Size	Amount Needed to Be Earned to Get Check Sent
Dreamstime.com	.84–11.69	50%	3 MP	$100
iStockphoto.com	.30–8.40	20%	1600×1200 pixels; 300 dpi 5"×7" is optimal	$100
BigStockPhoto.com	.50–3.00 flat fee		800 pixels across	$50 (You can request PayPal or Moneybookers payment at a $30 limit)
Shutterstock.com	.25 flat fee		4 MP	$300
Fotolia.com	Varies	30–44%	4 MP	$50

Copyrighting Your Photos

Once you print a photo on a printer (or have it printed) and/or upload it to the Internet, your photo is automatically copyrighted. But the truth is that doesn't matter much, because if someone takes it and makes money from it, you have to prove it's yours. You do that by filing a copyright form with the United States Copyright Office.

You can get copyright forms or copyright photographs online at www.copyright.gov/forms. You can get a collection of photographs (JPG-, TIF-, and PSD-formatted images, among others) copyrighted online for $35 by paying the fee online and uploading your photos.

There are copyright cases out there, and some get settled when the photographer and the person who infringed on the copyright negotiate. If you find someone using your work, you can send them a bill for three times what the photo cost for unauthorized usage. This works very well if you have had the images copyrighted by the government. Your case is weak if they aren't.

There is a way you can deter people from swiping your photos on the Internet. You can put the © (Option+G on a Mac; Ctrl+Alt+C in Windows) symbol followed by your name at the bottom of your Internet pages. (You can also make a copyright symbol in Word by typing a capital C within parentheses—Word will convert it into the copyright symbol.) Usually, when most people see that, they'll figure that you mean business about copyright, even though it's not required by law.

Finally, there is a way that you can make copying your photos very difficult for people online. You can add a watermark to your photographs. To do this, see the following "Adding a Watermark to Your Photos" sidebar.

ADDING A WATERMARK TO YOUR PHOTOS

To add a watermark to a photo, as shown in Figure 8.1:

1. Open your image in Photoshop or Elements.
2. Click on the T (Text) tool in the Tools palette. Remember that as soon as you type text into your image, you are creating a new layer.
3. Set your text color by double-clicking on the Set the Text Color swatch in the toolbar at the top of the window. Choose a color you want for your watermark in the dialog box that appears.
4. Type in your text.
5. Click and drag over your text and select font and font size. (Choose fonts and font sizes at the top of the window or in the Character palette.)
6. Navigate to Layer > Style > Blending Options. A dialog box will appear, and all you have to do is slide the Opacity slider to about 40%.
7. Navigate to Layer > Flatten Image.

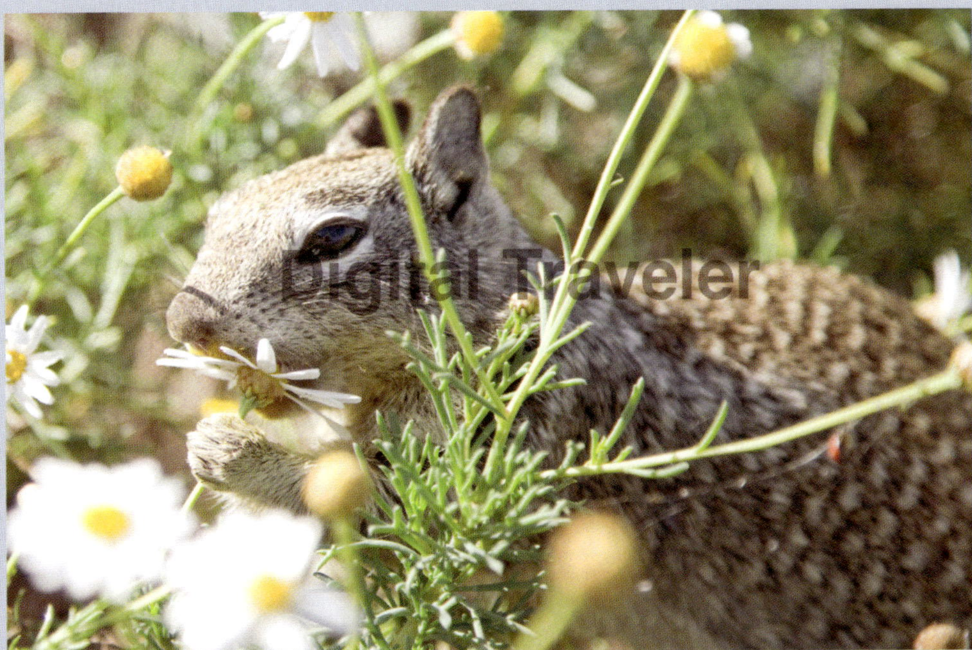

Figure 8.1 A watermark is some translucent text that covers your photos so people can't copy them.

To make putting a watermark on any photo easier, you can save the steps as an action.

1. Open a new file.
2. Navigate to Window > Action. This will bring up your Actions palette.
3. Click on Create New Action at the bottom of the palette, next to the trash bin.
4. In the dialog box that appears, give the action a name (Watermarks) and click on Record.
5. Repeat Steps 2 through 7 above.

After you've done your second watermark, all the rest will be a breeze. All you have to do is the Watermark action in the Actions palette and then click on the small arrow (Play) to run the action, which gets the watermark on your image.

Selling Your Photos as Postcards

There are a few ways to get postcards made so you can sell them. Here are some options:

- **Buy a backing.** One way you can make your photos into postcards is by buying a backing for them. The2Buds (www.the2buds.com) has backings for 4×6 and 5×7 prints. For 4×6, if you buy 10, they're 39 cents apiece; if you buy 500, they're 20 cents apiece. For 5×7, if you buy 10, they're 59 cents apiece; if you buy 250, they're 38 cents apiece.
- **Have postcards made and mailed online.** At PremiumPostcard (www.premiumpostcard.com), you can have postcards with your photo(s) made and mailed (the next business day) by U.S. Mail. All you have to do is follow prompts to help you upload a pic, fill out the return address and message, and then mail it to as many recipient addresses as you want.
- **Order printed postcards online.** If you want your photo put on a professionally made postcard, Zazzle's your place. At www.zazzle.com/custom/postcards, you can make and sell postcards with your photos on them. To experiment with this interactive product maker, you click on Create a Postcard. In the next window that comes up, click on Select Image and Make It Now. In the next window, click on My Computer and Select Images to Upload. Navigate to your image on your computer on the next prompt. Click OK. Click Make It Now. Your picture will then come up in an editing window, where you can tweak it so that it looks good on the postcard. Figure 8.2 shows you the editing window. At the bottom of the window, you have two options—Add to Cart or Post for Sale. Selling on Zazzle is covered in the next section.

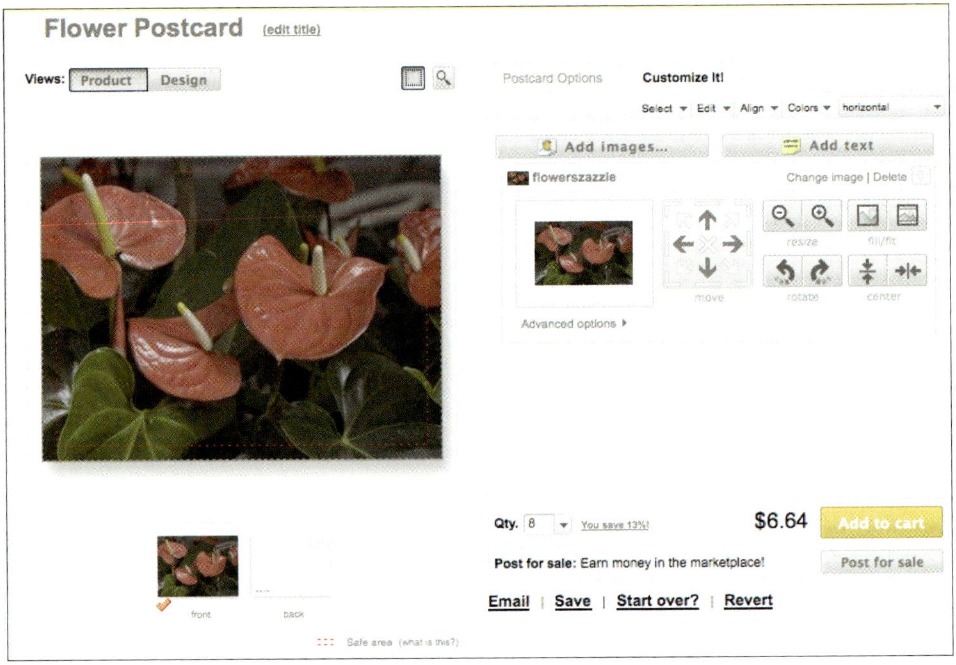

Figure 8.2 Zazzle.com has an online postcard maker.

Selling Your Photo Designs at Zazzle.com

In the previous section, you learned that you can make postcards at Zazzle.com. That's not all you can make there. You can make T-shirts, mugs, business cards, greeting cards, posters, and more. Basically, to make an item, you follow similar prompts to those shown in the "Selling Your Photos as Postcards" section. Best yet is that you can take what you make and sell it on their site.

At the top of the Zazzle window, there are the following tabs: Shop, Create, Sell, Community.

In the Shop area, you are taken to items people who have registered to sell at Zazzle have made. On the left side of the window, you'll see the categories of products. You'll see that some of the designs on the products have been made in Photoshop and/or have been scanned from prints. Be warned when you shop that some categories have thousands of products to browse. You can narrow your search on the product page by clicking on Narrow by Product (buttons, hats, and posters, for example), then Narrow by Topic (technology, events, and humor, for example).

In the Create section, there are clickable images from which to choose products you can make. After you click on T-shirts, for example, you're taken to an assortment of tees. You then click on one of those to be taken to the interactive product maker, where you upload your image.

In the Sell area, you sign up to sell products with your designs or images on them. To register, you enter the usual username, password, and email address. In addition, you give your birth date and agree to Zazzle's user agreement. That's all you do—there's no email confirmation or anything else to do except click Continue in one window and Create Store in the next.

> **NOTE**
> Your username will be contained in the URL you will receive for your store (www.zazzle.com/username).

The next thing you do is choose or customize a template. Then you can check out all the tabs at the top of the Appearance page: Dashboard, Account, Store, Products, Images, Favorites, and Earnings. Dashboard is where you create your products. Account is where you can edit your profile and upload an image of yourself. In the Store section, you can add a description of your store by clicking Basic Information on the left side of the window. The Products section lists the products you have up for sale. In the Images section, every image you've uploaded is stored. In the Favorites section, you record products you like. In the Earnings section, you see how much money you've made. To get paid by Zazzle, you need to earn at least $25.

> **NOTE**
> Zazzle supports both JPEG and TIFF files (as well as GIF and PNG).

> **NOTE**
> Other similar sites to Zazzle.com are CafePress.com and redbubble.com.

Selling Photos to Regional Magazines

Wanted: photos for regional magazines. As a freelancer, I've written articles and submitted photographs for local publications in the Palm Springs area of California. Figure 8.3 shows a photo taken on the same shoot as one that appeared in the regional magazine *Palm Springs Life*. It is similar to the one that appeared in the magazine.

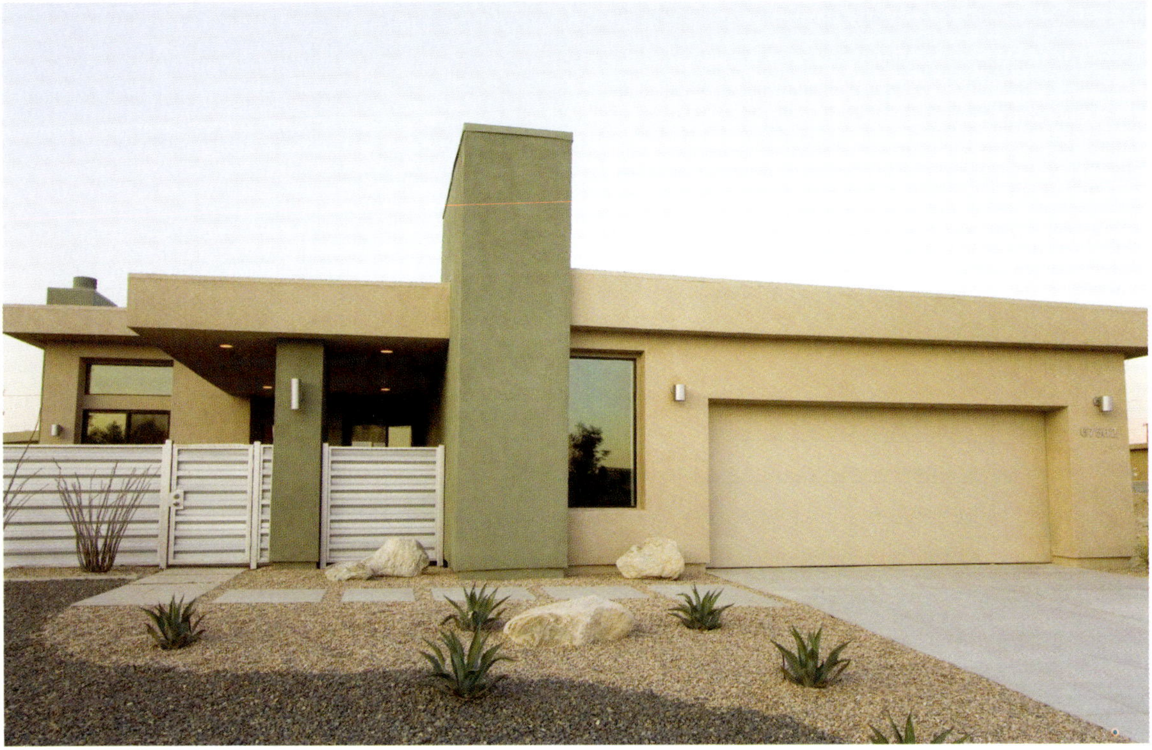

Figure 8.3 A photo similar to this appeared in *Palm Springs Life* a few years ago.

Regional magazines, such as *Arizona Highways*, *Vermont Life*, *Pittsburgh Magazine*, and *Ohio Magazine*, are just some that need photos from freelancers. When you think about it, regional magazines can't use stock photography because the photos that they use are location specific. Submission requirements vary from magazine to magazine. Some magazines, such as *Yankee Magazine* (New England states) and *Ohio Magazine*, give assignments to photographers based on work presented in their portfolio. Other magazines, such as *Arizona Highways* and *Vermont Life*, have pages strictly devoted to photographs. They'll look at any good photograph that has to do with their region.

Here's a comparison of how the photos should be delivered for two regional magazines:

Arizona Highways

- All images should be submitted to *Arizona Highways* on a CD or DVD with the following embedded profiles (note that these are default settings in Photoshop, so you won't have to change anything in that program): Adobe RGB (1998), 8 bit, RAW captures saved as TIFF files.
- Document should be a minimum of 300 ppi 12×18 inches.

- Include your name and copyright, with detailed caption information.
- Filename or number should begin with D_ and end with .tif.
- Also, submit a small guide print for each digital file submitted (contact sheets).

Vermont Life

- Digital photos should be sent on CDs or DVDs as RAW files (preferred), high-resolution TIFFs, or JPEGs without compression.
- Include low-res versions of all images. Note: RAW files with low-res JPEGs for viewing and with Adobe RGB color profile are preferred.
- Include color contact sheets of all images in a readable size and sharp resolution—no more than nine images per page.
- Include a simple caption sheet.

Donating Your Framed Photos to Charitable Institutions (and Getting Tax Deductions)

Don't let the IRS get you down. Get some tax breaks (if you itemize deductions) by donating your framed photography to charitable organizations, such as Goodwill and the Salvation Army.

Not all charitable institutions are the same. Goodwill notes on their website that when you donate to some thrift stores, only a small part of the donation goes to charity—sometimes less than five percent. Goodwill lets you know that 84 percent of their revenues goes to their employment and training programs.

While Goodwill can be a good choice to donate your photographs, there are also other places where you can donate, such as thrift stores run by the Salvation Army, City of Hope, St. Vincent de Paul, and other local organizations.

Before you donate your framed photography, the IRS requires that you determine the fair market value. To receive a deduction, you can only donate items that are in "good used condition or better." I often donate my framed artwork of signs (see Figure 8.4) to thrift stores run by the Desert AIDS project. I also donate my pictures to be sold at silent auctions at fundraisers for that organization. Finding the fair market value for these items is simple—I use the normal price I sell them for, which is anywhere from $60 to $200.

> **NOTE**
>
> The IRS assesses penalties if you overstate the value of items that you donate.

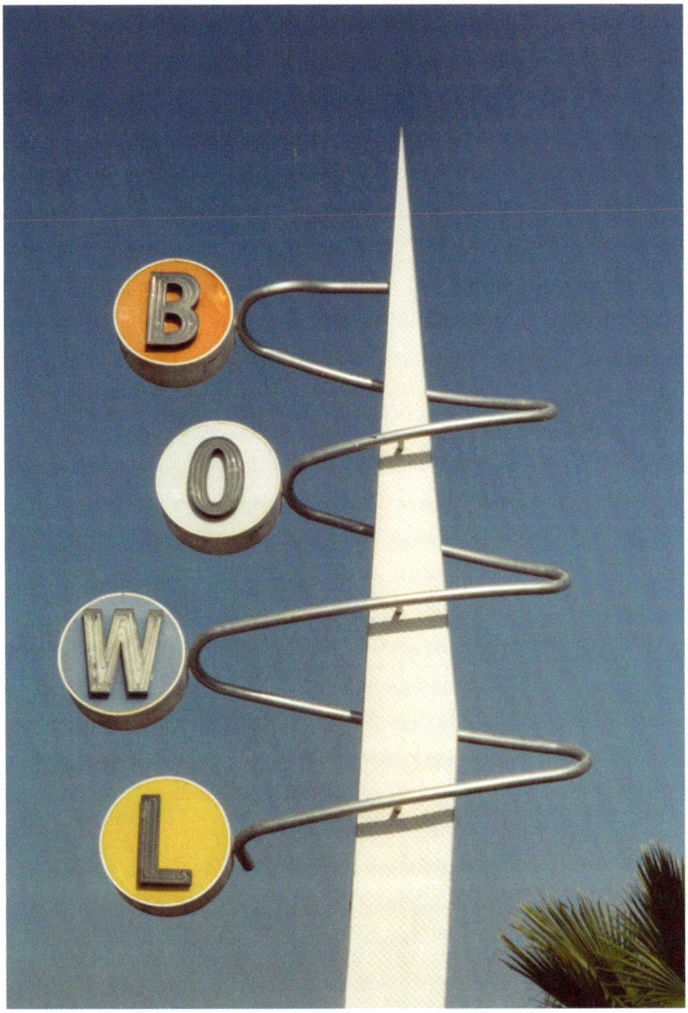

Figure 8.4 You can donate your photos to charity.

> **NOTE**
>
> You must keep good records, having a written acknowledgement that you donated to the charity.

There's another benefit to donating to charity, other than a tax deduction, and that's knowing you've contributed to a good cause—hopefully one that you care about.

Selling Your Photography on eBay

Selling your photos on eBay is one way you can make some cash (see Figure 8.5). At BermanGraphics.com, Chris Maher and Larry Berman report that they sold $2,000 of their photography in the first month that they put it on eBay.

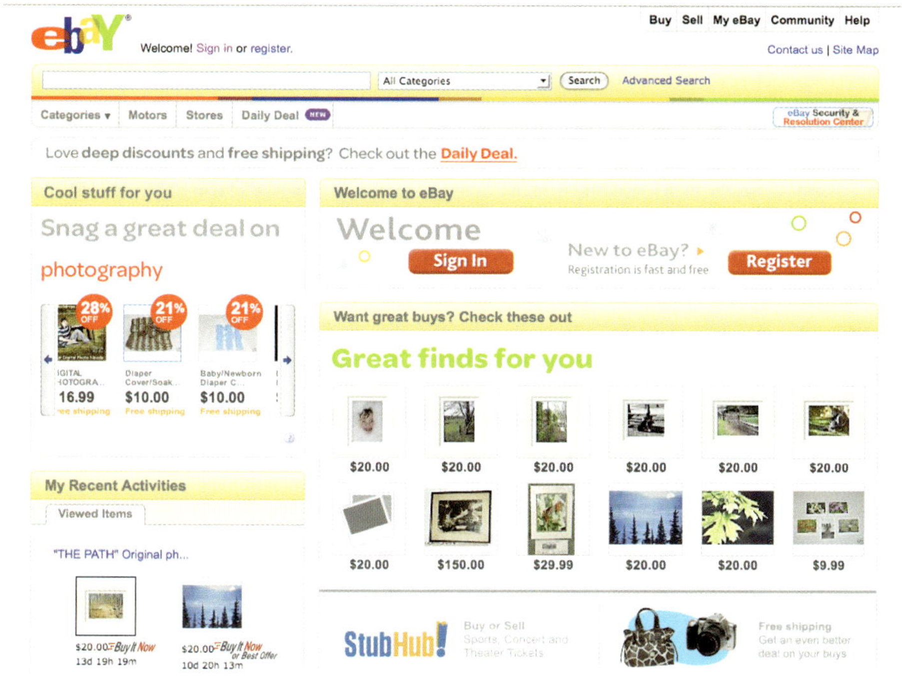

Figure 8.5 Sell high-quality prints at inexpensive prices on eBay.

To get started selling at eBay, you first have to register, and then you have to become a seller, give info about how you'll pay eBay for listings, and select payment methods you'll accept from buyers. Finally, you'll probably need a PayPal account so you can accept credit cards. To register there, go to PayPal.com.

After you've read everything at http://pages.ebay.com/help/sell/sell-getstarted.html, you're ready to list an item. To sell an item on eBay, they recommend that you read the information on this page: http://pages.ebay.com/help/sell/selling-basics.html. To start selling, click Sell > Sell an Item at the very top of the homepage window. In the next window, click Start Selling. You'll then be prompted through the process of selecting a category for your item, creating your listing, and reviewing your listing.

During the process you'll use drop-down menus to select details about your product. You'll also choose a description and a selling format (you'll choose Online Auction), as well as a starting price (other selections contain fees), quantity, duration of listing (five to seven days, including weekend days, is best), payment, payment method, shipping costs, and additional info (including return policy).

NOTE

Before you begin selling on eBay, make sure you research the item you are selling by finding a similar item for sale on the site. For framed photos, navigate to Art under where it says Shop Your Favorite Categories on the homepage, and then select Direct from the Artist > Photographs. You can then search for what type of photos you want on the right side of the page.

Next preview and/or edit your listing.

If you want a step-by-step tutorial on how to sell on eBay, go to pages.ebay.com/education/selling.html.

Again, don't forget the power of not reinventing the wheel when selling on eBay. See what others are selling and have sold. For example, I found the following clues as to what photographs are selling by searching for photographs and spotting the ones that have bids. I've found a seller, for example, who had a bid on three 8×10 framed photos of huge waves (taken in sequence using burst mode). The photos were bidded for $29.95 and $24.27 for shipping. The seller can't make a terribly big profit on these items, but she does sell them, as the bidding indicated. Once you've signed on to eBay and are in the process of selling an item, you have access to items similar to yours that have recently sold—a very helpful resource!

NOTE

You want to sell high-quality products at inexpensive prices. eBay is a good place to do this because there's very little overhead when you sell, so you get to keep all the profit.

One photography category that sells is nature photography. You'll find sellers offering dozens of different 8×10 nature photographs for, say, $17 with free shipping. There's also fine-art nude photography 5×7 prints for $7 (with $2 shipping).

Selling Your Photography on Craigslist

Craigslist offers classified advertising hosting for free. Got that? FREE! The site consists of close to 500 regions—usually cities and surrounding areas—each of which has its own website for classified listings for mostly that region only.

Perhaps the easiest, cheapest way to sell your photography is on Craigslist. There's no fee for posting an ad. Posting an ad takes less than five minutes. Before you post to sell, you have to register at https://accounts.craigslist.org/login/signup. All you do is type in your email and a verification code, and an email is sent to you with a confirmation link. After you click on that link, you create your password and accept the terms of service.

Although there are almost no existing ads for print photography on Craigslist, there are ads for framed prints (see Figure 8.6). For this reason, I suggest that you only try selling framed prints on Craigslist.

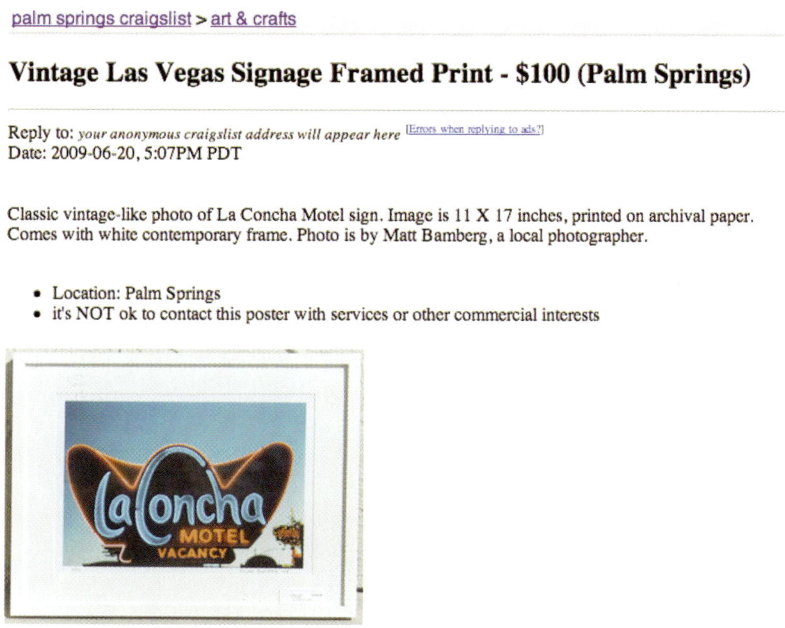
palm springs craigslist > art & crafts

Vintage Las Vegas Signage Framed Print - $100 (Palm Springs)

Reply to: *your anonymous craigslist address will appear here* [Errors when replying to ads?]
Date: 2009-06-20, 5:07PM PDT

Classic vintage-like photo of La Concha Motel sign. Image is 11 X 17 inches, printed on archival paper. Comes with white contemporary frame. Photo is by Matt Bamberg, a local photographer.

- Location: Palm Springs
- it's NOT ok to contact this poster with services or other commercial interests

Figure 8.6 An ad for a framed photo on Craigslist.

There are many category choices under which you can choose to sell your items. Probably the best choice for framed photography would be For Sale > Arts+Crafts. To post your ad, navigate to the city or region in which you reside. Click on Post to Classifieds at the top left of the window on that region's page. In the next window, there will be links below the question,

"What type of posting is this?" Click on For Sale > Arts/Crafts for Sale. This will take you to a window with a Create Posting form. Fill it out with a description of the photograph, including the size of the print. You'll also have to choose whether you want people to respond by emailing you directly or by "anonymizing" your email. (When you "anonymize," they send a response to a Craigslist email, which gets forwarded to your email.) Next, upload your image(s).

NOTE

Include a picture (or pictures) of your framed photo. You're allowed up to four. To avoid glare, don't use flash; use a high ISO to take the photo.

Now click Continue, and you'll see what your ad will look like.

Click Continue again, and you'll be led to a verification code page. Type in the code, and your ad will be posted.

NOTE

On the page where it asks for the type of posting you want, there's a warning to posters not to cross-post, which means you're not supposed to post the same ad in multiple cities or in multiple categories.

NOTE

If anyone is coming to your home to look at your work, be careful. Feel the person out in a phone conversation to make sure his or her purpose is to come and look at your artwork and nothing else.

Selling Your Photos at an Art/Street Fair

Selling your photography on the street or in a park can be great fun. To get to the point of selling your work at the big festivals, you have to build a body of work. You'll have to spend lots of time tweaking, printing, and framing your images. See Chapter 1 for details about those processes.

The first step in selling at an art show or street fair is to go to one and look at what's selling (see Figure 8.7).

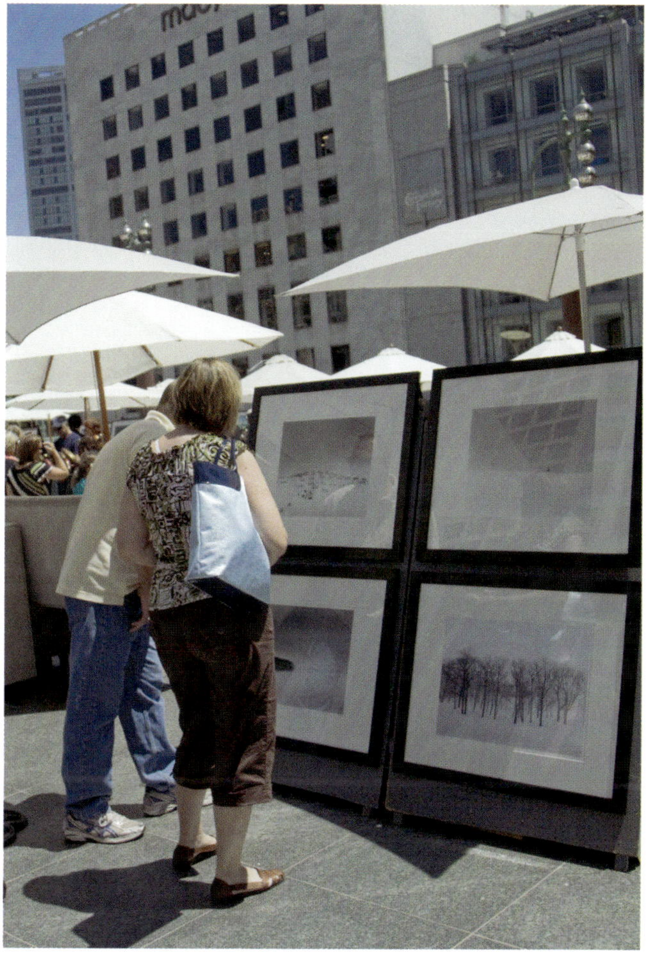

Figure 8.7 Photography in a San Francisco art show.

You'll probably see that artists who show at fairs are very experienced with continuity in their body of work. (In other words, their photographs have a similar look.) Some artists sell flower photos, for example; others concentrate on regional landscapes. I've even seen one artist whose body of work consists of golf-course photographs.

If you get on the big-show circuit, there's prize money to be had. Most of these festivals are juried shows, which means a jury (panel) chooses the work that goes into the show. Some big art festivals in the United States are the Sausalito Art Festival (Labor Day weekend), Coconut Grove Arts Festival (President's Day weekend), Cherry Creek Arts Festival (Denver, Independence Day weekend), and the Old Town Art Fair (Chicago, mid-June). For a list of the biggest art festivals, go to artfaircalendar.com and click on Best Art Fairs in the page links on the left side of the window.

Competition to get in the big art festivals is keen. There are more than 1,200 artists who apply for about 230 spaces at the Sausalito Arts Festival.

At most art festivals, you have to submit five images that are representative of your work—four of individual works and one of your work in a booth.

You have to apply early, too. The Sausalito Art Festival takes place on Labor Day weekend each year; applications are due no later than March 1. For the Old Town Art Fair in Chicago, which takes place in mid-June, you have to have your application in by mid-December the year before.

Other regulations for the Sausalito Art Festival include:

- Artists must have an artist statement.
- Only limited, signed and numbered works.
- Artist has to buy a Sausalito business license.
- Artists have to pay California sales tax on their sales.

Finally, you can't forget the booth fees. Single-booth fees can range from $750 at the Cherry Creek Arts Festival to $1,150 at the Sausalito Art Festival.

Street Fairs

Many street fairs are open to artists (which includes photographers). Art has become a mainstay, from yearly festivals, such as the Haight-Ashbury Street Fair in San Francisco, to weekly farmers' markets all over the country, which include local art into the mix of fresh produce and live performances. VillageFest in Palm Springs, California, takes place every Thursday night all year long. To get your digital photography included in that event, you have to write a letter of intent and include photos taken of the artist and showroom (including pictures of the process of making the digital photographs), photos of finished products (framed photography or matted photography), and a photo of your booth layout.

If you're not yet ready for the festival circuit, there are other things you can do to make money by selling your photography on the ground. Try smaller art shows sponsored by local organizations. Other ideas to sell your photos on the ground are discussed the next section.

Selling Your Framed Photos at a Café, Art Gallery, or Consignment Store

If you're not quite ready to dole out the bucks and time for one of the big art festivals, there are other alternatives for selling your photography on the ground. You can sell your photographs in cafés, consignment stores, art galleries, and even stores that sell home furnishings.

While you do, you can build up a unit of work so you can have additional items to sell when it comes time to apply for a spot in an art festival.

To get started, browse the local stores and small art galleries and see what's out there.

If you want to sell your photograph locally, take pictures of local landscapes, monuments, and attractions. For example, I live in the Southwest. My motel signs from this region of the country sell well. I've seen photographers in Los Angeles do well selling photos of beach scenes and palm trees, not to mention the Hollywood sign.

If you're selling photos on consignment, you'll usually get a form upon which the consigner will record what items you have given him, the selling price of those items, and the percentage he gets when they sell. Every month (more or less), you'll check with the consigner to see whether your images have sold. If they have, you'll get a check along with a form that lists the sold items, what price they've sold at, and the percent deducted for commission. You'll also probably have to replace the sold items with new items (so the store's walls are filled with your work).

There are other deals you can work out where you get paid for your work up front. I had a deal with a home furnishing store where I got a fixed amount of money when the store accepted my photos for sale and the rest of the money when the photos sold. In that case, I invoiced each time I dropped off the photographs at the store. The invoice included the photos that I delivered along with the photos that sold with the money I was to be paid. To find out how many photos I had sold, I had to call the store for them to count them up before I invoiced.

Although at first your business might not be all that lucrative, when you make that sale, it really puts a smile on your face.

PRICING YOUR PHOTOS

One of the big questions often asked when selling your photographs is how much you should charge for them. That depends on how much money you put into making them and how much commission you are being charged. My photos were not aimed at high-end collectors; they were strictly sold as home accessories. Since that was the case, I didn't go with costly framing and matting. I would purchase the most inexpensive acid-free mats I could find (usually $2 to $4 apiece). I would do my best to get frames wholesale from a dealer in LA (usually $15). When I considered these prices and added $3 per print for ink and paper, I found that I would spend about $20 for a framed image. I'd sell the framed images for $70 to $100. My profit without the commission would average $60. Usually the commission was 40 to 60 percent, making my final profit about $30 per framed photo.

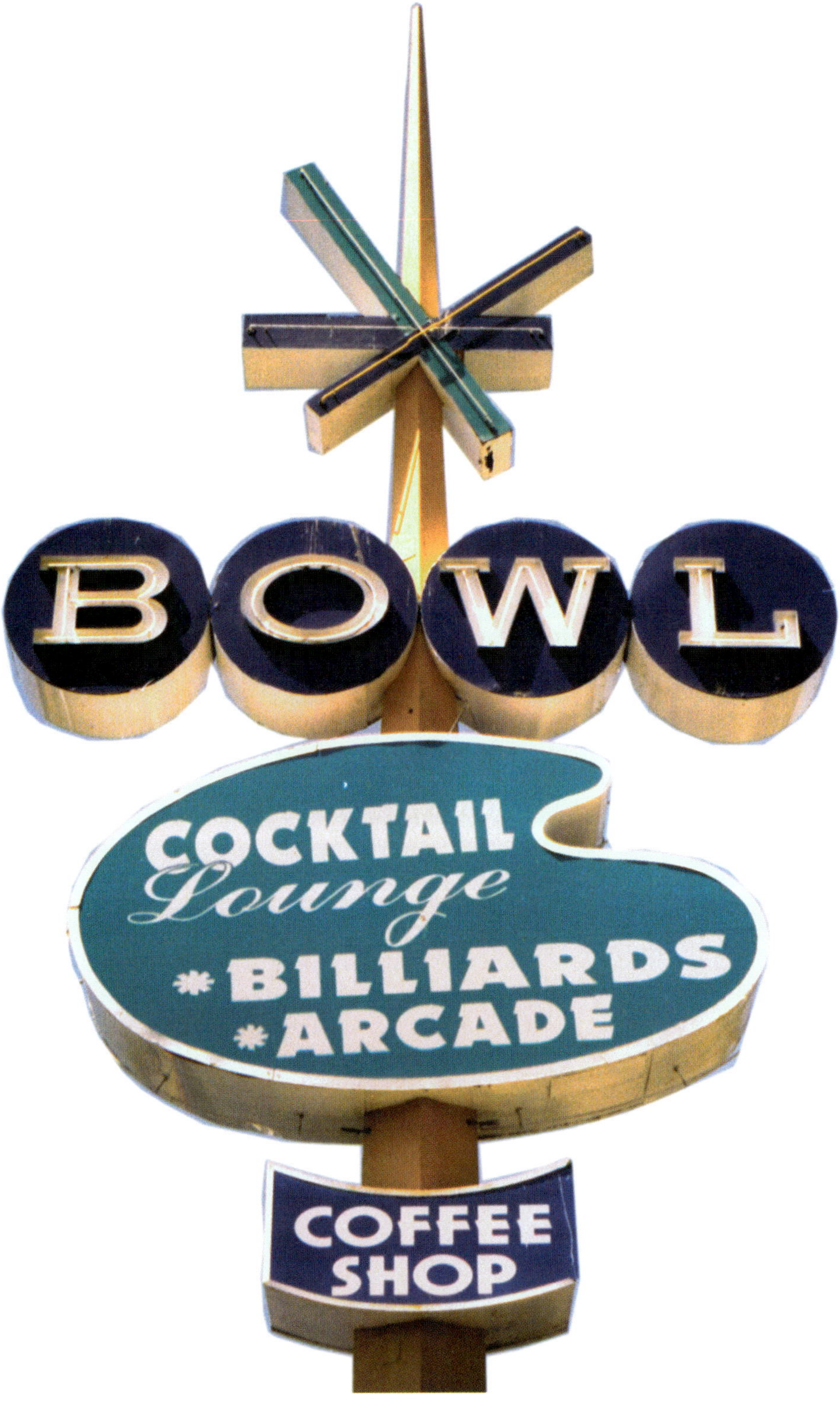
BOWL
COCKTAIL
Lounge
BILLIARDS
ARCADE
COFFEE
SHOP

CHAPTER 9

Personal Accessories

If the sight of your photos pleases you, you have nearly limitless opportunities to view them spontaneously during your daily activities. Look at one of your photos while having a cup of coffee, flipping a business card to a client, sending a holiday greeting card, and/or wearing a T-shirt. To create these pleasurable photo moments, just read this chapter, and you'll be able to set yourself up to have your photos presented on the spot at any given moment. Other people will see your photos, too, which can create more than a Kodak moment. When someone sees that you're wearing your photo on a T-shirt, for example, it could initiate a conversation that leads to a lifetime friendship. You just never know.

Putting Your Photos in a Traditional Photo Album

Displaying your photographs in a traditional photo album has changed from the days when your photographs turned yellow inside plastic enclosures. Almost all materials nowadays are acid free so that your photographs can last generations and stay relatively intact. Albums today offer clear sheets (enclosures) that are archival, which means that they don't contain acid, a substance that deteriorates photos over time.

There are many websites where you can buy photo albums. AlbumSource.com is one site that deals exclusively with photo albums (and portfolios for photographers). The site offers albums with slip-in pockets, scrapbook-style albums, wedding albums, three-ring binders, portfolios, and refills/accessories.

One popular album, Item A1 (click on Albums with Slip-in Pockets on the homepage, and it's the first album listed on the page), the Raika 102 leather double-page picture pocket album, holds 120 4×6 photos and is offered in 53 cover finishes. This album contains 30 archival sheets. The sheets are clear on one side and have a black background. This album is refillable, so you can get a maximum of 240 photos into it provided you buy extra sheets.

Other albums for smaller photographs range from mahogany and wood albums, to bonded leather albums, to the large leather oval-window album that holds 300 photos. They also have wedding albums. Some of these include the gold oval-frame album, the silver-plated wedding album, the Maude Asbury white silken fabric album, and European rose memory books.

Last are the portfolio offerings. Made by Prat, the outside cover is finished in black molded polypropylene finish. The archival pages are clear with black mounting inserts. Each binder comes with 10 sheets but will hold up to 30 sheets. The portfolios are offered in 8.5×11, 11×14, 14×17, 17×22, and 18×24. You can comparison shop for portfolios by going to portfolios-and-art-cases.com, which I mentioned in the "What about Storing Prints?" sidebar in Chapter 1.

Putting Your Photos on Coffee Mugs

You can design and then buy (as well as sell) your own mugs with your photos on them at Zazzle.com (www.zazzle.com/custom/mugs). All you have to do is use the same procedure as described for ordering printed postcards online in the "Selling Your Photos as Postcards" section in Chapter 8. Figure 9.1 shows a photo on a cup in the Zazzle editing window. Coffee mugs with your photo on them cost $12.95. If you want to sell a mug (or any other product on the site) with your photo on it, you earn a minimum of 10 percent royalty of the standard price ($1.29 on the mug, for example). You can set the royalty rate higher, and Zazzle will add the increase to its price. You earn all of the increase.

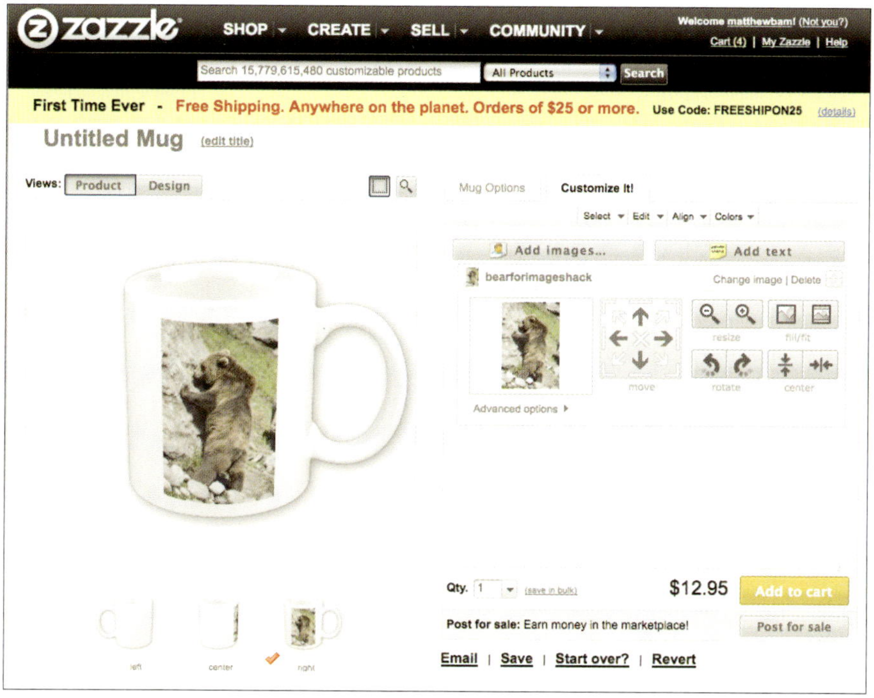

Figure 9.1 At Zazzle.com, you view your photos on coffee mugs before you order them.

You can also order mugs with your images on them at Shutterfly.com. If you go to Shutterfly.com, click on Photo Gifts (at the top of the window, below the My Shutterfly, My Pictures, Share, Community, and Store tabs), and then click on Mugs, you'll get to the window where you browse for the picture you want to be on your mug. When you click Browse, a navigation window will appear on your computer. Pick the image you want (in JPEG format) from your computer. After you click Next, your picture will appear on a page where you can edit it. You click Next again, and you're taken to a page where you can order the mug (from $11.19 to $12.79 depending on size and color). There is no feature where you can see your photo on the cup, like there is on Zazzle.com.

Oh, let's not forget Kodak. You can make mugs there in much the same way as you do on Zazzle. Go to kodakgallery.com > Shop > Photo Gifts. Cups go for $12.99 and up.

Ironing Your Photos on T-Shirts

Putting one of your photos on a T-shirt is easy. The first thing you have to get (other than a photo) is specialty iron-on printer paper. You'll also need an iron, an ironing board (or other flat surface), and a computer.

Then you just follow the directions on the box of specialty paper you are using. In a nutshell, you print your image on iron-on transfer paper (print preview on regular paper first) and then iron the image onto a T-shirt. Make sure you opt for T-shirt transfer paper (or photo paper if that choice isn't available) when choosing the paper for the printing process (usually under Advanced Options/Media Type or Paper Type). When you iron, choose the highest temperature your iron has (cotton setting), without steam, and press firmly on the iron so that the print adheres to the fabric.

NOTE

Iron-on specialty paper is called *transfer paper*. There is a transfer paper designed for both light and dark T-shirts. Make sure you get the right transfer paper that's compatible with the color of the T-shirt upon which you are ironing an image.

Finally, if you don't feel like making your own T-shirts, you can order one with your photo on it for $12.95 and up at Zazzle (www.zazzle.com/custom/tshirts). Zazzle handles PNG files. (See the note after the "Getting Rid of Your Background" sidebar.)

You can also create a T-shirt for $19.99 with your photo on it at Snapfish (www.snapfish.com/gifts/product=tshirt).

GETTING RID OF YOUR BACKGROUND

If you want to get rid of the background of your image, and you are printing on a T-shirt from an iron-on transfer, all you have to do is cut out the part of the image you want on the T-shirt. If you're ordering a T-shirt from an online seller, you have to upload a photo.

If you want to put an image on a T-shirt using an online interactive editing program, you'll have to cut out the background in Photoshop (or Elements) first.

To do this:

1. Open your image and save it with a new name. Figure 9.2 shows my original image.
2. In the Layers palette (Window > Layers), double-click the padlock, unlocking the Background layer.
3. Select the Polygonal Lasso tool and type **2 px** in the Feather field (in the Options bar).
4. Click the Polygonal Lasso tool around the part of the image you want cut out.

5. Choose Select > Inverse.
6. Click Delete on your keyboard. Figure 9.3 shows my image after clicking Delete.

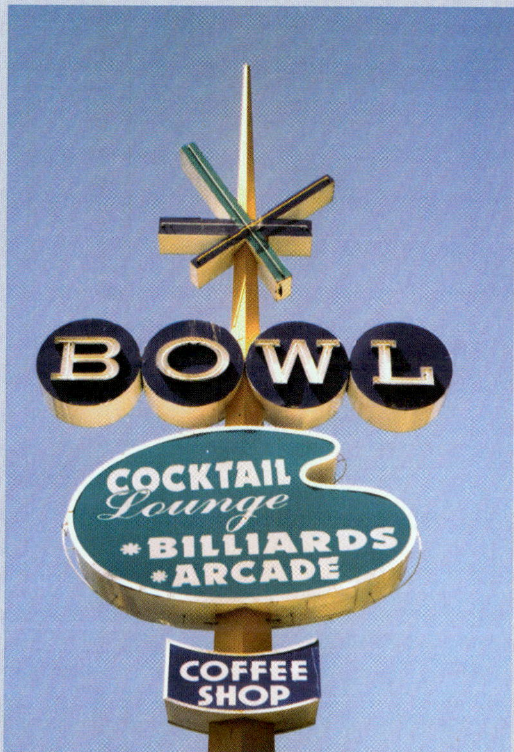

Figure 9.2 Bowl picture before deleting the background in Photoshop.

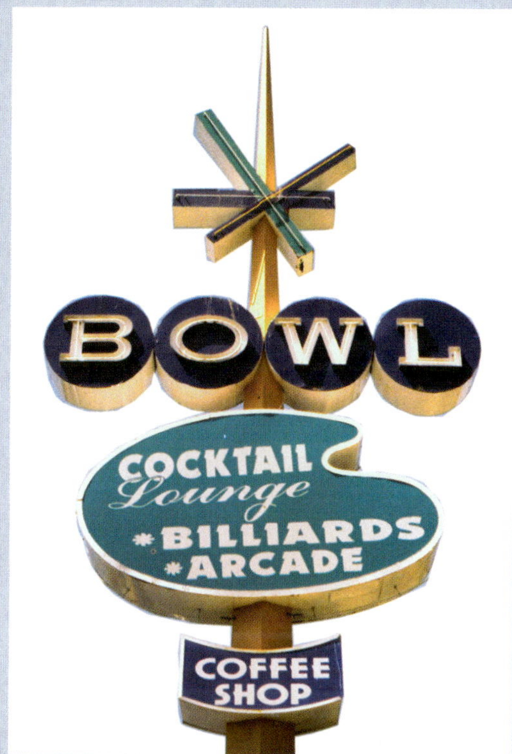

Figure 9.3 The bowl sign with the background deleted.

Voila! You have your image cut out with a transparent background!

NOTE

There will be two layers in this file. Don't flatten the image. If you do, your background will turn white. (The squares that indicate it's transparent will go away.) Save the file as a PNG file (which will convert the two layers to one)—a file type that handles images with transparent backgrounds with a one-layer non-flattened image. PNG files are compatible with many online platforms, such as Zazzle.

Making Business Cards with Your Photos at MOO.com

To be sure, you can make business cards at Zazzle.com ($16.95 for 100 business cards with the same image), but there's another site that lets you make each business card in a pack with a different picture ($21.99 for 50 cards).

You can upload photos from your computer or use the ones that you have on Flickr, Facebook, or Etsy. The business cards are printed on two sides—one side with your photo on it, and the other side with details of your business (text).

On MOO.com's homepage, you click on Choose a Product to Make and then in the next window, Make Business Cards. In the next window, click Upload Your Images (JPEG, PNG, GIF, or PDF). The site recommends that images be 300 dpi. Finally, click on Upload Your Images to MOO. In the selection box that comes up, you'll then do the usual picking of photos that you want from your computer. After you've selected your images (use the Shift/Command/Ctrl key to select multiple images, depending on your computer), click on Select. Your images will be uploaded right away.

After your images are uploaded (which will take a few minutes), click on Next Step. The new window will slowly display the front (image side) of the business card. The window will also contain how many cards of each picture will be in your pack. For example, I uploaded 16 cards, and the site calculated that I would get three of each card in each pack I ordered. Figure 9.4 shows how the sample cards are displayed in the window. You can click Edit This Card to rotate or enlarge the picture on the card. You can also click and drag the picture around in the window.

After you preview your images, click Next Step. This is the window where you can add text (and a logo or another image if you want). You can choose a layout for the text side of the card (which also has an option for putting another small image on it). After you do, the appropriate entry boxes for text will be displayed. Just type in your name, address, phone number, and so on. When you're finished, click Next Step.

In the new window that comes up, you pick your paper. You have a choice of a Classic or Green card. The MOO Classic card is smooth, sturdy paper with a matte laminate on both sides. The MOO Green card is uncoated, so the image will be less bright. After that choice, click Next Step. A preview of your business cards will come up. Check to see that everything is okay and then click Next Step. Check off the number of cards you want and then click Add to Cart.

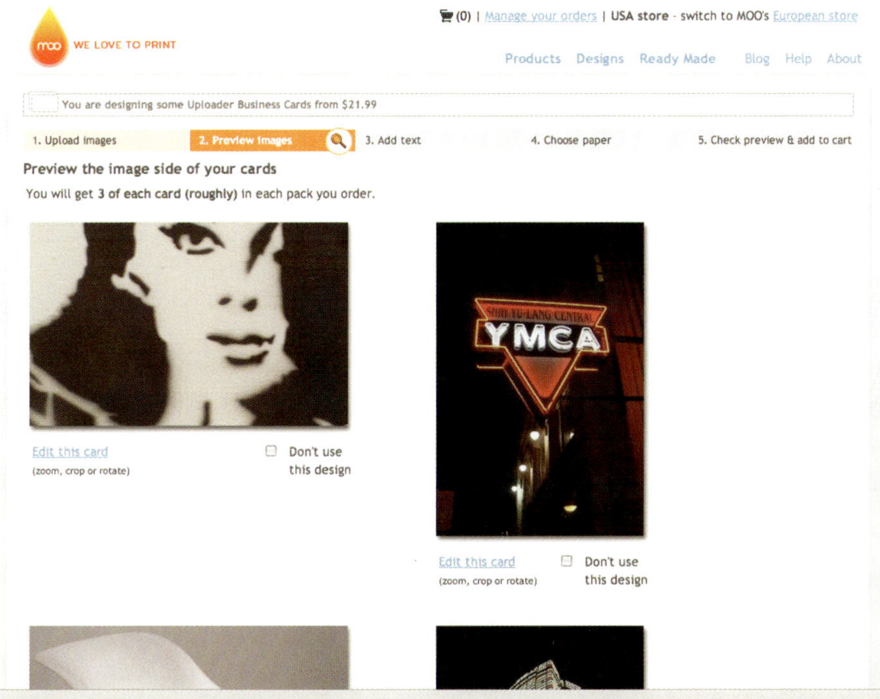

Figure 9.4 Your business-card images are previewed at MOO.com.

Burning Your Photos onto a Gift CD

Why not find and burn your best photos to make a gift CD for a friend or family member?

In Windows Vista, all you have to do to burn a CD or DVD is pop one into the CD/DVD recorder. After you do, a dialog box will come up. Click Burn Files to Data Disc. Next, a Burn a Disc dialog box comes up. Type a name for your disc and then click Next. An empty disc folder will then come up. Open a folder of images you want to burn to the CD/DVD and click and drag the images inside into the disc folder.

On a Mac, all you have to do to burn a CD or DVD is to insert it into the CD/DVD drive. Click OK in the prompt that comes up. Your CD will appear on the desktop. Open it by double-clicking on it. A blank window will appear. Click and drag the folders and files you want to burn to the disc. You'll see aliases in the window (folders/image files with arrows next to their icons). These connect the files to the originals so the originals aren't moved. Click Burn at the top of the window. In the dialog that comes up, give the disc a name, enter a speed (the maximum), and uncheck the Save Burn Folder To option. (Check it if you want the aliases saved.) Click Burn.

For more about CDs and DVDs, see "Storing Your Photos and Backups Properly" in Chapter 1.

Creating a Greeting Card Online

After searching the Internet and making cards on a couple of sites, I've found MOO.com and Snapfish.com to offer great features in their online photo greeting-card makers.

Here's the skinny on these two sites. MOO.com has greeting cards by the pack. (A pack of 10 folded cards with envelopes is $24.99.) Like the business cards described in the "Making Business Cards with Your Photos at MOO.com" section, you can opt for a different image on every card.

To access the greeting-card maker, click on Choose a Product to Make on the homepage. Then click on Make Greeting Cards. The next window gives you options to make 10 or 25 greeting cards. To make the greeting cards, click on Start Uploading Images. Again, as with the business cards, you can opt to choose images from your Flickr account. Once you upload your image(s), a new window will come up where there are templates (choose between landscape and portrait) you can select for the front of your card. You can opt to have your entire image be the template in this window. After you click on Next Step, a new window will come up where you design the front of the card. You can add any text you want to the front of the card. Figure 9.5 shows a card where I typed in Happy Birthday to make a birthday card. When you're finished, click on Save and Make Another and then click on Next Step again. A new window will come up where you make the middle of the card. After you're finished typing in the text for that, click Next Step again to personalize the back of the card. After that, you pick an envelope (white ones are free; color ones cost extra). Finally, they ask you how many packs you want, and then you go to payment.

NOTE

Your image will appear at the top of window; you have to click and drag it onto the card for it to appear.

Snapfish.com (www.snapfish.com/storecards2) has greeting cards in packs with 20 and more. The more you buy, the cheaper each card is. The cards are around $17 for 20 non-folded cards without envelopes.

The first thing you do at Snapfish to create a card is pick a template from dozens that appear on more than 12 pages on the site. After you click on one, you're taken to a new window where you choose your size and layout and the kind of paper you want. After you select these, click on Create This Card. In the left side of the window that comes up, upload your photo.

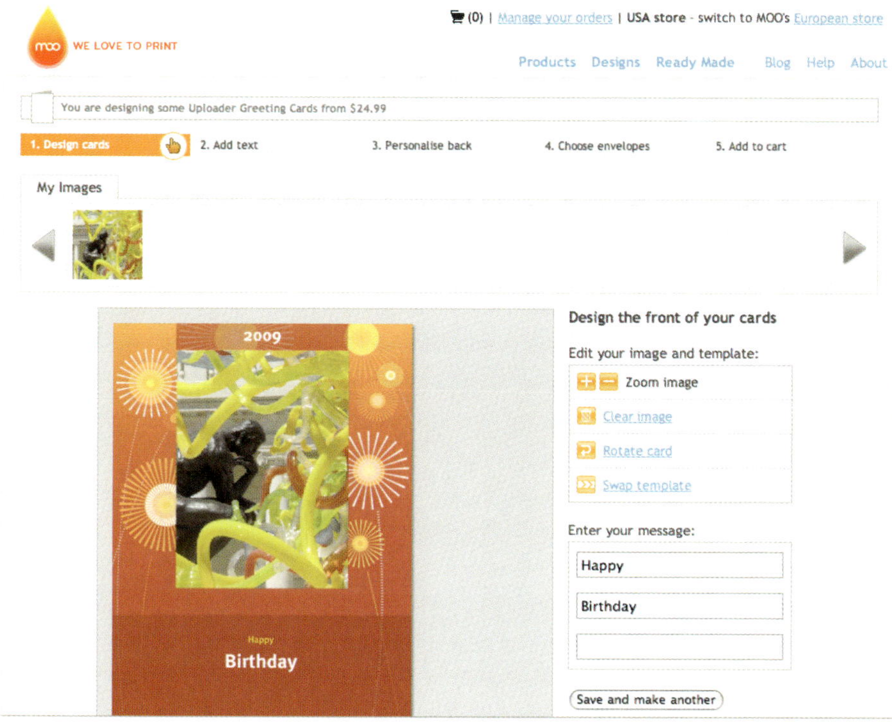

Figure 9.5 MOO.com has cards where you customize the front, the inside, and the back.

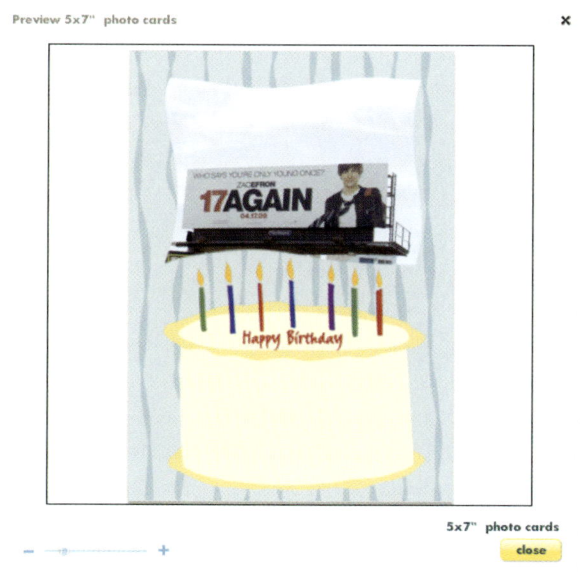

Figure 9.6 Snapfish.com has cards where you only customize the front.

A dialog box will come up, where you navigate on your computer to the photo you want on the card. Follow the prompts, and you'll be taken to the window where you customize your card. Your photo will appear on the right side of the window. You have to click and drag that photo onto the card. Then you can add text at the bottom of the card if you like. Next, click on Save Card and then Order Card. Figure 9.6 shows a preview of the card.

Creating Custom Postage Stamps with Your Photos at Stamps.com

When you arrive at the window after clicking PhotoStamps at the bottom of the stamps.com window, you can personalize your stamps with one of your own photos. Just click on Create PhotoStamps, and you'll be taken to a dialog box where you browse for the picture you want on your computer. After you've found the photo you want, you click Choose and then click Next. In the next window, you'll see your image on a stamp (see Figure 9.7). It is here where you can customize your stamp (edit it) using drop-down menus for border, color (of the number value of the postage), and postage price. You can also rotate and/or zoom into your photo. When you're finished customizing, click Continue. In the next window, your cart (your invoice) for 20 stamps (1 sheet worth) for $18.99 comes up. Click on Check Out Now to pay (or to register if you didn't when you got to the site; registration requires that you give your home address). When you're finished making your stamp template and you've chosen which shipping option you want, the stamps are sent to you by mail.

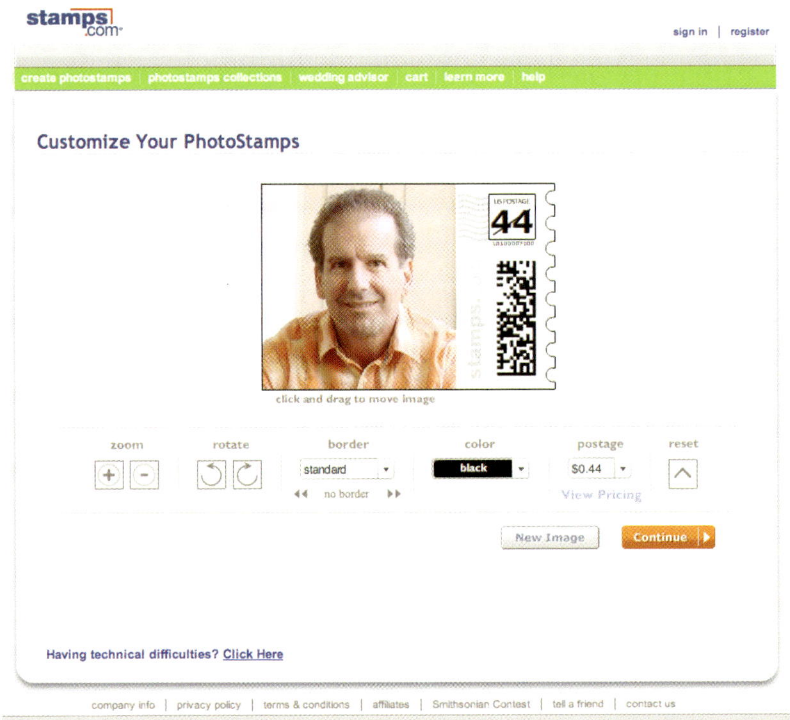

Figure 9.7 Put an image of yourself on a stamp.

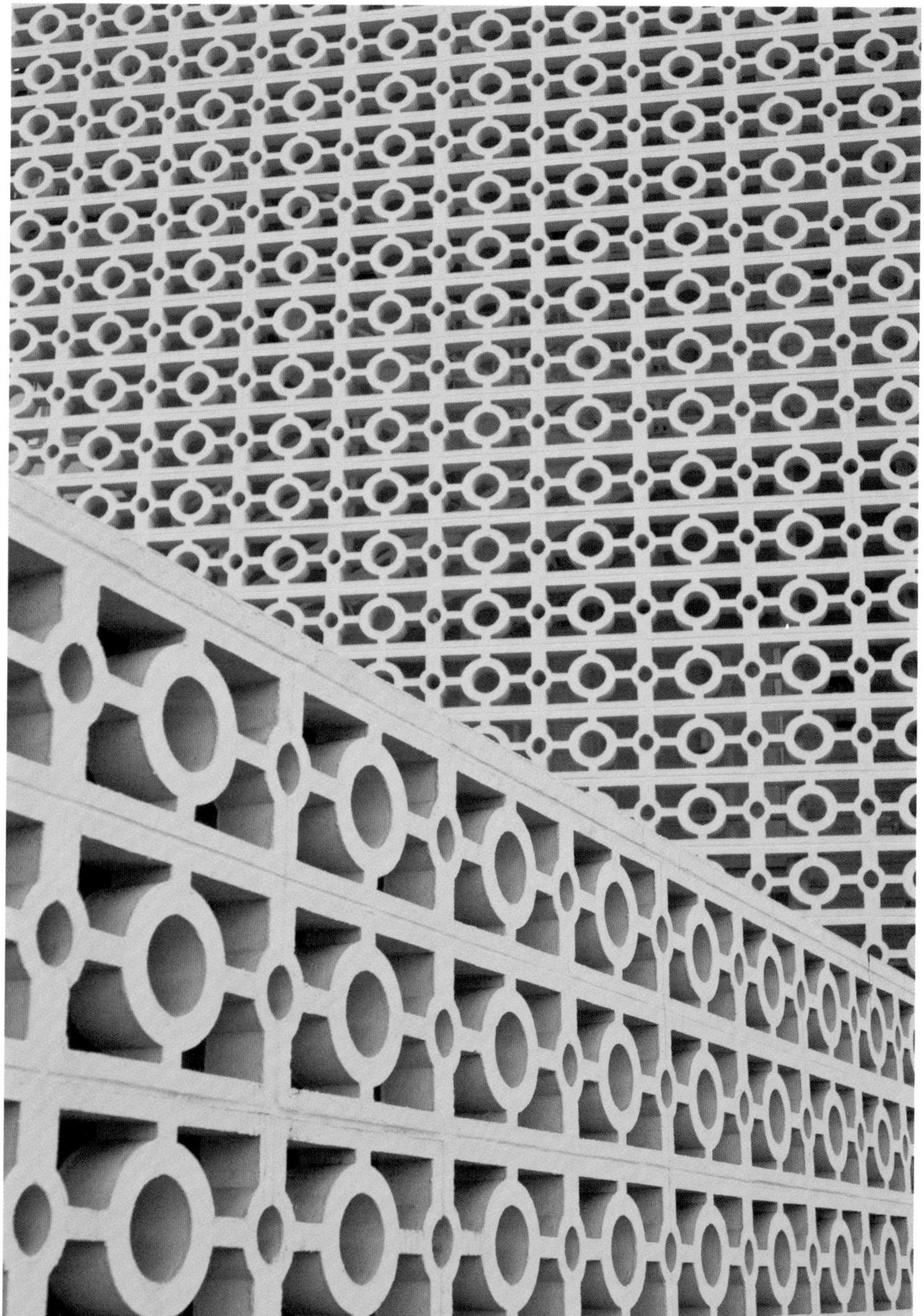

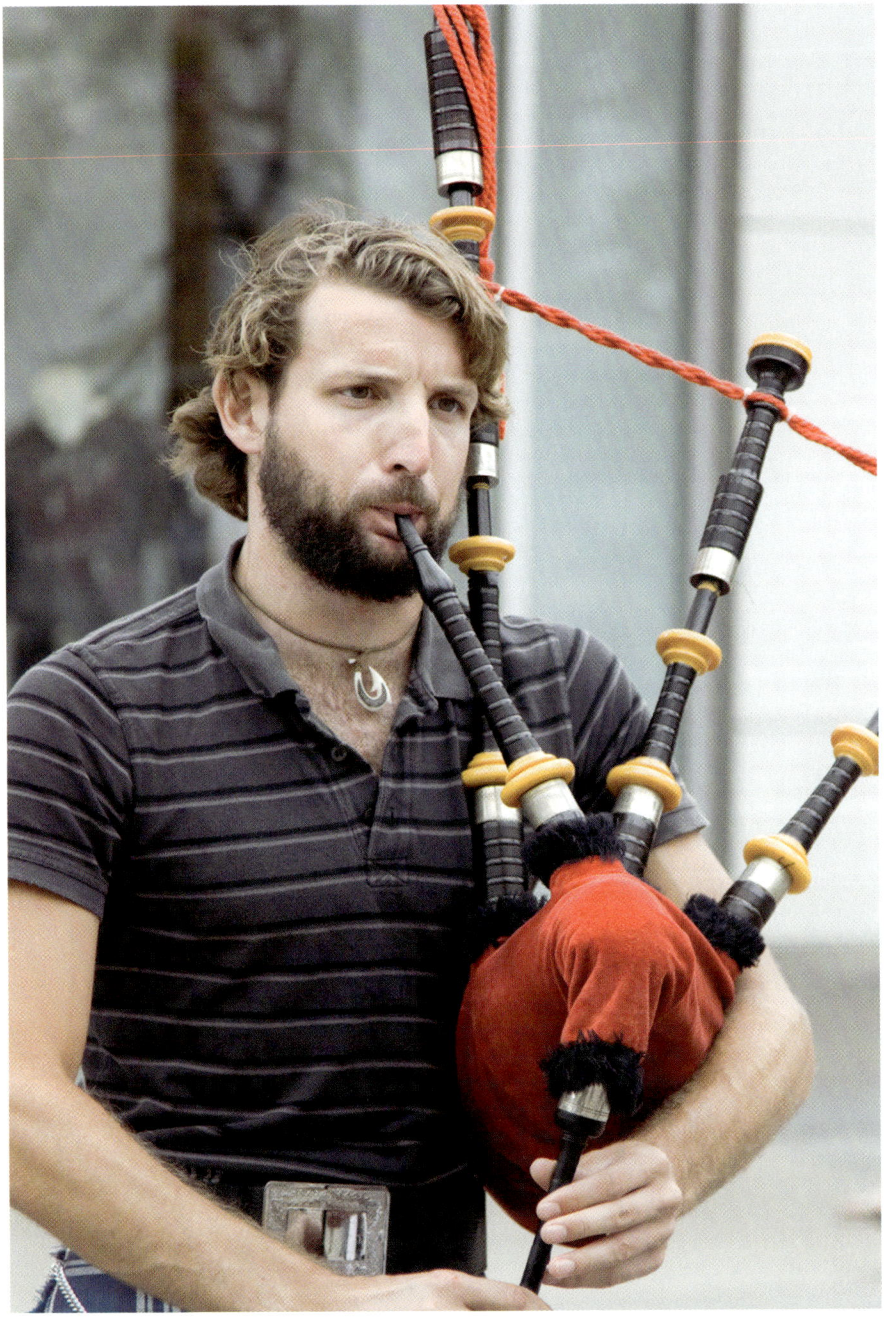

Chapter 10
Getting Published

There are many venues for having your photos published these days. Did you know that there are probably thousands of websites that could use your pictures? There are magazines and newspapers all over the world that devote a page (or pages) to amateur photographer photos. They also accept submissions from new freelance photographers (though you usually have to submit a portfolio and get it approved first). Then there are your own blogs and websites. There are easy things you can do to get search engines to list your photos to result in more hits (visitors) to them—things as simple as naming your photo files a certain way. If you're selling your photos, the more people who see them, the more who are likely to buy them. Publishing ideas are detailed in this chapter, with many novel ideas you can use right now.

Making Your Photos Web Ready

In the "Resizing Your Photos for Different Uses" section in Chapter 1, the resolution for web-ready photos is discussed, as well as how to resize them in Photoshop (or Elements) to make them web ready. After you resize an image, there are a number of things you can do to make it look good on the web.

If you shoot in Raw format, it's best to tweak your image as much as possible when you are viewing it in the Raw window. (See the "Using Image Processing Programs to Tweak Your Photos" section in Chapter 1.) However, you won't be able to resize it at that point because the Raw window contains no options to do that. It does, however, have options for cropping and rotating your photos. After you're finished tweaking in that window, you click on Open Image, and your image appears in a new window where you can tweak using the tools of Photoshop's main program, including the Resize option.

Once your photo is open in the new window, or if you've opened your image as a JPEG or TIFF file, you're ready to start post-processing to prepare your image for the web. If you've already edited your photo in Raw, you shouldn't have to do much tweaking of color, brightness, and exposure before you resize for the web.

Now, if you're opening an existing JPEG or TIFF file, you'll have to tweak using Photoshop's (or Elements') tools. If your image is fairly decent (meaning it's well exposed), you probably won't have to do much.

The first thing I do after opening an image and resizing it is make adjustments in the levels (Image > Levels). I can make the image have more contrast and/or make it brighter or darker using these options. Figure 10.1 shows the histogram, which you tweak by moving the right, middle, and left sliders. To get the image ready for the web, this particular picture has to be lighter. I made adjustments to do that by clicking and dragging the slider on the right to the left at the beginning of the histogram (see Figure 10.2). If I wanted to make the image darker (bring out the shadows), I'd click and drag the left slider to the right. The middle slider also can be adjusted, usually to the left to add tones in the midrange.

If the image doesn't look good (if it's soft or has too many blown highlights) after I've made adjustments in levels, I usually toss it and find a better one.

The last thing you want to do is save your photo for the web. To do that, navigate to File > Save for Web & Devices. Check Optimized and then pay attention to the Quality setting. When you move the Quality slider, check the size of the file (in KB) at the bottom left of the window. You'll notice that the file size gets smaller with diminishing quality. If you're working in an online platform that gives you a choice of photo sizes, that number matters.

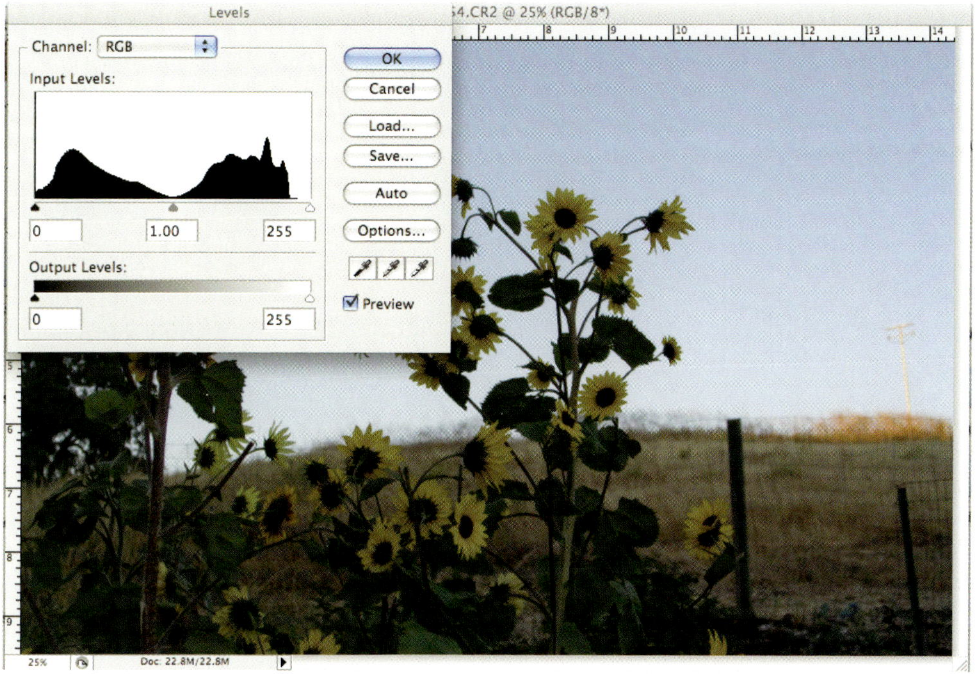

Figure 10.1 Image before tweaking Levels sliders.

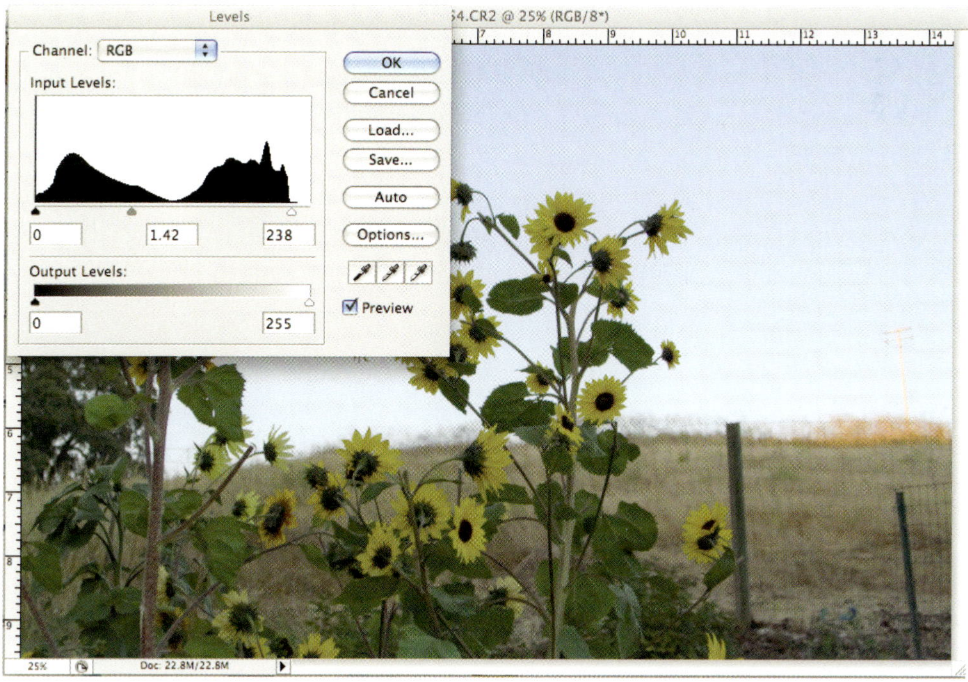

Figure 10.2 Image after tweaking Levels sliders.

If the photo is going to be displayed small, then your quality can be low (and thus your file size can be small). If you're going to display it large, then you'll want your quality high.

Making Your Photos Magazine Ready

In the "Resizing Your Photos for Different Uses" section in Chapter 1, there is a description of how to resize photos. In the "Selling Photos to Regional Magazines" section in Chapter 8, the requirements for magazine submissions are listed. *Arizona Highways* requires a 12×18-inch digital photo with 300 ppi resolution. That's one big photo. Most magazines don't require the resolutions to be that great. In order to meet that image resolution requirement, you'd need a camera on the order of the new Canon 21 MP EOS 5D Mark II. For a great megapixel/print dimension chart, check out http://design215.com/toolbox/megapixels.php.

No matter what the resolution of your photos is, you'd best be sure that when you view the photos you are going to be submitting at 100-percent resolution on your computer screen (in Photoshop, type **100** into the lower-left corner of the window in which your picture is displayed), they are sharp in every detail. If not, don't bother sending them, because magazines won't accept them.

Okay, so what if you don't have a 21-MP camera for taking photos fit for *Arizona Highways*? You can try other magazines, such as *Dog Fancy* (if you take pictures of dogs), most of which require a minimum of 300 dpi for a 5×7 photo.

To check how big your images are, you need to open an image (one taken with your camera set at its highest resolution, which would be the Raw setting on most dSLRs) and navigate to Image > Image Size. A dialog box will come up (see Figure 10.3). Uncheck the box next to where it says Resample Image. When Resample Image isn't checked, you can change the values of Width, Height, or Resolution, and Photoshop/Elements will proportion the photo accordingly without changing the file size. Now, delete the value that's for Resolution and type in **300**.

I find that for my 12.8-MP Canon 5D, the values that come up are 11.52 inches for the width and 7.68 inches for the height. I also find out that this size of image has a file size of 22.8 MB. Sadly, my image doesn't have enough resolution to submit to *Arizona Highways*. But it is big enough (greater than 5×7 at 300 dpi) for other magazines.

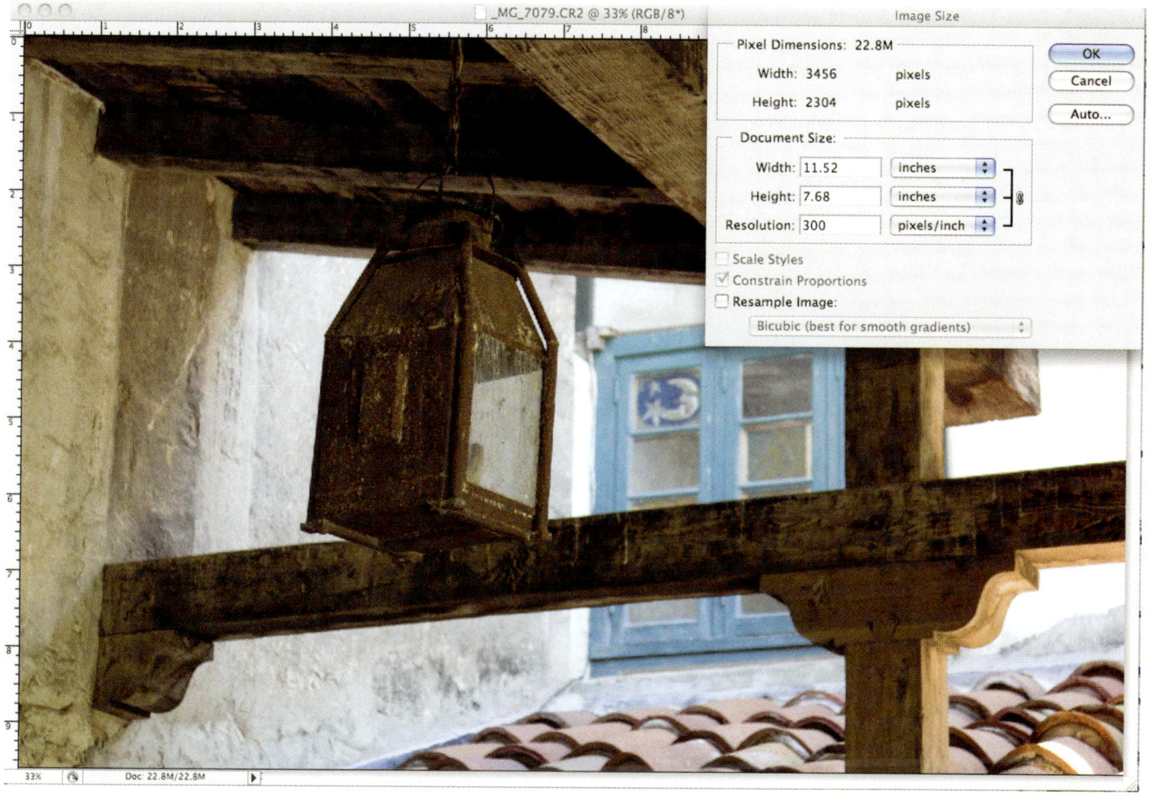

Figure 10.3 The largest resolution a 12.8-MP camera will shoot at is 7.68×11.52 inches at 300 dpi.

Writing a How-To Photo Book

With the popularity of digital photography increasing daily, more people than ever are purchasing digital cameras. Many of those people would like to learn how to use all of the options and settings these cameras offer. To meet the needs of digital camera owners who have an interest in going beyond auto mode, publishers have to put out a certain number of how-to photography books a year that teach people how to do so.

To write a how-to photography book, such as the one shown in Figure 10.4, you not only have to be an adept writer, you also have to have an eclectic collection of images. These days, how-to photography books not only teach readers how to use their cameras, but they also give readers a rich collection of sample images for them to learn the different skills needed to be a good photographer.

Probably two of the most important things publishers look for in a potential author are the ideas he has for a photography how-to book and the platform (public life) upon which he works. Publishers want novel ideas and good photographs to go with them. They also want a potential author to have the ability to reach the readers for whom a book is targeted. This platform should include that the author has a good presence on the Internet (blogs, websites, Twitter, Facebook) and that he is able to reach potential book buyers on the ground (through seminars, classes, and/or published articles).

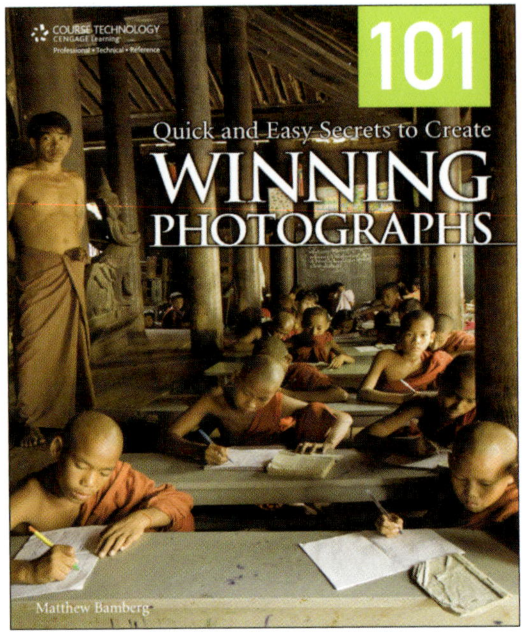

Figure 10.4 If you're a good writer and you have a diverse collection of images, you can try your hand at writing a how-to photography book.

So how does one go about beginning the process of pitching a book to a publisher? The first thing you should do if you have a good idea for any type of photography book is to get an agent. There are some agents who specifically handle photography books. Some handle only coffee table books, others handle only how-to books, and there are some who handle both. There are some agencies that deal specifically with technology books—a category that includes digital photography. Off the top of my head, there are two literary agencies that have gotten book deals for authors of books about digital photography. They are watersidesyndication.com and fresh-books.com.

Many large publishing companies—Wiley, for example—only accept submissions from agents. That means it's best to get an agent if you want to get a book deal. Agents don't usually cost anything (if they do, I'd be suspicious). They make their money from the money their client makes—15 percent of it, usually.

These two agencies accept query letters by e-mail for initial contact. (Watersidesyndication.com has a Query an Agent form, which you fill out online.) In your communication, you can introduce yourself and describe your idea. If any of the agents likes your idea, they'll probably have you write a proposal. Most proposals include a description of the audience, competing or related books, marketing, a description of the book, an outline or TOC (table of contents), and an author bio.

Entering a Photography Competition

There are a couple of big-name magazines that sponsor photography competitions in which part of the prize (aside from money and/or travel) is getting your photos published on their pages.

Popular Photography Photo Contest

Enter at www.popphotocontest.com

America's biggest photo magazine has a big contest. The winning images are published both in the magazine and on the website. The categories include action/sports, candid/humor, nature, architecture, people, and travel/places.

American PHOTO

Enter at www.iotycontest.com

The annual American PHOTO Images of the Year Competition is another biggie. The winning images are published in an issue of American PHOTO magazine and at popphoto.com. The categories for entries are photojournalism/documentary, commercial work: advertising/editorial, personal work, student work, portraiture, nature, and extreme.

National Wildlife

Enter at www.nwf.org/photozone/enterphotocontest.cfm

National Wildlife, the magazine of the National Wildlife Federation, sponsors a photo contest for wildlife photographers. Winners of the contest are published in one of their issues. There are seven categories in three different divisions (Pro, Amateur, and Youth). The categories are global warming, wildlife, mammals, birds, other wildlife, backyard habitats, connecting people and nature, landscapes, and plant life.

Smithsonian Magazine

Enter at http://photocontest.smithsonianmag.com

Every year, Smithsonian magazine sponsors a contest. There are five categories in which you can enter: natural world, Americana, altered images, travel, and people. Ten finalists from each category are chosen. The finalists' photos get published on the Smithsonian website.

PHOTO CONTEST LIST

Want to enter a different photo competition? Here's a list of some more of the bigger contests.

* Sony World Photography Awards: www.worldphotographyawards.org
* Travel Photographer of the Year: www.tpoty.com
* Nature's Best Photography Awards: www.naturesbestphotography.com
* International Photography Awards: www.photoawards.com
* The Everyman Amateur Photography Contest: www.theeveryman.com

Self-Publishing a Photo Book Using Blurb

Blurb lets you make your own photo book (see Figure 10.5). It isn't cheap. Prices range from $12.95 for a 7×7, 40-page softcover book to $186.95 for a 12×12, 440-page hardcover book. The site is probably not the place for making bulk orders. What it is, though, is a great place to see how a finished book looks and perhaps to print a few copies to see whether they sell. If all goes well, then you can bulk order through a print shop.

To download Blurb's BookSmart, the program with which you build your book, you have to register (username, password, and e-mail) at the site. The site then processes that info and determines what kind of computer you're working on (Mac or PC). From there, you can download the program.

Using the program is not all that difficult. You basically import your photos from your computer (or from Flickr, Photobucket, Picasa Web Albums and/or SmugMug). After they're uploaded, you'll see them as thumbnails in the right frame of the window. To place a photo in the book, you just click and drag a photo when the book page says Drag Image Here. To add text, just click in the textbox. The pages are organized in two-page spreads where the text is on the left page and the images are on the right. Thumbnails for the pages are numbered along the bottom of the window. To work on one, you just have to click on it.

These aforementioned directions will get you started on your book. There are numerous video and text tutorials that show you many of BookSmart's features when you navigate to the Help drop-down menu at the top of your computer screen.

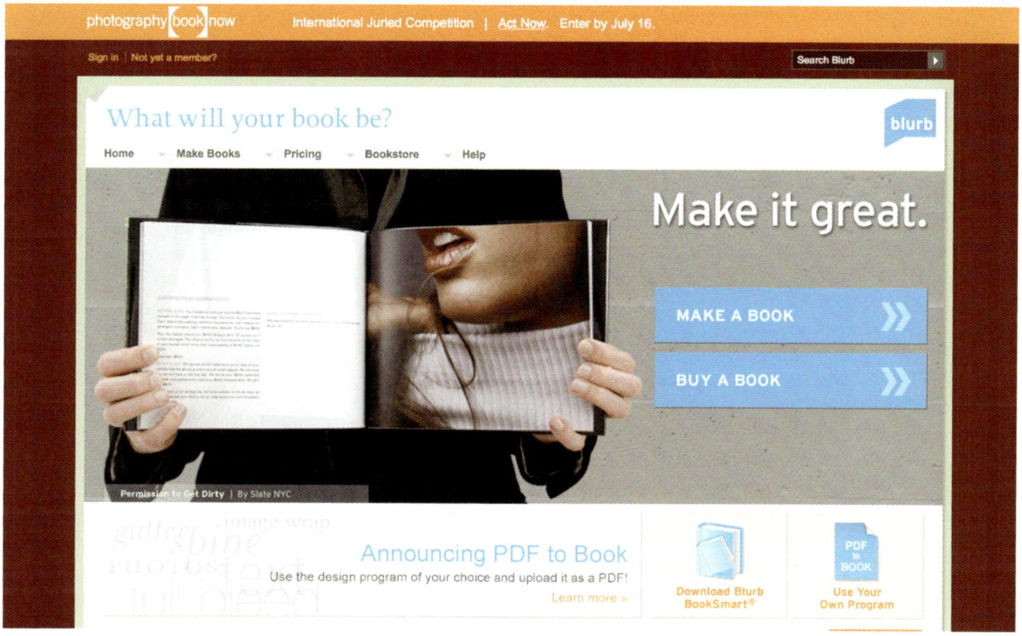

Figure 10.5 Blurb is a site where you self-publish books.

> **NOTE**
>
> Other self-publishing sites include mypublisher.com and lulu.com. They work in much the same way as Blurb does.

Submitting Photos to the Big-Time Media Outlets for Publication

* **Reuters/Yahoo!** Submit at www.reuters.com/youwitness. Reuters/Yahoo! news service is always looking for newsworthy photography. If the photos are published, you'll get paid! The photos also have the potential to be published in hundreds of news publications worldwide. All you have to do is upload and fill out the information prompts at www.reuters.com/youwitness/upload.

> **NOTE**
>
> You can spend hours looking at the images on the Reuters site, so be forewarned that they are riveting!

- **Your Scene *LA Times*.** If you live in or around LA, you can submit at yourscene.latimes.com. (Scroll to the bottom of the page and click on the tiny print that reads Submit Your Photo or Video.) If you want to get your feet wet and see your image as part of a big-city newspaper, submit your image to Your Scene. There are hundreds of images submitted there, which might deter you if you feel like a needle in a haystack, but consider this: If your image is good, it might get picked to be Editor's Choice or Best of Your Scene.
- **iReport.com.** Submit at ireport.com. (Where it says Upload Now, register and then upload your photo.) iReport.com is a site put out by CNN that it describes as "a place where the community decides what the news is" (see Figure 10.6). At the site you can submit video, text, or photos. Some of the content at iReport appears on CNN's newscast.

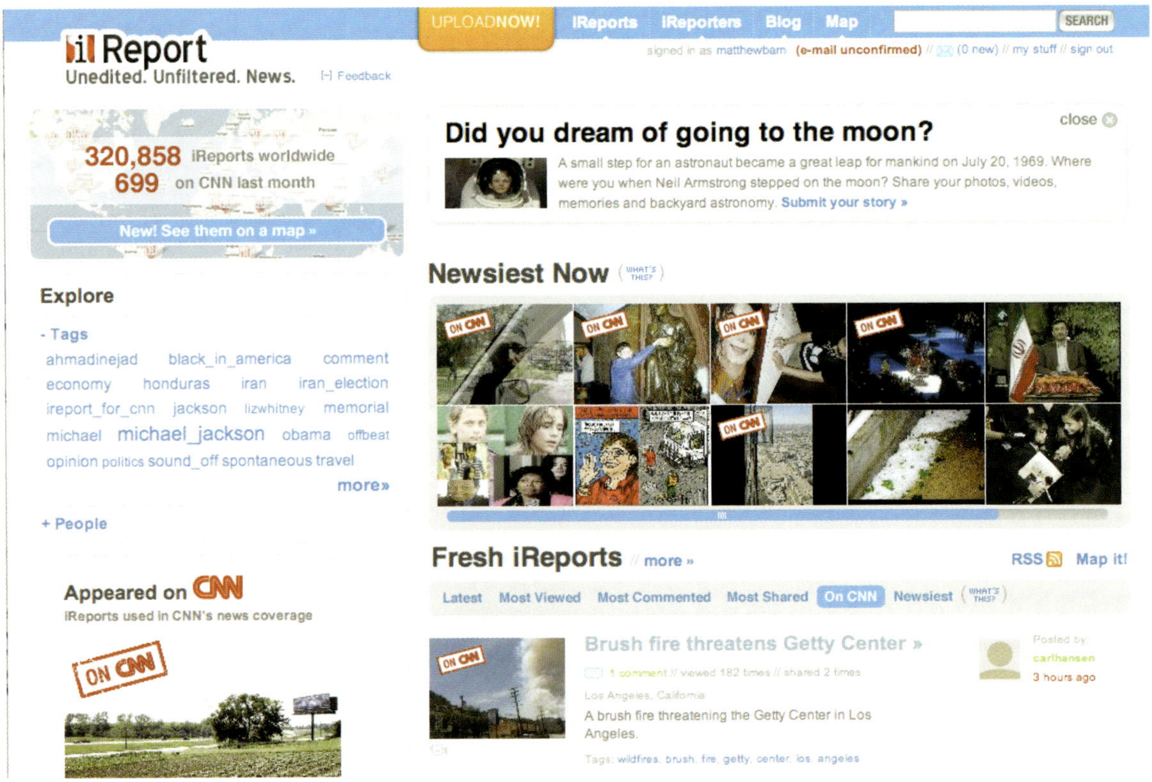

Figure 10.6 You can submit your photos on ireport.com for publication.

> **NOTE**
>
> When you register at iReport, you'll get a webpage with your profile and the items you uploaded listed.

To increase your chances of getting your work shown on CNN, take a look at the Assignment Desk. To get to it, scroll to the bottom of the iReport.com homepage. You'll see the link Assignment Desk among others that spread across the page. On the Assignment Desk page are topics for which you can submit photos. When you click on any topic, you'll be taken to a new page where the assignment is listed with a link called Share Your Story. When you click on that, you're taken to a page where you can input the photo and other necessary info.

For example, when you click on Travel Snapshots on the Assignment Desk page, the link will take you to a description of what CNN wants in terms of a photo. For this category, CNN wants photos of a different destination that it names each week.

NOTE

All images you submit appear on the website. If it gets marked with "On CNN," it means that it has appeared on the CNN newscast.

Getting Your Photo Noticed on Google

When you type keywords into Google Images, the images that show up come from websites and blogs. What bloggers and webmasters have done when they make their webpage or blog is use relevant keywords for the images they post. The Google Search software (called Googlebot) can't "see" pictures, but it can read the text associated with them. This is why using keywords relevant to the images you use helps Googlebot to find your images and list them in Google Images.

The first two things you should do when you're posting images to your blog or website are to resize (see Chapter 1) and rename your images. When you rename the files using relevant keywords, Google uses those names in its directory after you upload them (see Figure 10.7). When you post images on Blogger, for example, the images get their own URLs, which contain the keywords you've given them. (For more about making blogs, refer to Chapter 6.)

Blog surfers get to my blog through the pictures I post on it. Google is finding many of my images from the keywords I give their filenames when I create them. These keywords are then used at the end of the URL Blogger gives my image. For example, I get hits from a picture of an opera singer that's listed on Blogger because the keywords that I've given it are listed in the picture's very long URL:

http://4.bp.blogspot.com/_tGRbgaFgWh4/R_Rosf7YF9I/AAAAAAAACBI/E2NzX-uEJC0/s400/opera_singer.jpg.

When Internet surfers key in the words "opera singer," they might just find my image among the thousands that come up in a Google image search.

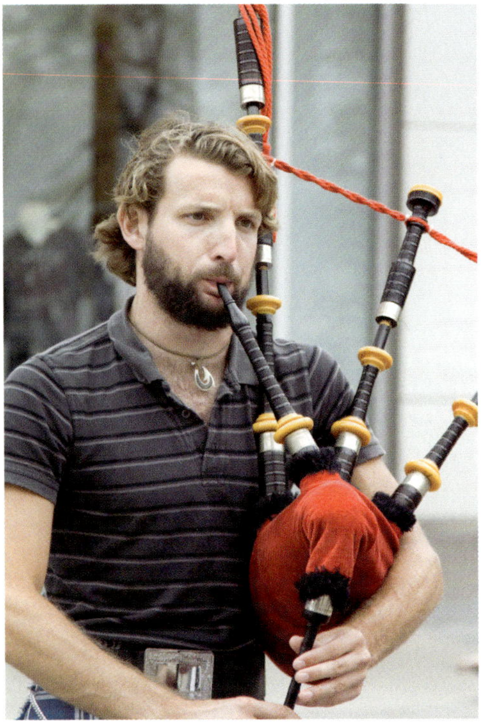

Figure 10.7 Keywords for this image would be bagpipe player; the filename should be bagpipe_player.

> **NOTE**
>
> When naming files, never leave spaces in the file name. In Internet-land, a blank space is read as a % sign. Googlebot will then not know that the two words belong together. To let Googlebot know the words go together, use a dash or underscore between words.

Finally, I have a service on my blog that tells me where my hits are coming from. It's called Site Meter. (See the following "How Do I Know Who's Looking at the Pictures on My Blog?" sidebar.) When I access it by clicking on the icon for it I have put on my webpage, I can see what pictures are being found by looking at the keywords in the URL. Some keywords for images Google has found on my blog are Bob Hope, Mexico house, orchid, motion blur, Galapagos finch, yellow lotus, heart graffiti, tree house, 60s architecture. There are hundreds more, but I think you get the picture.

HOW DO I KNOW WHO'S LOOKING AT THE PICTURES ON MY BLOG?

Many bloggers and/or webmasters want to know information about who is visiting their website. They want to know how many hits they are getting, what websites they are coming from, how long they are spending at the website, and what links they are clicking on their website. There are free meters (website counters) for which you can get HTML code to include in your website or blog template. These website meters then appear as a link on the blog/website. When the owner of the website or blog wants to know the comings and goings of his website/blog, he just clicks on the meter. One of the best meters can be had at sitemeter.com. It's free and easy to install on your website/blog.

Using BigHugeLabs to Publish Photo Posters, Jigsaw Puzzles, Comicbook Captions, and More

If you're not into having a general public audience for your photography, yet you want something published to show your friends, then BigHugeLabs is the place to be (see Figure 10.8).

The site has generators for making the following with your images: motivator posters, magazine covers, movie posters, David Hockney–like posters, mats, trading cards, wallpaper for computers, Andy Warhol–like posters, and mosaic posters.

To make any of these creations, you just click on one of them on the homepage. For example, when you click on Motivator, you'll click on Browse for the file you want to upload from your computer. (That's all you have to do; there is no Upload button to push.) Then you click on the listed options you want for your photo (cropping, orientation, border), choose the color of your text, type in the text you want the poster to have, and then use a drop-down menu to select the text style you want. Finally, you click on Create. Your poster will be shown in the next window, where you'll have options to Add to Cart, Edit, Start Over, Save, Upload to Flickr, Share, Email, and Create High Res.

The site lets you save your new creation, but it only saves it in low res (72 KB). To get a high-res file of your image, you have to join the site. (You'll be prompted for what to do after you click on Create High Res.) It costs $5 per week/$10 per month/$25 per year to join, and you get to make as many high-res images as you want during that period of time. High-res is only available for Calendar, Hockneyizer, Jigsaw, Magazine Cover, Mosaic Maker, Motivator, Movie Poster, Scout, and Warholizer features.

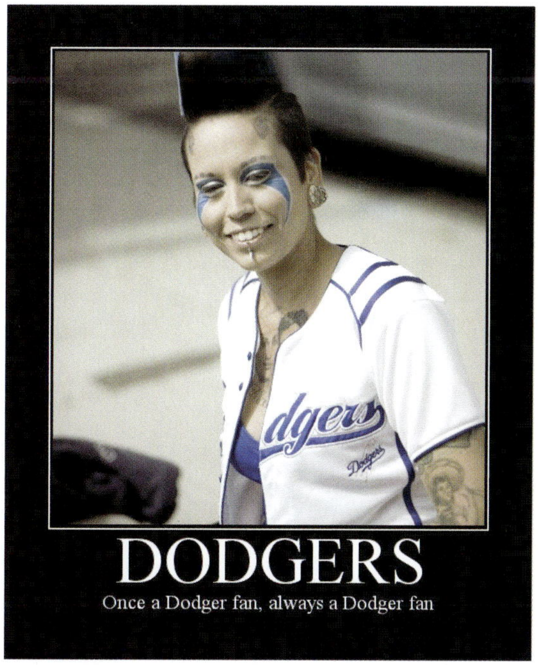

Figure 10.8 BigHugeLab motivator poster with uploaded image.

You do not have to join the site to buy a print of an image you've made. Prices for prints are:

- 8×10: $15
- 11×14: $20
- 16×20: $30

You can also have the jigsaw image made into a jigsaw puzzle for $40.

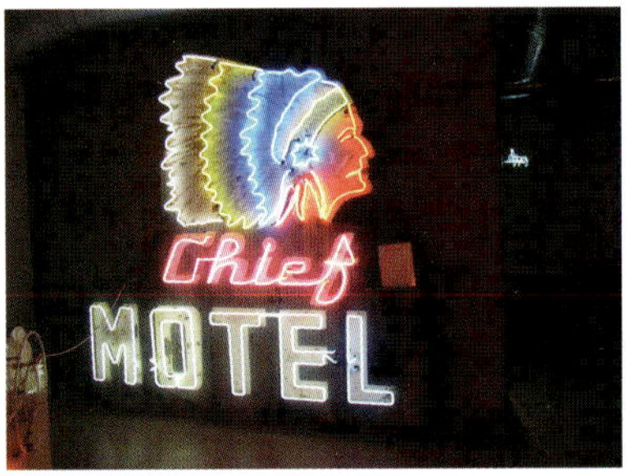
Chief
MOTEL

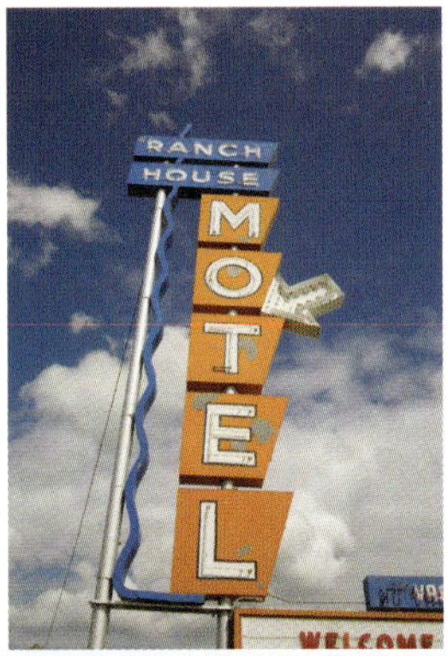
RANCH
HOUSE
MOTEL

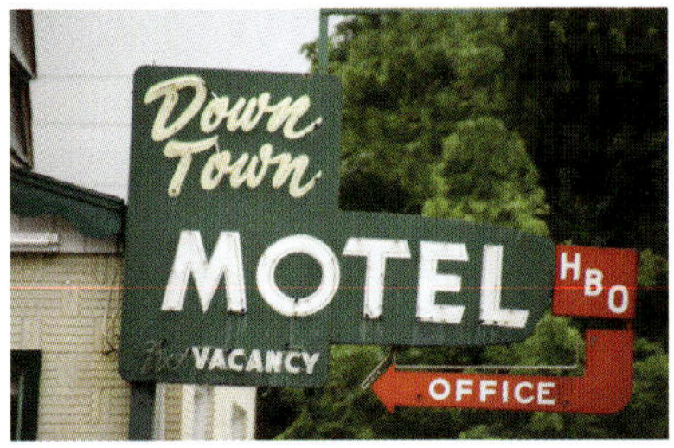
Down
Town
MOTEL
HBO
VACANCY
OFFICE

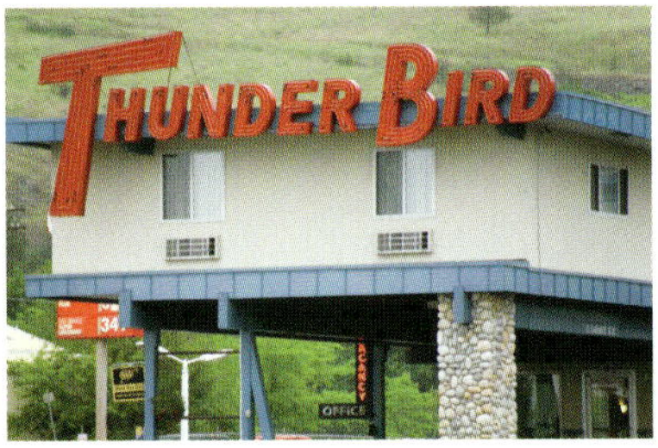
THUNDER BIRD

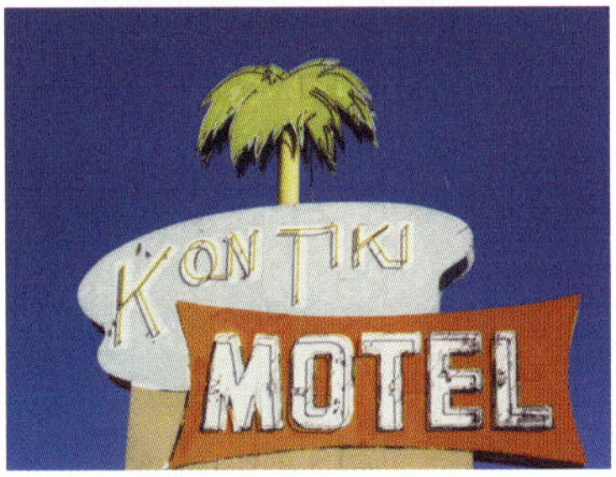
KON TIKI
MOTEL

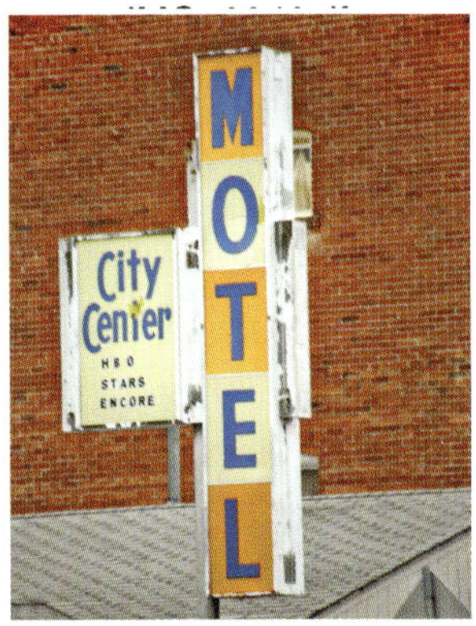
City
Center
HBO
STARS
ENCORE
MOTEL

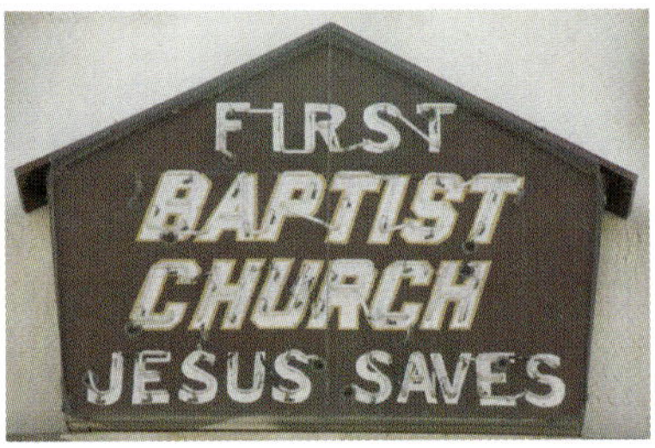
FIRST
BAPTIST
CHURCH
JESUS SAVES

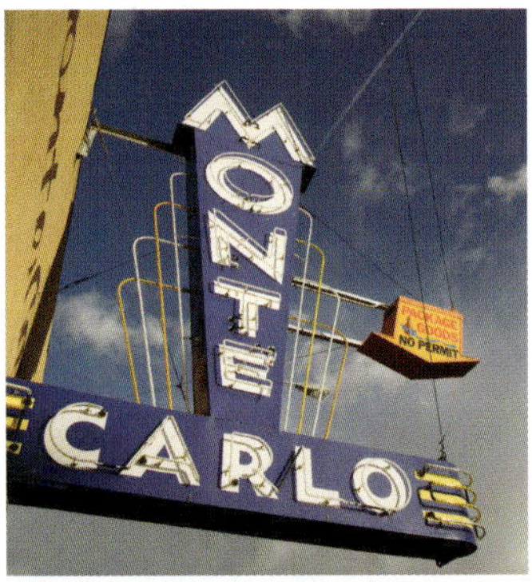
MONTE
CARLO

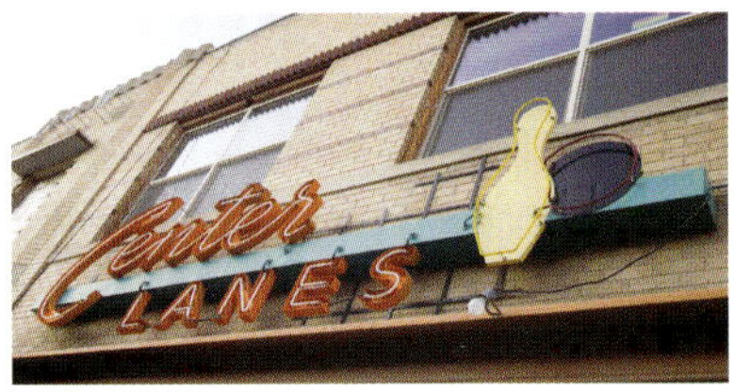
Center
LANES

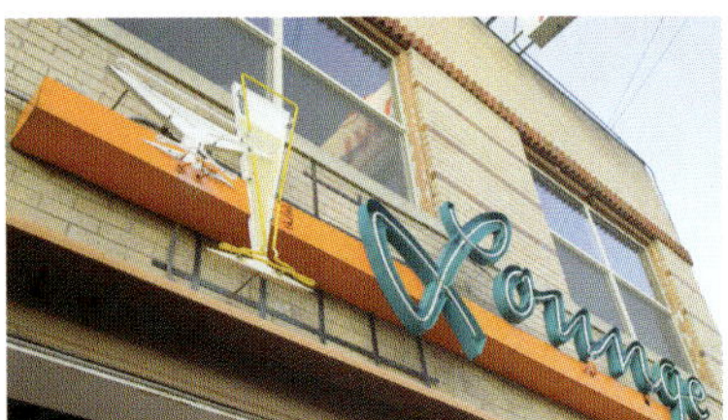
Lounge

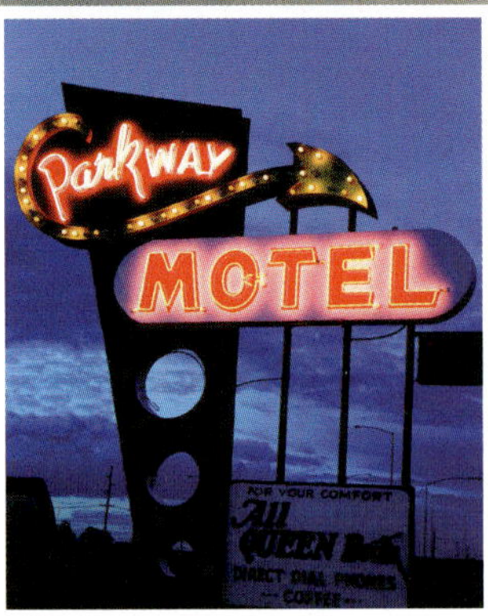
Parkway
MOTEL

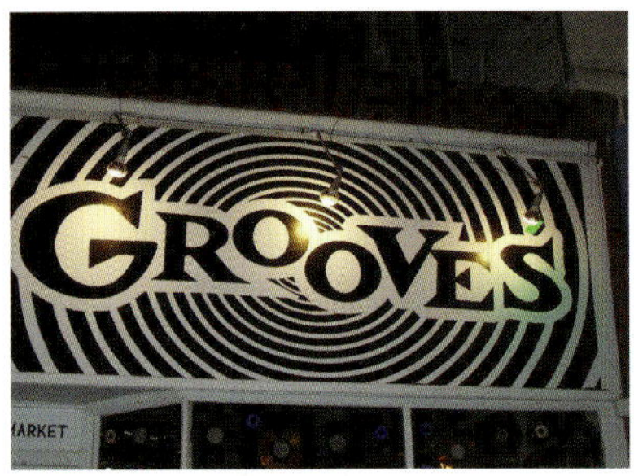
GROOVES

Chapter 11

Promoting Yourself

If you want people to know about your work, you have to let them know what you've got. From making prints for your images and showing them to people on the ground, to sifting through the Internet to find people interested in your photography, promoting yourself will keep you busy. When you're putting your work out there, you'll have to consider your budget. The most logical place to start is to build a website on one of the free web-hosting sites. In this chapter, I'll tell you how to build one that's within your budget. You'll also get a look at the best photography websites out there to build a wish list of what you want on your site as your budget allows. Remember, you don't have to reinvent the wheel when you are promoting yourself. Many people have done it well before, and with the Internet, you can see what they've done.

Building a Website That Respects Your Budget

A website can be as simple as one page made with Weebly (refer to Chapter 3), or you can go full steam ahead with a site where the content constantly changes—one filled with numerous articles to help photographers shoot better pictures. (Take a look at bobatkins.com and also at Figure 11.1.) It can also have a store for website visitors to purchase photos.

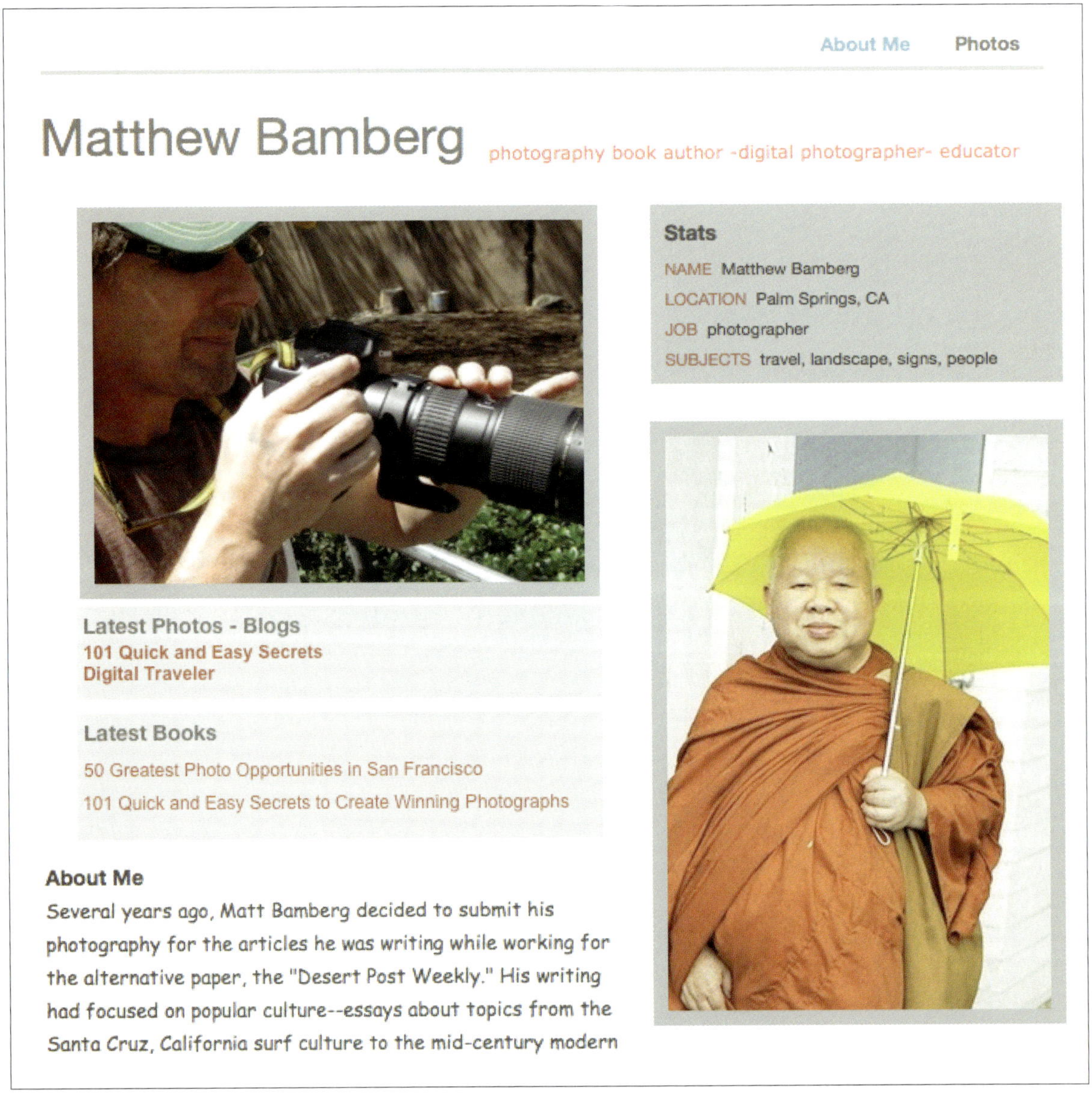

Figure 11.1 Building a website can be quick and easy.

There are basically three quick and easy ways you can go about building a website. The first is to use a free website host, such as weebly.com. There are also other free web-hosting sites at fortunecity.com and bravenet.com. The second method is to buy hosting and online web-building tools at a site such as BetterPhoto.com. And the third is to have a professional make a website for you. However, many professional webmasters require that you have them make all the changes you want to your website, which can get expensive.

Here are three options for building a website that are easy on the budget.

- **BetterPhoto.com.** BetterPhoto offers two photography website options. The first is Deluxe BetterPholio, and the second is Pro BetterPholio. Both offer uploading of unlimited photos. Delux BetterPholios costs $199 for the first year and $169 per year afterwards. It includes a domain name (a name you create for your site if that name is available) and has options for making different designs. Pro BetterPholios cost $349 for the first year and $299 per year after. It includes all of what Delux BetterPholios does and adds on blogs, analytics (site statistics), and image sales. The site uses a PayPal interface for payment. See the upcoming "Selling Images on Your Website or Blog Right Away with PayPal" sidebar.
- **PhotographyWebmasters.com.** Photography Webmasters sets its options by the number of photos you upload. The prices range from $29.95 for 2,000 photos to $99.95 for 20,000 photos. They offer a wide range of web designs. It costs $100 to get your site customized and $499 for them to create a ready-made website. You can make advanced slideshows, music videos, QuickTime movies, flip-album shows, and more. The site includes the option to sell your images.
- **PhotoBiz.com.** PhotoBiz.com sets its options by the number of photos you have uploaded. All websites include image sales. The prices range from $15 for 200 photos to $100 for 12,000 photos. They also offer the following extra products for a one-time fee: online proofing/ordering system for $125, Flash website template for $125, HTML website template for $45, and client mini sites for $175. The site uses a PayPal interface for payment.

NOTE

If you're into building your own website with software, there are many options. Some are listed at www.digitalphotographywebsite.com/easywebsitebuilders.html.

SELLING IMAGES ON YOUR WEBSITE OR BLOG RIGHT AWAY WITH PAYPAL

PayPal is a site you can register on that allows your customers to pay for their goods with a credit card. When the buyer wants an item on your website, he can go to the PayPal site and pay with his credit card. It's quick and easy to sell images on your blog using PayPal. You can make a button for the image that states its name and price and that will link to PayPal so the customer can use his credit card to buy it. (You can also make multiple-choice buttons that allow you to sell the same image at different sizes or in black and white versus color.) To make the button go to PayPal, click on the Merchant Services tab at the top of the page. Then click Buy Now Button. Fill out the form and then click on Create Button. You'll be given some HTML code to put in your blog post (in the HTML section). Put it under the image, and your image will be for sale. After that, they can click the button and pay, and you can deliver, say, a high-res image by e-mail.

Knowing What You Want on Your Website

One of the biggest challenges of making a website is deciding what content you will have.

To decide that, it's always a good idea to take a look at what others have done. You want to know what links are on the homepage; what they sell (including services), if anything; and what other extras they have. Table 11.1 presents a wide range of photographer websites and the content they contain.

Notice that there is a trend toward websites that contain blog posts (see Figure 11.2). It makes sense because when you write a blog post for your webpage, you have fresh content that will keep people coming back. You'll find that all the sites have great photo galleries and that some don't sell anything. Most of the time, if they're not selling anything, they'll have ads to make money.

NOTE

You can make money on your website or blog by putting ads on it. Google (https://www.google.com/adsense) has an AdSense program where you can put ads on your site with HTML code. LinkWorth (www.linkworth.com) also has a good program for putting ads on your site.

TABLE 11.1 PHOTOGRAPHER WEBSITES AND CONTENT

Website	**Main Homepage Links and Content**	**Items Sold at Site**	**Ads**
Photocritic.org	Home, About, All Articles, and Search, as well as blog posts	On About page, link to his book on Amazon: *Macro Photography Photo Workshop*	Google Adsense
Tony Sweet Photography (Tonysweet.com)	Gallery, Workshops, Bio, Events, Blog, Store	Fine art prints, notecards, DVDs, and books	None
Author Gunther Photography (aguntherphotography.com)	Home, Store, Limited Edition, High Resolution Murals, Contact, Copyright, Galleries, Links, Tutorials, Wallpapers (free), as well as daily blog posts	Fine art prints, limited editions	Amazon
Jill Greenberg (manipulator.com)	Portfolio, Names (she photographs celebrities), Bio and Press, News, Publications, Exhibitions/Events, Contact	None	None
Wow Photo Art (wowphotoart.com)	Home, Statement, Reviews, Exhibits, Buy, Care, Links, Contact	Prints, prints on canvas	None

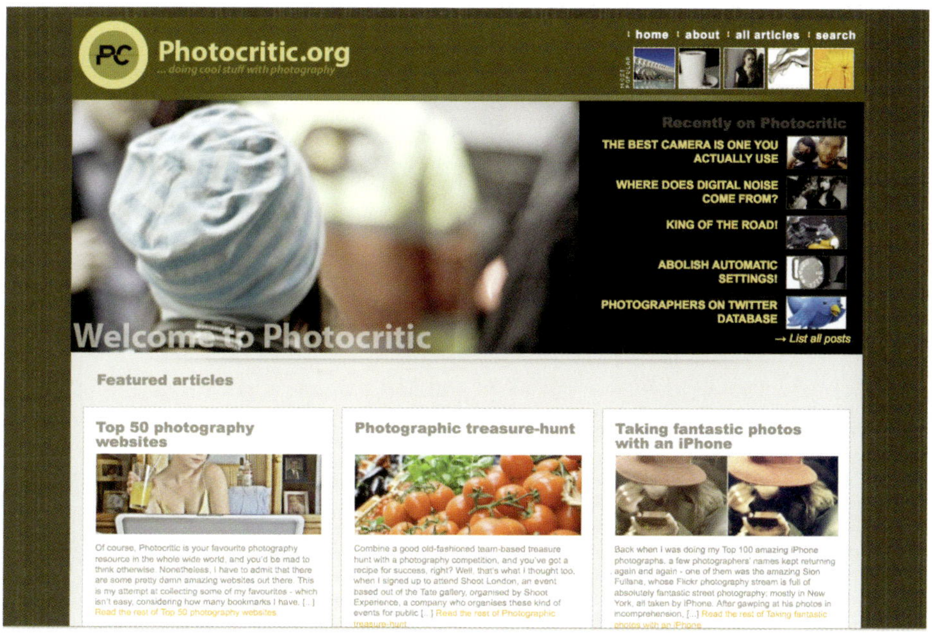

Figure 11.2 Many websites today contain blog posts.

Letting Others Know about Your Website/Blog

Once you have your website up and running, how are you going to let people know it's there?

There are myriad ways to do that—no one way is an easy bullet. It takes time and perseverance to get people to come to your website and/or blog. In the "Getting Your Photo Noticed on Google" section in Chapter 10, there is information about one way to get people to come to your webpage/blog—making filenames for your pictures that the Googlebot can find. If you recall, when you make a blog or website with an online program such as Blogger or Weebly, you'll have to upload the images to that website/blog. The programs convert the insertion of images into a website/blog into language the web can understand, which is HTML. Here are some other ways to get your website/blog noticed:

- Get popular blogs/websites to link your blog/website to theirs. Many blogs/websites have a Links section. Your goal is to get to be one of those links. The more links you have, the more the Googlebot will notice that your site's out there, and the higher ranking it will give it in the search results.
- Submit your blog/website directly to the search engines. Google's is at www.google.com/addurl, and Yahoo!'s is at https://ecom.yahoo.com/dir/submit/intro/. It'll cost you, though—a tidy $299 per year.
- When you name the new pages to your website or new posts to your blog, use the right keywords. In Blogger, it asks you to name your blog as well as describe it. The words count in your ranking. For example, I named one of my blogs "Digital Traveler." When you type those words into Google, my site comes up first (out of some 11 million sites). If your site comes up number one for the keywords "digital photography," then you know you're probably going to get millions of hits a day. Digital Photography Review (www.dpreview.com) has that honor; it's a site you should count on for great reviews about cameras, lenses, and other photo accessories.
- Submit your blog posts, webpage, webpage articles, or even your best images to social bookmarking sites, such as delicious.com, shoutwire.com, and digg.com. People on those sites can vote on whether they think your submission is a good one.
- Keep content fresh. Post on blogs as often as you can and/or add fresh content to your website. Search engines like to pick up new stuff.
- Submit your site to directories such as photo.net and photographydirectory.org.

Using Twitter to Announce Your Events/Activities

Keep in mind that getting word about your photography out there will get more people to a gallery when you have a show, draw more readers to your photography book if you've written one, and send more people to your blog/website to see and either buy your photography or click on the ads on your site/blog.

Twitter is a social networking site where you post short messages (140 characters max). You can choose to follow other people by searching for them. (To search, click on Find People at the top of all Twitter pages.) After you do your search, a list of people will come up with a Follow link. Just click on that link to follow them. Once you start following people, you'll find that they'll start following you. See Figure 11.3.

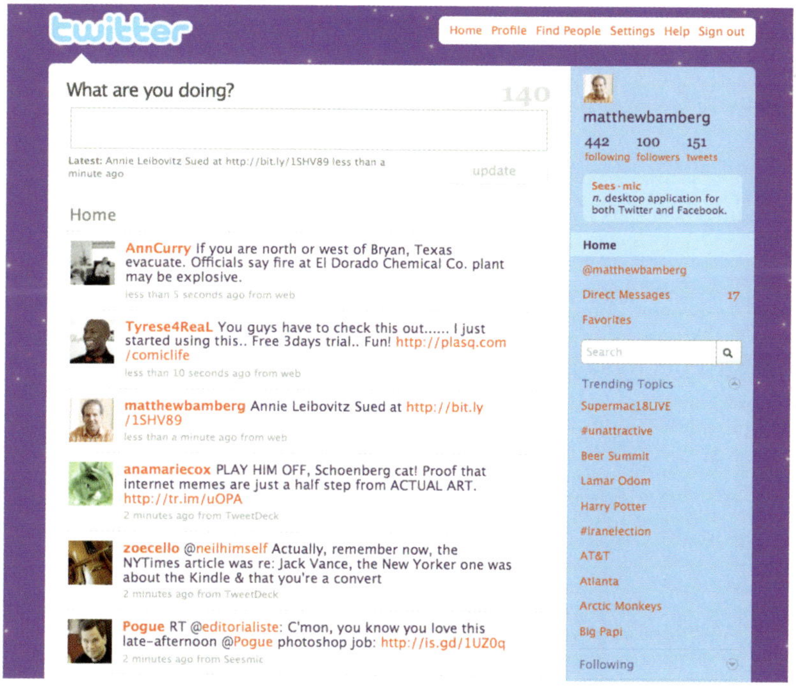

Figure 11.3 An entry on Twitter is called a "tweet."

Every time you post on your blog or other site and/or find an interesting photo article/blog post/website, let people on Twitter know. (This is called "tweeting" it.)

If you're writing a book, you can put out a chapter bit by bit (140 characters max per post) on Twitter. It's easy to become a member; just sign up at twitter.com. When you start being active on Twitter, you'll find you gather followers quickly.

NOTE

You can let people on Twitter know about photos you post by giving them the URL in your post. Flickr gives you a URL for each photo you post. Navigate to your homepage and click on Your Photostream under your image/greeting at the top of the window. Then, in the next window, click on the picture for which you want the URL. It will appear with a single enlarged version of your image. Blogger also gives you a URL for each photo you post. (Click on the photo in your post to get the photo's URL.)

NOTE

It doesn't hurt to follow other photographers, too, as you'll come to find out new techniques and goings-on in the photography world.

Finally, you can link your Twitter posts to your blog. This will put your Twitter posts on your blog every time you tweet. When you do this, your blog and social networking accounts will be more active, drawing more interest. To do this, log into Twitter and click on Settings. In the More Info URL category, click on the link that says You Can Also Add Twitter to Your Site Here. A new window will come up with a choice of blogs and social networking sites (MySpace, Blogger, Facebook, and TypePad). Click on one of them and then click on Continue at the bottom-right part of the window. Last, in the new window, choose the number of updates you want on your blog and then follow the directions for putting the updates on the blog/social networking sites you want.

Creating a Print Photography Portfolio

Creating a print portfolio is one of the best things you can do with your photos, which often sit in your computer without anyone physically seeing them in print form. Printing your images makes sense because no one knows what will happen to technology in the years to come, possibly making what's in your computer today obsolete 20 years from now. (You can review the "What Will Your Images Look Like in 10 Years?" sidebar in Chapter 1 to see what the possibilities are.) When you print your photos out, they become a permanent record of what you've done. With today's archival inks and paper, your printed images are likely to last generations.

Another reason why you might want to print out samples of your best images is so you can show your work at photo festivals around the country when there are photographers available to review it. Some festivals, such as Palm Springs Photo Festival (palmspringsphotofestival.com), have seasoned photographers that you can pay to review your work. One thing is for sure, they won't want to look at your work on a computer, as printing is part of the photography process, and they will want to critique that as well as other aspects of the photography.

The last and most important reason (for aspiring artists) to print out your photos is to show them to different gallery owners after you've set up a meeting with them. If they are serious about accepting your work into their gallery, they will first look at your digital images, and then if they like those, they will want to see them in print in a portfolio.

NOTE

You can also print out contact sheets of your body of work in Photoshop by navigating to File > Automate > Contact Sheet. You can then give these to gallery owners. See Figure 11.4.

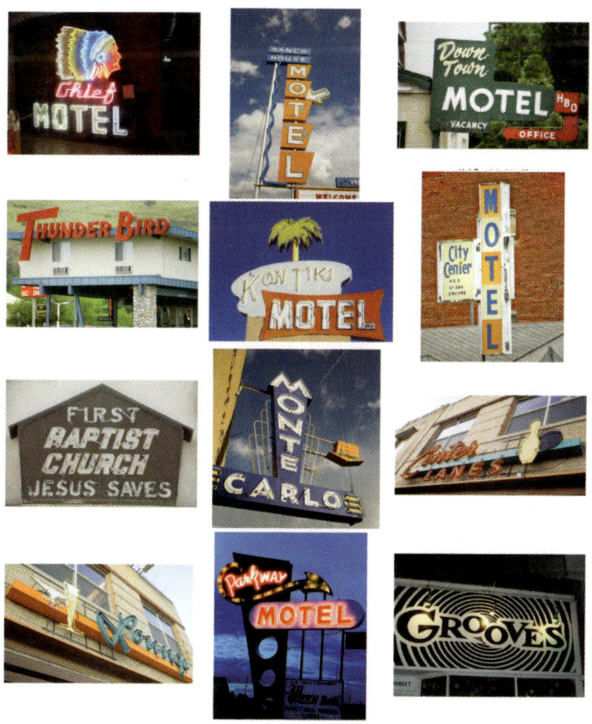

Figure 11.4 A contact sheet made in Photoshop.

A portfolio should have no more than 25 images. It should contain images as large as ones you would include in a gallery show if possible, so if the gallery owner likes them, all you have to do is mat and frame the images. In addition to portfolios-and-art-cases.com, mentioned in Chapter 1, www.lightimpressionsdirect.com also has different professional portfolio options.

The most important thing you can do with your portfolio is make sure it contains a body of work—that is, a group of images that relate to one another. Remember, if you want an art show of your own, it's best to have some kind of theme. For more about themes in photography, see *101 Quick and Easy Secrets to Create Winning Photographs* (Course Technology PTR, 2009).

Creating a Google Knol

A knol (knol.google.com) is an article platform put out by Google. (A knol is a unit of knowledge.) You can write an article and post pictures. When Google lists your knol, it includes your Google profile in the left-hand corner, so be sure to have a complete profile with links to all of your publications, websites, blogs, and whatnot.

The first thing to do if you haven't already is to create a Google account (https://www.google.com/accounts/NewAccount).

To write a knol, click Write a Knol on the homepage. A prompt will come up, where you should click Create. A page will come up that looks like a word processing program (and works like one, too). All you do is type in or copy and paste an article into the document provided.

You can insert an image into your knol by navigating to Insert > Image. You can also put in a Picasa slideshow. (See "Making a Slideshow Using Picasa" in Chapter 12 to learn how to make one.)

Finally, you publish your knol by clicking Publish in the left side of the window. A sample one is shown in Figure 11.5.

Knols are unique because you can leave them open for anyone to edit (in that way, it kind of works like Wikipedia). You can also set it for only people you know to edit, or you can set it so no one is permitted to edit it. Comments are also permitted on knols.

Interacting with Others Online

Okay, then. So this promotion stuff isn't all about people coming to you. Make it part of your daily ritual to reach out to others. Make it a goal to reach out to at least 10 others a day. This can be done by:

- **Commenting on other blogs.** Most blogs have comment sections at the end of their posts. Many comments are open to Everyday Joe; anyone can comment on that blog. Some comments are moderated; that is, you can write a comment on a blog, but in order for it to be displayed, it has to have the blog owner's approval. Finally, some blogs require that you register in order to comment. That's usually an easy process of filling out an online form. Sometimes you might already be registered. Any blogs that use Blogger as a host let Google members comment by logging into their Google account right there in the comment dialog box. Make sure your comments don't just pitch your photography. Remember, this process really isn't about you as much as it is about the person who is the host and has displayed his work. Comment about what they've written in their post. Then, if you want to, you can include a link to your blog, Flickr page, or website.
- **Be active on Flickr.** Keep posting those images on Flickr. Comment on others' images. Join a group. (Choose Group > Search for a Group and then type in the type of photography you like—for example, candid photographers.)

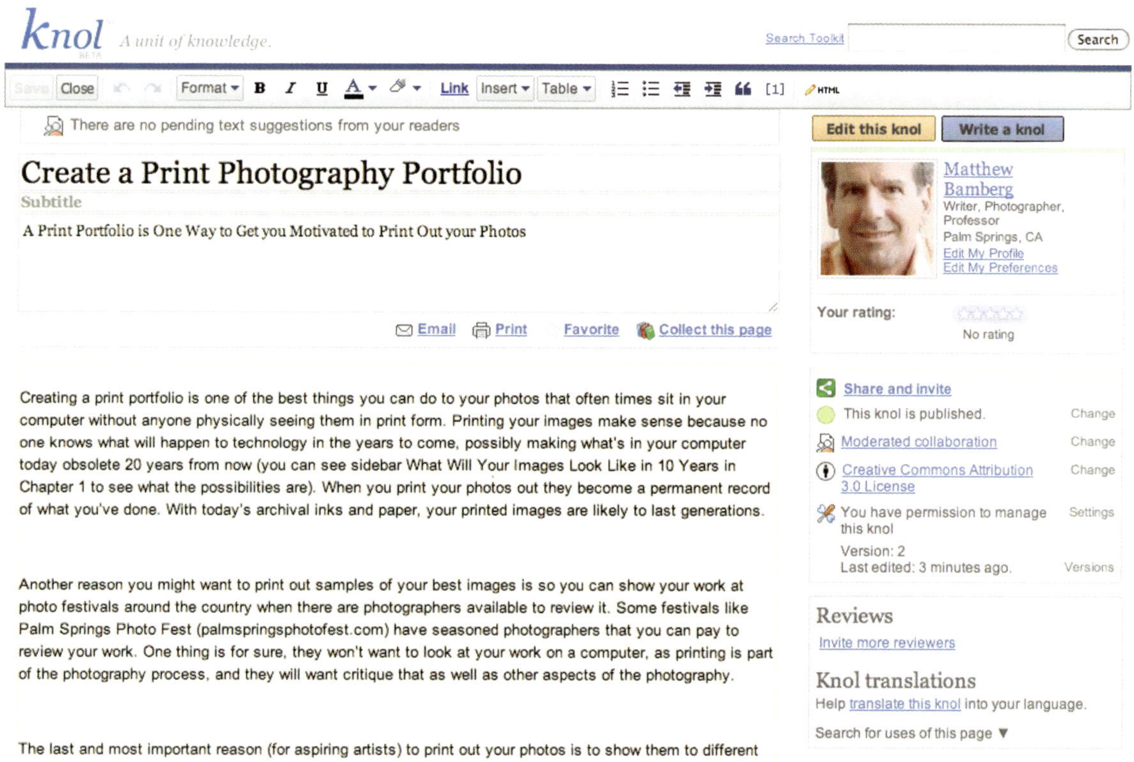

Figure 11.5 A knol is an article platform by Google.

- **On Twitter, reply to others when they post a photo and tweet your own.** To reply, move your cursor over the tweet and click on the arrow icon that says Reply To and then type in your message. To tweet your own, just copy and paste the photo's URL into the message box.
- **Join a Facebook group.** You can upload your images there for people to view. To find a group, just type what you are interested in into the Search box, and groups will come up that contain that word. For example, type in the word **photography**, and many photography groups will come up.
- **E-mail, e-mail, and e-mail some more.** Find anyone who might have an interest in what you're doing and e-mail them about it. To find e-mail addresses, type in a keyword (such as **photography**) and then the word **email** and/or @. Browse through the listing summaries and copy and paste the e-mails in the To field of your e-mail message. Keywords I might use with e-mail and @ to let people know about my books are "photography professor" (for university professors who might want to know about my books) and "holiday gift guide" (to get e-mail addresses of the people who have gift guides). (It's always nice to have your stuff in a gift guide.)

NOTE

If you put your link in too many times when writing messages in groups in Facebook, you'll get a note saying you've overdone it.

Pounding the Pavement

Don't forget the power of selling the old-fashioned way, going from door to door with your work or portfolio. To get your work out there on the ground, at some point you might have an inclination to go on the road with your goods and sell door to door.

If you go this route, it's best to be prepared. Call the places first; initial contacts are everything. Make an appointment if you can. I've been successful many times cold calling, making an appointment, and then showing up with my work at furniture stores, coffee shops, galleries that work with emerging artists, and galleries that have just opened.

NOTE

It used to be that most art galleries didn't accept photography, but that's changing quickly as photography becomes more and more popular.

High-end galleries are another story. They almost always want to see your work via JPEG files. When you send those, make sure you send an artist statement, and in those JPEGs, include a cohesive body of work. Even if a gallery asks you to send your work, go and visit several times anyway. Study the images there, talk to the people who work there, and, most important, have a tear sheet or sample image to show them if someone there expresses an interest in you.

NOTE

Once you're out there meeting people, you'll find some gallery owners will know of places where your art will work (or make a good match). They might even refer you there. And then, when you go to the gallery they mentioned, you can say you were referred by so and so from another gallery.

Don't expect to get a high profit the first time you have a show. The gallery will take about 50 percent of the price you ask for your image. The gallery doesn't pay for matting and framing either, so you can expect to earn less than 50 percent of your asking price.

DON'T FORGET THE PHOTO SHOWS

One of the highest honors you can achieve is to have your art in one of the big art shows around the country. At these shows the leading galleries display their art wares, and photography is becoming extremely popular at the shows. There are also shows just for photography. When you attend these shows, you might find that you have similar images, or they might give you ideas for new ones. Here's the scoop on some shows:

* Association of International Photography Art Dealers (AIPAD) in New York in March: www.aipad.com
* The Armory Show in New York in March: www.thearmoryshow.com
* Photo LA in January: www.artfairsinc.com
* Photo Miami in December: www.artfairsinc.com
* Art Basel in Basel, Switzerland, in June: www.artbasel.com
* Art Basel in Miami Beach in December: www.artbasel.com
* Paris Photo in January: www.parisphoto.fr
* FotoFest in Houston in March/April: www.fotofest.org

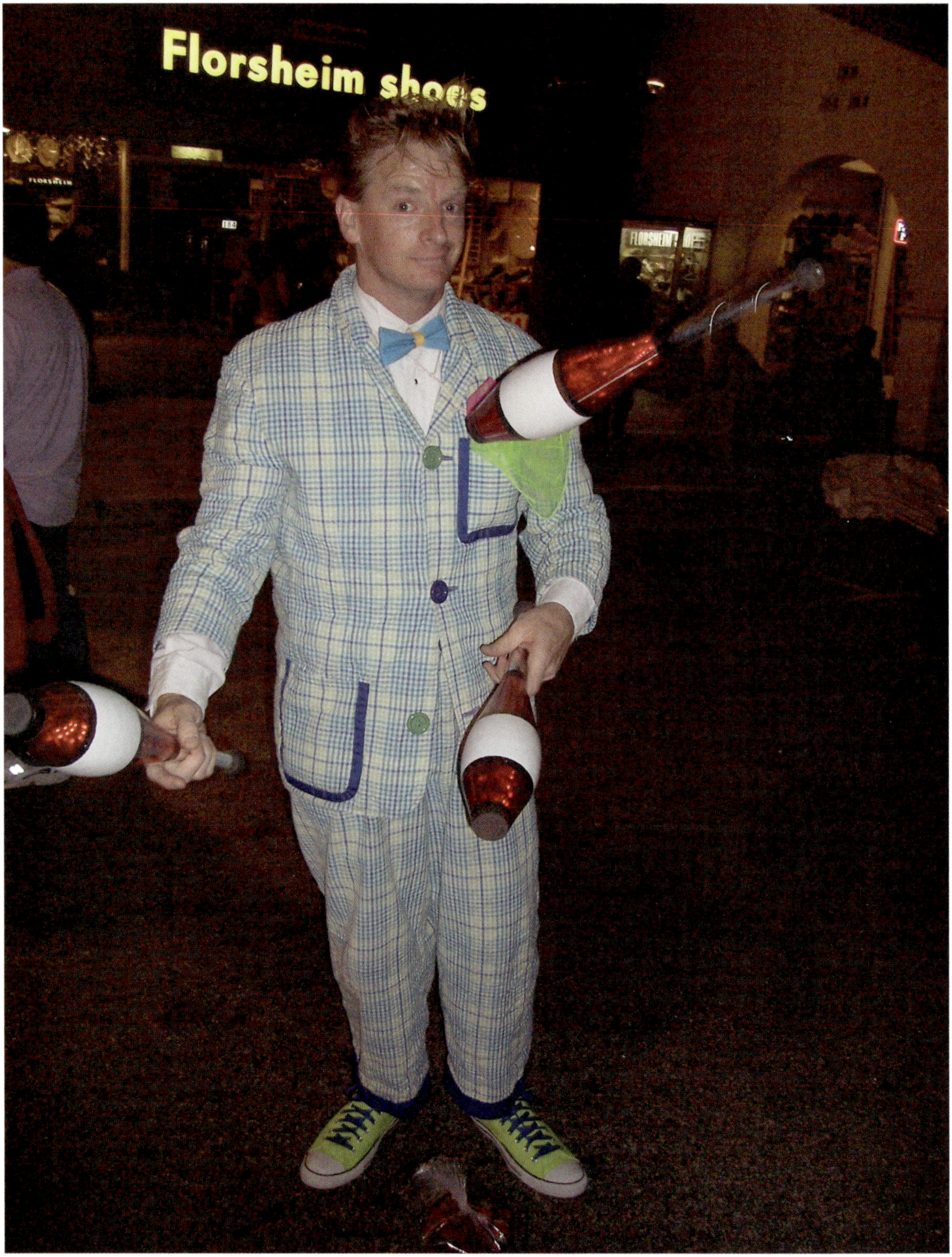
Florsheim shoes

Chapter 12
Working with Slideshows

Everyone loves a good slideshow, so why not get into the business of making them? You can, you know, by using your images and music. There are several ways you can do this, from making a slideshow using an online platform, to making one with software that comes with most computers (Macs or PCs). Not only can you make slideshows, you can also share them on YouTube, your blog, Facebook, and MySpace. Each platform has a different set of options to put together your slideshow. On many you can add transitions; on some you can add text on top of your images. Finally, if you opt to show one of these slideshows at home on your TV set, it's easy to connect your computer to it so that you can show it to your friends and family.

Making a Movie from Your Images Using iMovie

For you Mac users, there is software that comes with your computer that allows you to make a slideshow with your images, set it to music, and save it as a movie file or upload it directly to YouTube.

To do this, find iMovie in your Applications folder, open it, and navigate to File > New Project.

Click and drag your images from the appropriate folder into the area where it says Drag Media Here to Create a New Project. When you are dragging images, a light-green line will let you know where they are going. After you're finished dragging your images, you can change the order by clicking and dragging them around. To view your show, click on the Play button at the bottom of the thumbnail display.

NOTE

To delete, make a selection and navigate to Delete > Selection.

To change the timing of the slideshow, drag the cursor over the first slide and click on the timer icon that comes up. Input the duration for each slide in the dialog box that comes up.

To add music, click on the musical note icon. The music files that you have on iTunes will come up. Click and drag the song you want up to the first photo thumbnail in your iMovie. You'll then see the name of your music file in a green strip below your thumbnail images.

NOTE

To control the amount of time the music fades in at the beginning of your show and fades out at the end, click on the speaker icon and adjust the Fade In and Out sliders, respectively.

To add text to your first slide (make a title slide), click on the T icon. A choice of text options will appear for the layout of your text. They will include images, but those images are only samples. They will not be used when your text comes up in your project. To add text to your first slide, just click and drag one of the text sample frames on top of your first slide. You'll see a text frame appear above the frame for your image. In the viewer portion of the window, select the text by clicking and dragging over it and then type in the text you want. Figure 12.1 shows you what your window will look like when you type in your text.

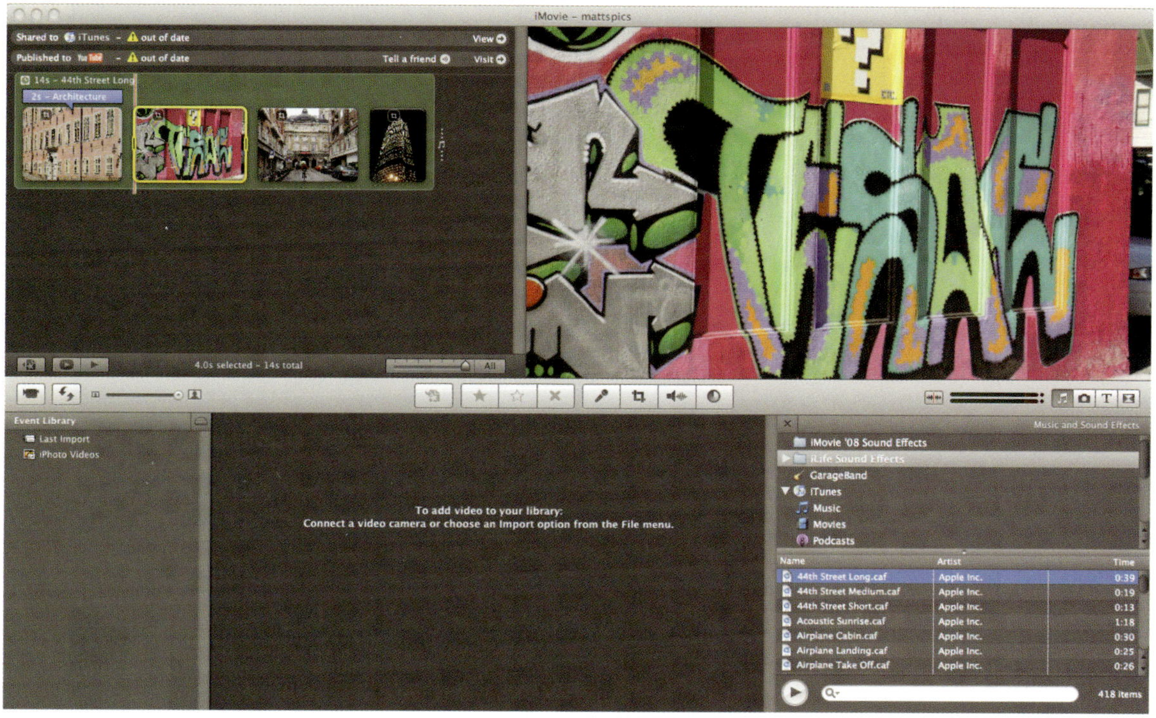

Figure 12.1 You can add text to your slideshows with iMovie.

To save the movie as a .m4v file, navigate to Share > Export Movie. To save the movie as a .mov file (one that can be read in Windows using QuickTime), navigate to Share > Export Using Quicktime.

Making a Movie from Your Images Using Windows Movie Maker

Movie Maker comes free with Windows Vista. It has all the nuts and bolts to make great slideshows with your images (see Figure 12.2).

To make a movie, navigate to Start, then type **Movie Maker** in the Search box, then click Windows Movie Maker when it comes up under Programs.

Click on Pictures under the Import heading. If you put the pictures you want for the slideshow in your Pictures folder, you should see them in the window (Import Media Items) that comes up. If you don't, navigate to them. Select the pictures you want in your slideshow; use the Shift key to select multiple files. Click on Import when you're finished.

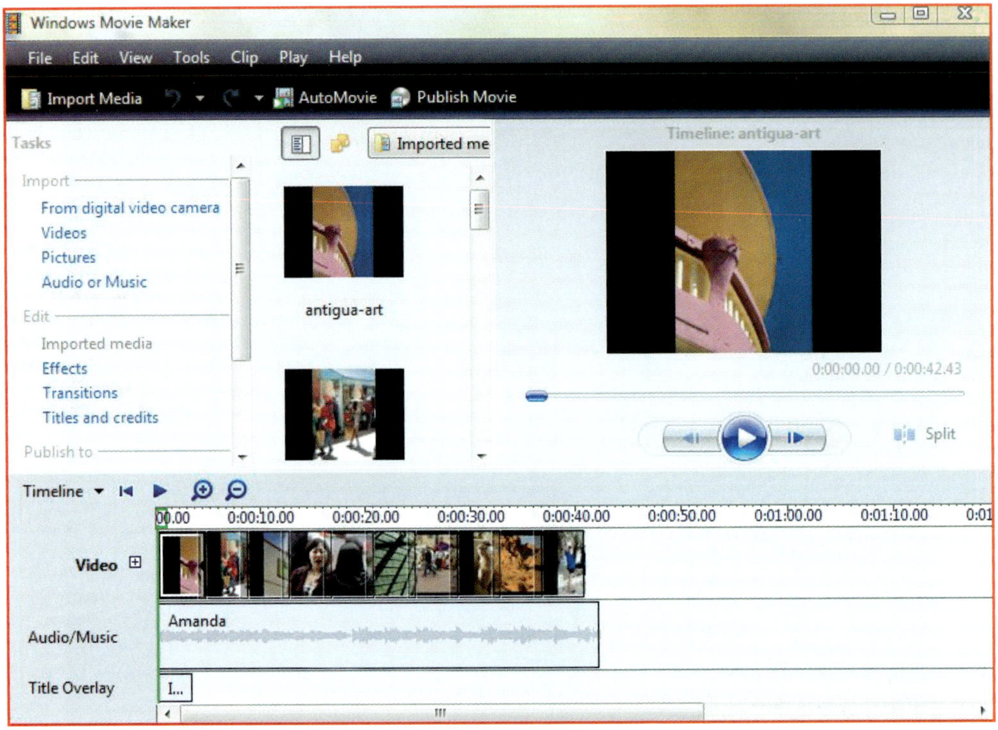

Figure 12.2 Windows Movie Maker lets you make slideshow movies.

Your pictures should now be visible in the Task and Content pane (the frame in the middle of the window). Make sure Timeline is selected from the drop-down menu in the frame at the bottom of the window. Click and drag your pictures to the video part of the timeline. If you make a mistake, right-click and select Remove. You can change the order of the pictures once they are on the storyboard. You can also preview your show by pressing the right arrow button below the Preview window. Finally, you can change the time each slide shows on the screen by navigating to Tools > Options. In the Options window that comes up, click on the Advanced tab and change the time in the input box.

To add music, click Audio or Music and navigate to the music files on your computer and then click Import. Click and drag the music file you want into the audio part of the storyboard. If your music's too long for your show, click and drag it to your last slide. To get your music to fade in and out, go to the beginning of your show and navigate to Clip > Audio > Fade In and then Clip > Audio > Fade Out.

To add a title for the first slide, click on Titles and Credits under Edit. In the next window, click on Title on the selected clip. Choose your first image in the timeline and enter text for the title (you'll see a preview on a slide other than your own) and then click on Add Title.

NOTE

If you want transitions in your movie, click on Storyboard in the drop-down menu in the bottom frame of the window and then click Transitions in the middle of the window. Click and drag your transitions between the pictures on the storyboard.

To add a title, click on Titles and Credits on the left side of the window. Then click on Title at the beginning. Enter your title in the space provided. You can change the font and color by clicking on Change the Text Font and Color below the space where you typed the title. Once you're finished, click Add Title.

Switch back to the timeline to finish your slideshow. If your music runs longer than your images, click and drag it from the ending inward to where your images end. To get the music to fade at the end, right-click on Song and click Fade Out.

To save your show as a .wmv movie file, click on File > Publish Movie and then choose This Computer. Click Next. Name your file. Click Browse and navigate to your desktop and then click Next again. In the next window, save at high quality. Click Next again. Your movie will be saved as a .wmv movie on your desktop, making it easy to upload to YouTube. (See the upcoming "Putting Your Slideshow on YouTube" section.)

Making a Slideshow Using Picasa

You can create a slideshow in Picasa if you've downloaded the program from the Internet. (Refer to the "Sharing Using Picasa and Picasa Web Albums" section in Chapter 2 for use and download info.)

Open Picasa and choose a folder from the right frame of the window. Select Movie from the Create menu. In the new window that comes up, you'll see your images from the folder you picked at the bottom of the window.

To choose an image for a slideshow, click on the one you want and then click on the green thumbtack (Hold Selected Items icon). You'll see the image appear in the lower-left corner of the window. Repeat the step for each image you choose. To select multiple images, click and drag over them and then click on the green thumbtack icon.

NOTE

To delete an item you've chosen, select the image from the icons and then click on the button with the red circle on it (Clear Items from Selection Item) to remove it as a selection.

When you're finished choosing images, click on the album icon (Add Selected Items to an Album). In the drop-down menu that appears, click on New Album. In the dialog box that comes up, name your album, click on Music, and then browse for an MP3 file on your computer. Then click OK. Next, click on the album that you made in the left frame of the window.

To make the movie, choose Create > Movie. A tab will come up with options for your movie. Your audio selection should show up in green under where it says Audio Track. If it doesn't, click Load and navigate to an MP3 file on your computer. To experiment with the audio, choose one of the three options from the drop-down menu (Truncate Audio, Fit Photos into Audio, Loop Photos to Match Audio). Click on the drop-down menu to choose a transition. Choose how much you want one slide to overlap another and then choose the dimensions you want the video to appear on your screen. Last, click Create Movie. Then wait. It takes a few minutes for Picasa to make the movie. To edit the movie, click on Edit Movie at the top of the window. To save it, click on Export Clip. Your movie will be saved in Pictures > Picasa > Exported Videos.

NOTE

Your movie filename will be the same name (with .mov added) as your Picasa album that contains the images you chose for the movie.

Putting Your Slideshow on YouTube

It's easy to post your video on YouTube. All you do is click on that option when it comes time to save your slideshow. After it's uploaded, YouTube gives you a URL for your video. The URL looks something like http://www.youtube.com/watch?v=HFA_a37Qi-0. (This happens to be the URL of the video slideshow I made using Picasa; see Figure 12.3.)

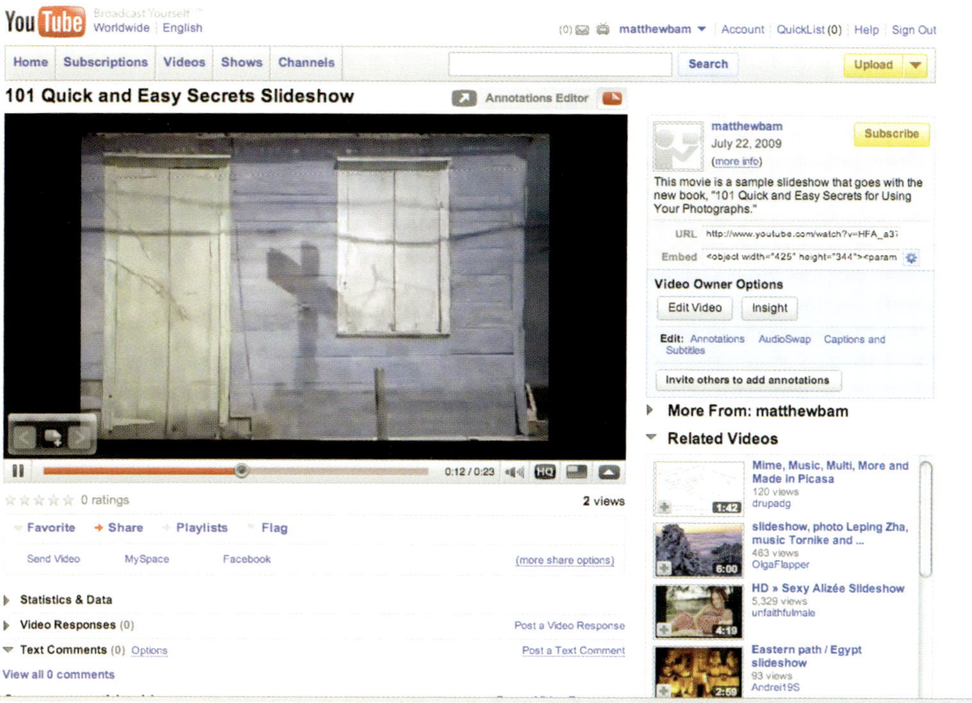

Figure 12.3 From most slideshow programs, your slideshow can automatically be uploaded to YouTube with one click.

From iMovie

To save to YouTube, navigate to Share > YouTube. (You have to be connected to the Internet so iMovie can contact YouTube.) Then fill in the prompts in the next window (your account, which is usually the e-mail address you have registered with Google, password, category from drop-down menu, title, description, and tags). When you're finished, click Next and then, in the next window, click Publish. It will take some time for your movie to upload to YouTube. When it's finished, you can view it on there.

From Movie Maker

In Movie Maker, publish your file to your desktop. (Refer to the "Making a Movie from Your Images Using Windows Movie Maker" section.) Go to YouTube and sign in with your Google account. Scroll over your username and then click on My Videos from the drop-down menu. In the window that comes up, scroll over Upload and click on Upload Video File. In the next window (the Video File Upload window), click on Upload Video. Navigate to your desktop and double-click on the .wmv file of your movie.

From Picasa

To upload a movie you made in Picasa, all you do is click on the Upload to YouTube button in the window that appears after Picasa finishes making your movie. You can also navigate to that button by double-clicking on the movie's thumbnail in the Picasa Library. After you click Upload to YouTube, a dialog box will come up in which you fill in the following prompts: title, description, video category, and tags (same as the dialog box in iMovie). You also have an option to make your movie public. Next, click on the Change User button at the top of the dialog box. A prompt will come up, asking for your username and password.

> **NOTE**
>
> Google owns YouTube, so use your Google username and password to log into YouTube.

Finally, click on Upload Video. After your video has been uploaded to YouTube, to view it, click the tiny Click to View Online icon that appears on your computer screen.

Embedding a Slideshow on Your Blog

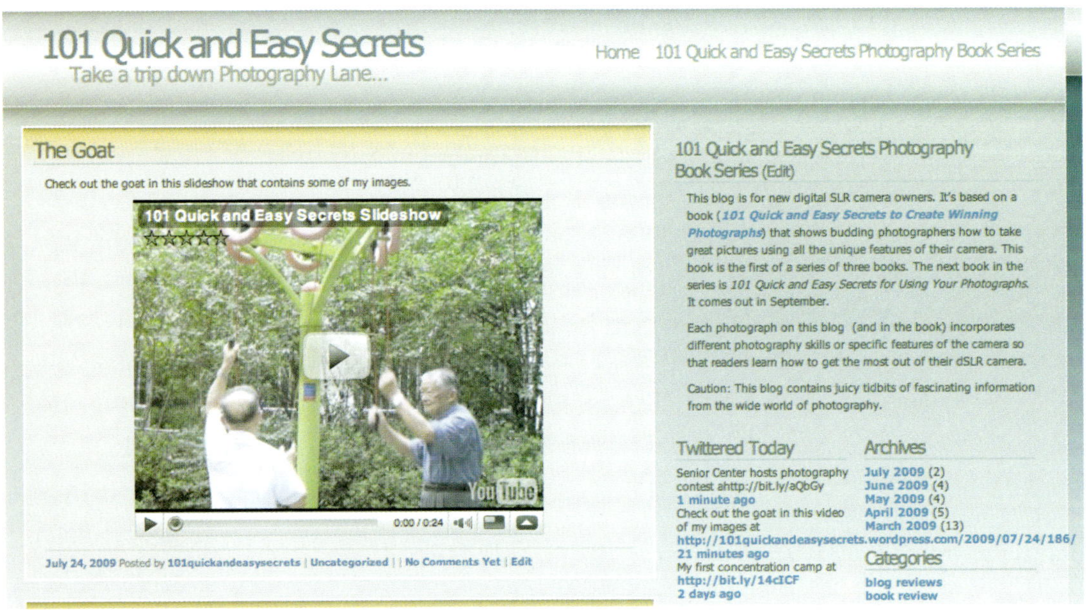

Figure 12.4 You can embed YouTube videos into your blog posts.

Two free blog hosts, Blogger and WordPress, make it easy for you to put YouTube videos on your blog.

> **NOTE**
>
> You can put any video from YouTube on your blog in the same way as you put your own on there—just copy and paste the HTML code into the HTML window of your blog.

On Blogger

Sign into YouTube with your Google account. Move the cursor over your username at the top-left part of the window (User Name > My Videos). Click on Play for the video you want to put on Blogger. In the frame on the right side of the window, you'll see text boxes for URL and Embed. The URL box gives you the URL of your YouTube video. You don't want to use that to get a YouTube video on your blog; you can only use that to provide a link to your video (or someone else's). What you *do* want, however, is the HTML code in the box next to where it says Embed. Select and copy the code and sign into Blogger with your Google account. Click on New Post for the blog where you want the YouTube video (slideshow) to go. In the next window (the Posting tab), click on the Edit HTML tab (if it isn't already selected). Paste in the HTML code you copied from YouTube. Click on Publish Post.

After you're finished, go ahead and type text, upload images, and create links as you would do normally. It looks nicer if you have space between the video and your text, so leave a blank space or two between your text/image code and the code for the video.

On WordPress

Follow the directions for signing into YouTube and getting the embedded code that's described in the previous section. Then sign into WordPress and navigate to your Dashboard. Click on Posts and, in the next window, click on Add New under where it says Posts. In the next window (the Posting tab), click on the HTML tab (if it isn't already selected). Paste in the HTML code you copied from YouTube. Click on Publish Post.

> **NOTE**
>
> To embed a video on your blog, you have to choose to make the video public on YouTube.

Using Slide.com to Make a Slideshow

You can make a slideshow from your photos on Flickr, Facebook, MySpace, and other sites using slide.com (see Figure 12.5). You can also make a slideshow from new images that you have on your computer.

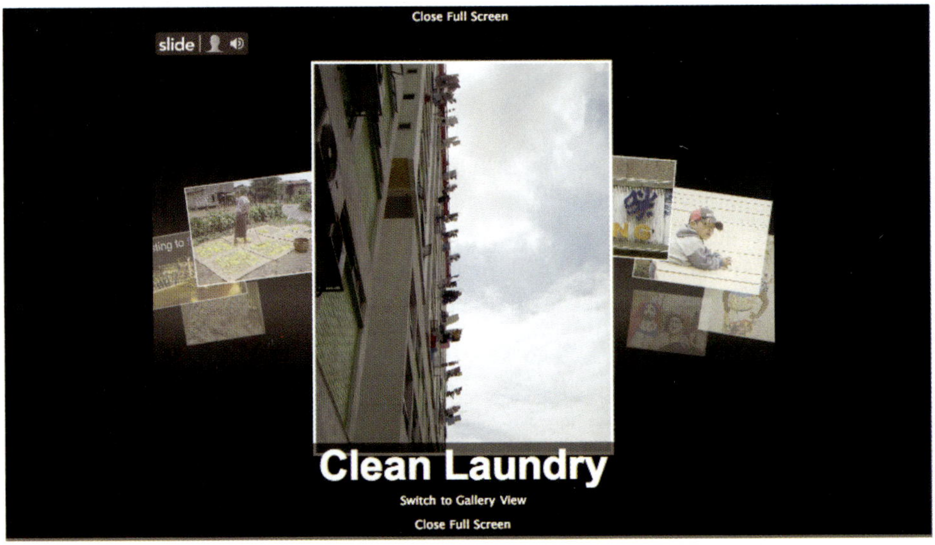

Figure 12.5 Revolver slideshow made with slide.com.

The first thing you do is go to slide.com and select Make a Slideshow. Then click on the place where you want the images to come from. You have a choice of My Files, Search, Friendster, Bebo, MySpace, Slide, Facebook, Photobucket, Flickr, or Image URL. Say, for example, you click on Flickr. You'll be prompted to sign in using your screen name. Then you'll be asked to select a folder to import. If you want all the pictures in all the folders, click each folder once.

> **NOTE**
>
> Select a folder only once, or else you'll get duplicates of the images in your slideshow.

In the Edit Photos window, click Next for each image you want in the slideshow. After you've selected the images, click Done. You can customize the design by clicking on one of the style choices in the left part of the window. Each time you click one, a preview of your show will come up. You can also add skins, themes, music/video/background, and effects to your show or change the size.

To add music to your show, click on Music/Video. Then click on View More Music/Videos for the maximum number of choices and categories.

NOTE

To delete the music selection, click Remove beneath the song's name.

When you're finished, click Save. A new window will come up, asking you for slideshow details and credits. Finally, click Save Slideshow.

You can automatically add the show to Facebook, Twitter, MySpace, and other social networking sites. You'll be given a URL for your show. When you go to it, you'll find links on the left side of the window to link to the show, embed the show, and e-mail the show. If you click on Embed, you'll get code to put the show on your blog or website.

NOTE

To edit a show you've already made, go to slide.com, click on your username, then scroll over to Options and navigate to Edit.

Making and Sharing Your Slideshow at Slideroll.com

Slideroll.com is another online platform where you can make and share photography slideshows.

The first thing you have to do is register to join. It's free. After that, you can upload photos by clicking on Upload Photos and then, in the next window, Select Photos to Upload. Navigate to the appropriate location on your computer and pick the file(s) you want.

After the uploading is finished, a new window will come up with the photos you've uploaded. You can rotate photos there if you want to. Be cautioned that this is the only place you can do that, so make it a point to rotate your photos in this step. When you're finished, click Done.

NOTE

You're only allowed to upload 100 photos and only those in JPG format.

You'll then get a prompt asking whether you want to upload the photos right now. Click No, and you'll be taken back to the My Photos page. When you click on a photo on that page, a window will come up with the option to delete it.

To make a slideshow, click Make a Slideshow on the My Photos page. You're given three options: Upload Photos, Load a Saved Slideshow, Import Flickr Photos.

Choose Start a New Slideshow, and your photos will come up. You can select more than one photo by holding down the Apple key on a Mac or the Ctrl key on a PC. To select all of them, hold down the Shift key and select the first and last photo. Next, click OK.

The slideshow creator will come up. Figure 12.6 shows how it looks.

NOTE

If you choose Import Flickr Photos, you'll be taken to a new window or tab where you'll have to sign into your Yahoo! account, confirm that you've come from slideroll.com, and authorize it. When you're finished, go back to the slideroll.com window/tab and click OK to be taken to the slideshow maker to make a slideshow with your Flickr photos. These photos will not be put in your Slideroll gallery.

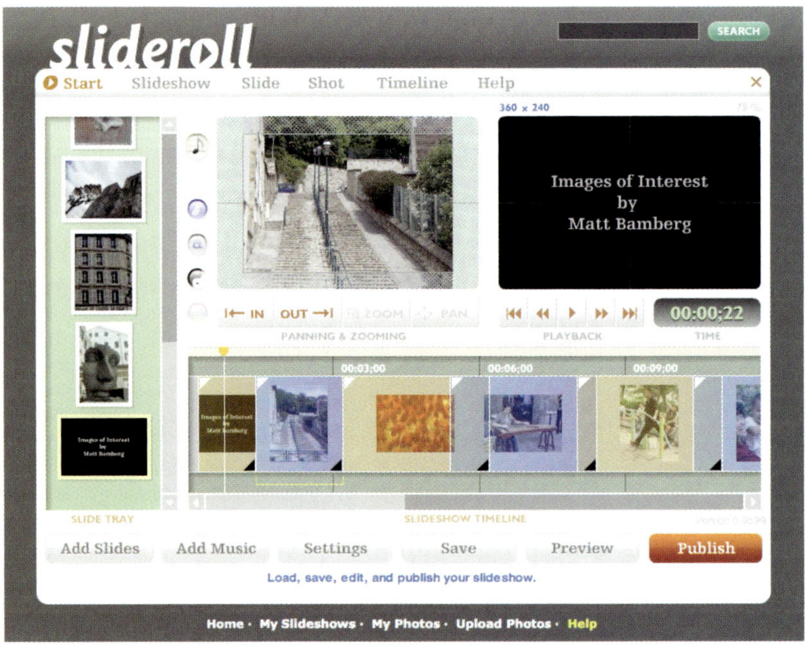

Figure 12.6 Slideshow creator in slideroll.com.

There are five button icons in the slideshow creator. To learn what they will do, move your cursor over each button and then read the bottom of the window.

> **NOTE**
>
> What's cool about this platform is you can link a slide to a webpage using one of the buttons.

First add your titles, navigating to Slide > Create Text Slide. Click and drag that slide into the timeline.

> **NOTE**
>
> Adjust the title slide and the first slide so they both fit into the timeline equally.

Next, add music by clicking on Add Music. Music will be automatically added with fade ins and fade outs. Finally, click Publish.

Showing Your Slideshows on TV

You can hook up your computer to a television set to show your slideshows on TV. In the Chapter 3 sidebar, "Connecting Your Computer to Your TV," there are directions for hooking up your computer to your TV.

Another way to get your slideshows on your TV is to use TiVo DVR or Apple TV.

- **Apple TV.** While Apple isn't pushing this appliance, it's still available. When you use this box that attaches to your TV, you can watch videos you've made on YouTube as well as show the images you have on Flickr, Shutterfly, and other photo-hosting sites—provided you have Wi-Fi. You can also stream photos wirelessly from your computer to Apple TV so that they show up on your TV screen.
- **TiVo.** Just like Apple TV, TiVo lets you view YouTube videos via a wireless Internet connection. You can also view images on your computer by first publishing them so they can be picked up by TiVo.

So what's the basic difference between TiVo and Apple TV? TiVo connects not only to the Internet via Wi-Fi; it also connects to your cable TV. Also, Apple TV can't access photos on a PC, and TiVo can be used with both PCs and Macs.

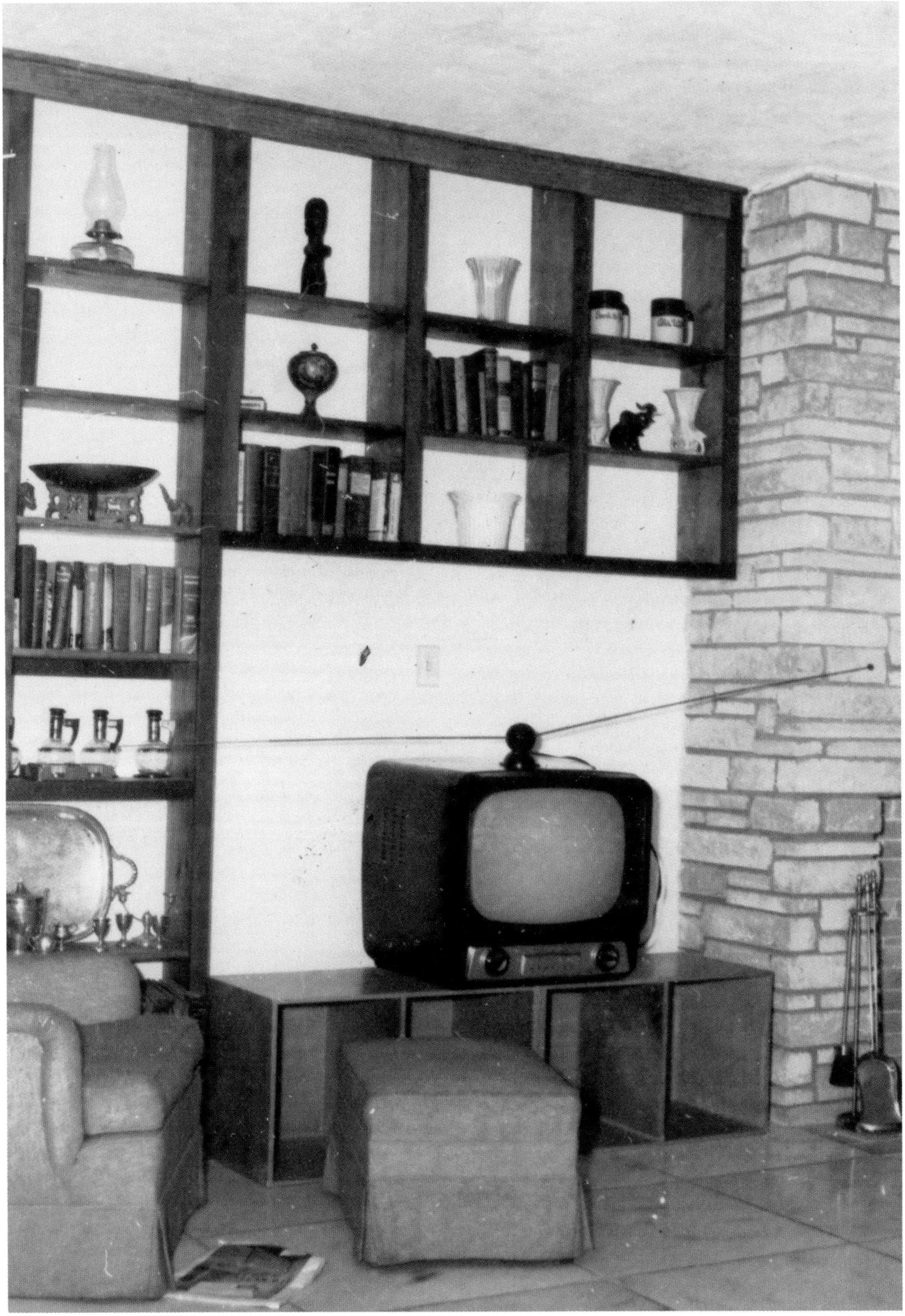

Chapter 13
Film to Digital

The last chapter of this book focuses on your prints, negatives, and slides. Almost everyone has them sitting around the house in a drawer, a basement, or an attic. There, they're certainly bound to be mold bait, waterlogged, or worse. If they're very old (more than 10 years), they'll certainly yellow, because back then they didn't make acid-free products.

Once you get to the job of getting your photos digitized, it can be great fun, like taking a time machine back to the future. There are two ways to digitize your photos. You can have someone else do it, or you can do it yourself. This chapter will show you how to do both and help you decide whether you want to do it yourself or have someone else do it.

Sorting through Your Old Photos to Prepare Them for Scanning

Sorting through all your old photos can occupy hours of your time. You'll find yourself enveloped in a variety of feelings about family, life, and the passage of time. It's a rewarding activity in which you might find some very compelling images.

The first thing you'll want to do is store the photos in acid-free materials. Remove them from cardboard boxes and get storage containers that will preserve them.

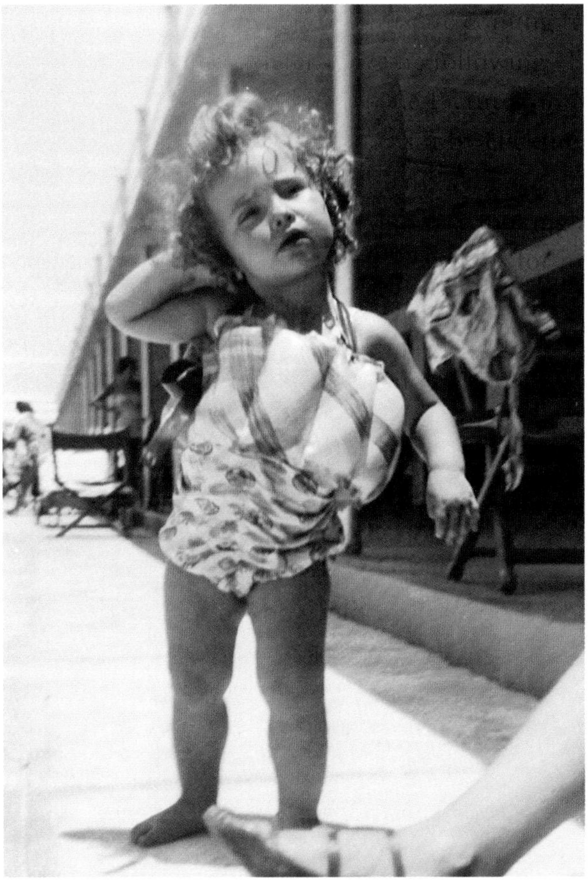

Figure 13.1 This photo was scanned from a 3×5 black-and-white negative.

NOTE

Use white cotton gloves when handling photos, slides, and negatives. They come by the dozen, and you can get them cheap at uline.com. (Type **cotton inspection gloves** in the Search box.)

For more about storing your old photos, refer to the "What about Storing Prints?" sidebar in Chapter 1.

Here are some of the types of photos you might find in an old photo collection:

- *Cartes de visite* and cabinet cards (card-backed photos).
- 8×10 black-and-white and color prints shot professionally.
- 35mm negatives.
- 4×5 black-and-white negatives.
- Polaroid Instamatic prints.
- Kodacolor prints made from negative film.
- Kodachrome slides. These, too, are square and enclosed in cardboard, but they're positives and can be scanned.

To look at negatives and slides, consider getting a light box. They're inexpensive and save you the effort of straining your eyes in front of a light to see the slides and/or negatives. You can also get a loupe (magnifying glass) so you can see the details of the image. B&H Photo (bhphotovideo.com) has both.

Next, you might want to look for pictures that will catch people's interest. They were described in the "Posting Retro Family Photos on Your Blog" section in Chapter 6.

Finally, you'll want to scan the images, which is described in the following section.

Scanning Prints, Slides, and Negatives

The sidebar "Scanners: What Type Should I Use?" in Chapter 6 provided a brief overview of the scanners you can buy for simple scanning jobs for prints. However, if you are seriously considering scanning your entire collection of photos—prints, slides, and negatives—you're looking at a big job. Believe me, I've done it, and although it's fun to see what you have on the computer screen, it takes hours to scan just 100 negatives.

A flatbed scanner, such as the Epson 4490, is good for scanning prints. Although it may have attachments to scan negatives and slides, it's not the best option for them. You're better off with a dedicated scanner, such as the Nikon 9000 ED.

When you scan negatives and slides on any scanner, there are holders you put the film into. Both flatbed and dedicated scanners can scan more than one negative/slide at a time.

NOTE

Scanning more than one slide or print is called *batch scanning*. No image is really scanned correctly, since you're getting an average scan/exposure for the batch. You should scan images individually to get optimum results.

Most scanners have full auto modes where the scanner software deals with all of the adjustments of the image. Sometimes this mode will let you customize your resolution and have you opt for dust removal and/or color restoration.

There are also professional modes where you can select options for your image. First, there's the type of image you have—48-bit, 24-bit color, and 16-bit and 8-bit grayscale—which affects your file size. If you're going to do a lot of tweaking in Photoshop, it's best to use 48-bit. However, if you do, your file size will be really big—so big that Photoshop will be slow. Personally, I don't find that there's much difference, and I usually go with the smaller file size that comes when you choose 24-bit. Then there's resolution (see Chapter 1), document size, target size (for negatives, slides), and a series of adjustments. If you check Unsharp Mask, your picture will be sharper without any added pixelization.

To get the best results, preview your image and then tweak using the options (curves, histogram, and so on) that are usually provided with most scanners. Tweaking is especially important when you're scanning negatives and slides. The last thing you do is click Scan to scan the image.

DIGITAL ICE TECHNOLOGY

Many scanners have Digital ICE (Image Correction Enhancement), which is a technology that gets rid of the fine dust particles imprinted on your image, as well as tiny scratches. Newer technology is now available that lessens the film grain that shows up when you enlarge 35mm negatives. Use this technology with care, because using it too heavily will create a soft image.

Getting Your Photos (Including Negatives) Professionally Scanned

At some point in your digital life, you're probably going to want to get your old negatives scanned. You can get your negatives scanned inexpensively by professionals who know what they are doing. Here are a couple of ideas:

- **ScanCafe.com.** This photo service can do everything from scanning prints, negatives, and slides to restoring their color. You place your order online (pay half upfront) and then send the items you want scanned. They scan them, put the results online for you to check (you can delete up to 50 percent of the ones you don't want, and they don't charge for those), and then send you a CD/DVD with your images at high resolution (600 dpi, 3000 dpi for negatives/slides). Scans are 29 cents apiece for prints, negatives, or slides.

> **NOTE**
>
> If you know Photoshop, it's probably best to do the tweaking yourself; otherwise, your scans can get very expensive ($6.95 basic to $40 or more for extreme fixing).

- **BritePix.com.** Similar to ScanCafe.com is BritePix.com. The pricing is the same for prints scanned at 600 dpi, but it's less if you're getting your images scanned at lower resolutions. (150 dpi is 19 cents and 300 dpi is 24 cents.) For negatives, it's also the same at 3000 dpi. They also scan at 4000 dpi (39 cents). They have a minimum order requirement of $50 plus shipping, and there's no upfront payment.
- **Digitalmemoriesonline.net.** Also in the business of scanning is digitalmemoriesonline.net. Their price for scanning a negative/slide at 3000 dpi is 59 cents (39 cents for 2000 dpi). They don't scan prints.

Index

M

N

O

P

Q-R

S

T

U-V

W

Y-Z